'The most dramatic centenary account of the Balfour Declaration.'

Robert Fisk

'Like his other books, David Cronin's latest work sheds light in the dark corners of western imperialist policies that wreak havoc in most of the world. This one about British policies over the 100 years since Balfour is worthy of reading not only by every British person interested in truth but all humans who yearn for peace and justice.'

Mazin Qumsiyeh, Professor at Bethlehem University

'It is not surprising that each year the November anniversary of the Balfour promise is celebrated by British friends of Israel and mourned by millions of dispossessed Palestinian refugees. Speaking the truth about the catastrophic consequences of British support for Zionism, this amply documented book shows how Britain erected and for decades maintained the scaffolding that gave birth to a settler-colonial state in Palestine and the Palestinian Nakba. Acknowledging Britain's moral responsibility towards the Palestinians is a key message of this timely and courageous book. A must read for those seeking truth and reconciliation in the Middle East.'

Nur Masalha, editor, Journal of *Holy Land and Palestine Studies*

'"Journalists", David Cronin tells us, "have a duty to cause trouble for the powerful." This sense of duty informs every word of Balfour's Shadow. From Foreign Secretary Balfour's illegitimate 1917 promise to the Jews of a homeland in Palestine to Tony Blair's global grandstanding and profiteering on Israel's behalf in the twenty-first century, Cronin exposes Britain as an enabler of Israeli apartheid. Cronin blends indignation with meticulous objectivity in an alternative history that is concise but comprehensive.'

Raymond Deane, Composer

'David Cronin describes vividly how, by deception, Britain's imperial designs and perceived need for international Jewish support in wartime gave birth to the Balfour Declaration of November 1917, which handed Arab Palestine to the Zionist Movement, as a "Jewish national home" or Jewish state. Cronin examines Britain's continuing pernicious, deadly and lucrative relationship with Israel, its political support for Israel's war crimes and theft of Arab land and the mutual arms trade.'

Tim Llewellyn, former BBC Middle East Correspondent

'Theresa May vowed in a recent speech to the Conservative Friends of Israel to mark the centenary of the Balfour Declaration "with pride" and to take the UK–Israeli relationship to "the next level". *Balfour's Shadow* challenges May's propagandist celebration through its exposure of the declaration's fundamental illegitimacy, supported by a wealth of factual detail on arms and money transfers, methods of repression, and the racist discourse through which the British Mandate prepared the establishment of Israel and ethnic cleansing of the Palestinian people.'

Rosemary Sayigh, author of *Palestinians: From Peasants to Revolutionaries and Too Many Enemies: The Palestinian Experience in Lebanon*

'*Balfour's Shadow* is a passionate, cogently argued presentation of the tragic and devastating consequences of the 1917 Balfour Declaration. Cronin's work provides a unique insight into the historic and current relationship between Britain, Israel and the Palestinians.'

Selma Dabbagh, novelist and playwright

'This superb book is a revelation, uncovering the dreadful history – and present – of Britain's connivance with Israeli atrocities. It is also badly-needed given the silence that has largely prevailed, in both academia and media, on the crucial relationship between British and Israeli governments. It really deserves to be widely read and understood.'

Mark Curtis, author of *Secret Affairs: Britain's Collusion with Radical Islam*

Balfour's Shadow

Balfour's Shadow

A Century of British Support for Zionism and Israel

David Cronin

PLUTO PRESS

First published 2017 by Pluto Press
345 Archway Road, London N6 5AA

www.plutobooks.com

Copyright © David Cronin 2017

The right of David Cronin to be identified as the author of this work has been
asserted by him in accordance with the Copyright, Designs and Patents Act 1988.

British Library Cataloguing in Publication Data
A catalogue record for this book is available from the British Library

ISBN   978 0 7453 9944 7   Hardback
ISBN   978 0 7453 9943 0   Paperback
ISBN   978 1 7868 0107 4   PDF eBook
ISBN   978 1 7868 0109 8   Kindle eBook
ISBN   978 1 7868 0108 1   EPUB eBook

.

Typeset by Stanford DTP Services, Northampton, England
Printed and bound by CPI Group (UK) Ltd, Croydon, CR0 4YY

Contents

Timeline of key events

November 1917	British government declares its support for the objective of establishing a 'Jewish national home' in Palestine.
December 1917	British Army captures Jerusalem.
April 1920	San Remo conference of allied powers agrees to place Palestine under British administration.
June 1920	Herbert Samuel arrives in Palestine as Britain's first high commissioner.
May 1921	Riots in Jaffa; Britain responds to this and subsequent unrest by sending extra security forces to Palestine.
May 1922	Winston Churchill, then colonial secretary, publishes a white paper on Palestine. It reconfirms commitment to Balfour Declaration but denies that Britain wants Palestine to be 'wholly Jewish'.
August 1929	British forces suppress riots in Jerusalem and other Palestinian cities.
October 1933	British forces attack Palestinian protesters in Jaffa.
April 1936	General strike declared by Palestinians' political leadership; revolt against Zionism and British administration begins.
June 1936	British authorities destroy Palestinian homes in Jaffa's Old City.

July 1937	Commission appointed by the British government recommends mass transfer of Palestinians – 'voluntary or otherwise' – so that Jewish state may be established.
March 1939	British government drafts white paper recommending that Palestine become an independent state, where 'Jews and Arabs share government', within a decade.
Summer 1939	British Army states that the Palestinian revolt has been 'smashed'.
November 1944	Armed Zionist group, the Lehi, assassinates Walter Guinness, a British politician, in Cairo.
July 1946	Another Zionist group, the Irgun, bombs British government offices in Jerusalem's King David Hotel.
September 1947	UN General Assembly votes for separate Jewish and Arab states to be formed in Palestine.
Spring–Summer 1948	Zionist forces undertake major ethnic cleansing campaign in Palestine.
May 1948	British rule in Palestine ends; state of Israel formally established.
May 1950	Britain, the USA and France sign Tripartite Declaration on limiting arms supplies to the Middle East.
October 1956	Israel attacks Egypt, implementing a secret plan drafted with Britain and France.
January 1959	Britain signs contract to supply Israel with Centurion tanks; various similar deals follow.
June 1967	Israel goes to war with Arab neighbours, making heavy use of weapons supplied by Britain.
October 1973	War between Israel, Egypt and Syria.

June 1980	Supported by Margaret Thatcher's government, the European Economic Community issues declaration on Israel–Palestine conflict.
September 1982	Thatcher condemns massacres by Israel's proxy forces in Lebanon as 'barbaric'.
May 1986	Thatcher undertakes first official visit by British prime minister to present-day Israel.
December 1987	First Palestinian uprising – or *intifada* – begins.
September 1993	Israel and PLO sign Oslo accords; Britain declares full support for this 'peace' deal.
September 2000	Second *intifada* begins.
August 2005	Contract signed to supply British Army with Israeli-designed drones.
November 2005	European Union launches first policing mission for the West Bank and Gaza, with significant British involvement.
July 2006	Israel attacks Lebanon, with support from Tony Blair, then Britain's prime minister.
June 2007	Blair named as representative for Middle East Quartet (the EU, USA, UN and Russia).
July 2008	Gordon Brown becomes first British prime minister to address Israel's parliament, the Knesset.
December 2008	Israel launches Operation Cast Lead, a major attack on Gaza, almost certainly using British weapons.
July 2014	Israel launches Operation Protective Edge, another offensive against Gaza.
December 2016	Theresa May promises to mark centenary of Balfour Declaration 'with pride'.

Text of Balfour Declaration

On 2 November 1917, Arthur James Balfour, then Britain's foreign secretary, signed a letter to Walter Rothschild, an aristocrat and committed Zionist. The letter – which became known as the Balfour Declaration – read:

Dear Lord Rothschild,

I have much pleasure in conveying to you, on behalf of His Majesty's government, the following declaration of sympathy with Jewish Zionist aspirations which has been submitted to, and approved, by the cabinet.

'His Majesty's government view with favour the establishment in Palestine of a national home for the Jewish people, and will use their best endeavours to facilitate the achievement of this object, it being clearly understood that nothing shall be done which may prejudice the civil and religious rights of existing non-Jewish communities in Palestine, or the rights and political status enjoyed by Jews in any other country.'

I should be grateful if you would bring this declaration to the knowledge of the Zionist Federation.

Yours,

Arthur James Balfour

Introduction

Boris Johnson has described the Balfour Declaration as 'bizarre', 'tragicomically incoherent' and 'an exquisite masterpiece of Foreign Office fudgerama'.[1] He is correct. Britain's 1917 pledge to help build a 'national home for the Jewish people' in Palestine struck a false balance. Despite resolving to respect the rights of everyone concerned, it accorded incoming settlers a higher status than the indigenous people. The world's pre-eminent power was sponsoring a project aimed at establishing a Jewish state in a land where most of the inhabitants were Arabs.

The irony is that Johnson has added to the incoherence. About a year after his critique of the declaration was published – in his 2014 biography of Winston Churchill – Johnson, then London's mayor, led a trade mission to Israel and the occupied West Bank. During his trip, he hailed the Balfour Declaration as 'a great thing' that 'reflected a great tide of history'.[2] Since then, Johnson has been appointed foreign secretary, a post held a century ago by Arthur James Balfour. Johnson has not repeated his 'fudgerama' claim since taking up that job.

Other Conservative politicians have publicly rejoiced in what William Hague has called the party's 'unbroken thread' of support for Zionism since the days of Balfour (such support is by no means confined to the Tories).[3] Visiting Jerusalem in 2014, David Cameron said the Balfour Declaration was the 'moment when the state of Israel went from a dream to a plan'.[4] Towards the end of 2016, Theresa May – Cameron's successor as prime minister – praised the declaration as 'one of the most important letters in history' and gave a commitment to mark its centenary 'with pride'. May is the latest in a series of British political leaders to prefer myths to reality. A sober assessment of events leads to the unavoidable conclusion that the Balfour Declaration enabled the mass dispossession of Palestinians, an injustice that persists. Rather than recognising that fact, May has celebrated Israel as 'a thriving democracy, a beacon of tolerance, an engine of enterprise'.[5]

Britain's relationship with the Zionist movement has not always been harmonious. At one crucial juncture in the 1940s, Britain was treated as the arch-enemy by some Zionist paramilitaries. The British administration in Jerusalem was even the target of Zionist bombing.

Viewed in its totality, the relationship has nonetheless proven to be resilient. That is despite the fact that the Zionist movement does not need Britain in the way it did 100 years ago. Then, convincing Britain to back the colonisation of Palestine was deemed to be vital by leading Zionists, notably Chaim Weizmann (later Israel's first president). With the USA now transferring billions of dollars in military aid to Israel each year, the notion that Zionists once pinned so much hope on receiving a brief letter from the British government might appear quaint.

The significance of the Balfour Declaration lies not only in its carefully weighed, though misleading, words – arguably, it lies more in the follow-up action. Soon after the letter to Walter Rothschild was dispatched, work began on laying the foundations of the coveted 'national home'. When the declaration's core tenets were enshrined in the League of Nations mandate under which Britain ruled Palestine between the two world wars, the 'home' began to take a discernible shape. It was not a place that made all its residents feel welcome. A pattern of discrimination against Palestinians developed – in access to land, employment and more besides. It led to the Nakba – Arabic for 'catastrophe' – the expulsion of 750,000 Palestinians around the time of Israel's foundation in 1948.

Boris Johnson is one of the many British politicians and diplomats to have voiced reservations about either the manner in which Zionism was embraced or whether the embrace was prudent. Yet the embrace has remained sufficiently tight for Britain to either directly crush resistance to the Zionist project – as occurred during the 1920s and 1930s – or, in more recent decades, to endorse Israeli repression.

The roles have, in some respects, been reversed. About 50 years ago, Britain supplied the tanks on which Israel would rely heavily during the Six-Day War of June 1967. Today, Israel designs the drones that are officially regarded as critical to Britain's future 'defence'. Yet it is not simply a case of a retailer turning into a customer. The occupation of the West Bank and Gaza, which began in 1967, has been treated as a business opportunity by Israel. The arms and surveillance equipment that Israel exports around the world have been tested out on the victims of that occupation. By supplying the hardware used in the initial invasion of those territories, Britain helped the Zionist colonisation project to enter into a new phase. There is a logic behind how Britain buys in bulk the products invented by its protégé and seeks to adapt them for its own ends.

Does the legacy of Arthur James Balfour matter in the era of Donald John Trump? The short answer is: yes. Israel's settlement activities have been one of the hot topics in the first few weeks of the Trump presidency (at the time of writing). The expansion of those settlements illustrates how the colonisation project that Balfour applauded in 1917 has never ceased. With Trump and his hard-right entourage now installed in the White House, there is a strong possibility that the project will accelerate.

Balfour could not have foreseen all of the project's consequences. He died in 1930 – 18 years before the State of Israel came into being, implicitly claiming that it held the title deeds to the 'Jewish national home'. Balfour did, however, know of the main risks entailed in building that 'home'. As this book demonstrates, he and his peers were fully aware that the pursuit of Zionist objectives endangered the fundamental rights of Palestinians, regardless of the caveats inserted into his declaration.

Israel's top politicians and diplomats continue to invest a great deal of energy towards maintaining strong relations with Britain. They do so in the expectation that their British counterparts will be receptive. Many Zionists of the twenty-first century still crave the respectability brought by endorsement from big players in global politics. Balfour casts a very long shadow.

I

Laying the foundations

The foundations of Israel were laid in London.

In November 1917, Arthur James Balfour, then Britain's foreign secretary, signed a letter that was just three sentences long. The brevity of the document did not detract from its impact.

Addressed to the aristocrat Walter Rothschild, it was a letter of support to the British Zionist Federation. It declared that the government viewed 'with favour the establishment in Palestine of a national home for the Jewish people' and promised assistance to realize that goal.

Through this declaration, Balfour set in train a process whereby colonisers would be treated as superior to the native population. A caveat – that 'nothing shall be done which may prejudice the civil and religious rights of existing non-Jewish communities in Palestine' – was really an insult. While Jews scattered across the world were accorded the status of belonging to a nation, Arabs living and farming on the land under discussion were merely described as 'non-Jewish communities'. The idea that they could constitute a nation was not entertained.

The declaration was very much a product of its time. Currying favour with the Zionist movement to establish a Jewish state in Palestine was deemed advantageous to Britain's strategy during the First World War. Balfour said as much during the war cabinet meetings at which the surrounding issues were discussed. In early October 1917, he inferred that Britain should try to win the sympathy of the Zionist movement before its enemy, Germany, did. At that meeting, he was given the go-ahead to take the 'necessary action'.[1] The war cabinet returned to the theme on 31 October 1917; the minutes of that meeting record Balfour as claiming 'it was desirable that some declaration favourable to the aspirations of the Jewish nationalists should now be made.' Balfour is reported to have claimed:

The vast majority of Jews in Russia and America, as, indeed, all over the world, now appeared to be favourable to Zionism. If we could make a declaration favourable to such an ideal, we should be able to carry on extremely useful propaganda both in Russia and America.[2]

Rumours and conspiracy theories about Jewish influence were influential in that era. Mark Sykes, a politician and diplomat who was considered a leading expert on the Middle East, had contended that Britain could not win the war if what he called 'great Jewry' was against it.[3] Robert Cecil, then the parliamentary secretary of state for foreign affairs, had remarked: 'I do not think it is easy to exaggerate the international power of the Jews.'[4]

The declaration's supporters have, however, long propagated the myth that Balfour was acting benevolently in offering a haven to persecuted Jews. Far from being a benevolent individual, Balfour was a man of imperial violence; that was proven by his stint as chief secretary in Ireland between 1887 and 1891. When a protest was held in Mitchelstown, County Cork, against the prosecution of the political leader William O'Brien, Balfour ordered police to open fire. Causing three deaths, the incident earned him the nickname 'Bloody Balfour'.[5]

Balfour should not be regarded as a saviour of the Jewish people; arguably, he was an anti-Semite. As prime minister, he pushed for a tough anti-immigration law in 1905 for the express purpose of stopping Jews fleeing Russia's pogroms from seeking refuge in Britain.[6] The Aliens Bill of that year allowed Britain to refuse refugees entry if they were deemed 'undesirable'. While the law was being debated, Balfour voiced fears about 'an alien immigration that was largely Jewish'. It would 'not be an advantage to the civilisation of the country,' he contended, to 'have an immense body of persons' with a different religion to the majority and 'who only intermarried among themselves'.[7] It is not as if Balfour discarded his prejudices towards Jews as his connections to the Zionist movement got stronger. In 1917, the same year as his eponymous declaration, he claimed that the persecutors of Jews had a 'case of their own'. Because a Jew 'belonged to a distinct race' that was 'numbered in millions, one could perhaps understand the desire to keep him down,' Balfour stated.[8]

Balfour's backing of the movement to establish a Jewish state in Palestine is not irreconcilable with his apparent anti-Semitism. Indeed, he dropped strong clues that his support for Jewish settlement in Palestine may have been motivated by a desire to see Europe emptied of Jews. In his introduction to a Nahum Sokolov book, Balfour praised Zionism as:

> a serious endeavour to mitigate the age-long miseries created for western civilisation by the presence in its midst of a body which is too long regarded as alien and even hostile, but which it was equally unable to expel or absorb.[9]

Rumours of Russia

The rumours of Jewish influence were taken especially seriously when they related to Russia. There was a perception that numerous Russian Jews were communist. *The Times* went even further by alleging that the Bolshevik leader Vladimir Lenin and 'several of his confederates are adventurers of German-Jewish blood and in German pay, whose sole objective is to exploit the ignorant masses in the interests of their employers in Berlin.'[10] By siding with the Zionist movement, Britain's elite felt it could win a majority of Russian Jews over to its side. A 1917 telegram from the Foreign Office to British envoys in Petrograd read:

> We are advised that one of the best methods of counteracting Jewish pacifists and socialist propaganda in Russia would be to offer definite encouragement to Jewish nationalist aspirations in Palestine. [The] question of Zionism is full of difficulties but I request your views in the first instance as to whether declaration by the Entente of sympathy with Jewish nationalist aspirations would help or not insofar as concerns [the] internal and external situation of Russia.[11]

Another senior figure in the Foreign Office, Ronald Graham, treated speculation as fact. In October 1917, he briefed Balfour about 'the very important role the Jews are now playing in the Russian political situation.' Although 'these Jews are certainly against the Allies and for the Germans, almost every Jew in Russia is a Zionist,' he claimed. If Britain convinced Russian Jews that the success of Zionism depended on 'the support of the Allies and the expulsion of the Turks from

Palestine, we shall enlist a most powerful element in our favour,' Graham added.[12]

Earlier in 1917, Britain's war cabinet had approved a memorandum detailing some of its key military objectives. One goal identified was to ensure 'continuity of territory or of control both in East Africa and between Egypt and India.'[13] Palestine was located close to the Suez Canal, which Britain relied on for shipping to and from many of its imperial 'possessions', as well as to coveted oil resources in Persia.

Chaim Weizmann was the leading Zionist in England at this time. Originally from Belarus (then part of the Russian Empire), he was a chemist, who taught at Manchester University and headed the British Admiralty Laboratories from 1917 to 1919. His scientific knowledge proved valuable to the British arms industry during the war. At a time when acetone (an important ingredient of cordite) was in short supply, Weizmann devised a method of manufacturing the solvent with maize. Rather than being paid for his breakthrough by the British government, he is reputed to have asked David Lloyd George, the then prime minister, for help in advancing the Zionist project.[14]

Weizmann was introduced to Lloyd George by C.P. Scott, editor of *The Manchester Guardian*. More a lobbyist than a journalist, Scott used the editorial section of his 'liberal' newspaper to support Zionism. Some of Scott's comments about Palestine's indigenous inhabitants verged on the racist. A 1917 leader described Palestinians as being 'at a low stage of civilisation' and containing 'none of the elements of progress'. In turn, Lloyd George arranged for Weizmann to see Balfour (as it happened, Balfour had had a previous conversation with Weizmann during a 1906 visit to Manchester).[15]

The Balfour Declaration was the product of discussions between Weizmann, a few other Zionists and the British government. Weizmann had appeared certain that Britain would become the main sponsor of his movement for months, if not years, prior to the declaration being published. At a May 1917 Zionist gathering in London, he said:

> Palestine will be protected by Great Britain. Protected by this power, the Jews will be able to develop and create an administrative organisation which, while safeguarding the interests of the non-Jew population, will permit us to realise the aims of Zionism. I am

authorised to declare to this assembly that His Majesty's government are ready to support our plans.[16]

Various drafts of the statement which Balfour eventually signed were considered by both sides. Scholars have pored over each draft, analysing, for example, how one advocated that Palestine be 'reconstituted' as the 'national home' of the Jewish people, whereas the final version merely envisaged a 'national home' being established in that country. Bearing in mind subsequent events, the differences between the various drafts appear less significant than they probably looked to those directly involved in the negotiations. Nahum Sokolov, one of the Zionists involved in the drafting, had his wish of having a declaration that would be 'as pregnant as possible' fulfilled. He wanted a statement that would be concise and express Britain's 'general approval' of Zionist aspirations.[17]

Unknown in international law, the phrase 'national home' has been attributed to Max Nordau, a founder of the World Zionist Organization. At an 1897 conference in Basle, he advocated that Zionists find 'a circumlocution that would express all we meant' but avoid provoking the Turkish rulers of Palestine. Nordau proposed 'national home' – *Heimstätte* in German – as what he called a 'synonym for "state"'.[18] The minutes of the key war cabinet meeting on Halloween in 1917 also acknowledge as much, albeit in a circuitous fashion. Balfour is recorded as explaining that a 'national home' meant:

> some form of British, American or other protectorate under which full facilities would be given to the Jews to work out their salvation and to build up, by means of education, agriculture and industry, a real centre of national culture and focus of national life.

Balfour added that 'it did not necessarily involve the early establishment of an independent Jewish state.' But he hinted that such a state could be formed 'in accordance with the ordinary laws of political evolution.' Leonard Stein, a Zionist and Liberal Party politician who wrote a bulky tome on the declaration, has confirmed that 'the conception of the eventual emergence of something in the nature of a Jewish state or commonwealth was, in fact, in the air when the declaration was published.'[19]

The golden key

The ambiguities in the declaration did not stop the Zionist movement from exploiting its potential. Weizmann stated as much when he wrote 'we ought not to ask the British government if we will enter Palestine as masters or equals to the Arabs.' In his words, 'the declaration implies that we have been given the opportunity to become masters.'[20] Weizmann was far less coy than his friends in government. During a public event in London, he said that 'a Jewish state will come about' and called the Balfour Declaration 'the golden key which unlocks the doors of Palestine.'[21]

Despite how it paid lip-service to civil rights, the declaration's effect was to formalise an alliance between the British Empire and a movement motivated by a sense of supremacy. Weizmann summarised the outlook of Zionists by stating: 'There is a fundamental difference in quality between Jew and native.'[22] (Perhaps it should be remarked that some of the politicians he courted used language that was even more pejorative. Lloyd George's war memoirs, for example, refer to the presence of 'nigger policemen' in Jerusalem.[23])

Britain had no moral or legal authority to make pledges on Palestine in November 1917. Palestine was not one of its imperial 'possessions' – British forces did not capture Jerusalem until a month after the declaration was published. Yet that did not stop the British government from acting as if it owned Palestine and, therefore, was entitled to dictate the country's future.

On occasion, Balfour acknowledged that he had negated the rights of Palestinians. Corresponding with George Curzon, a former viceroy of India who went on to succeed Balfour as foreign secretary, he admitted in 1919 that Britain's stance on Palestine was at odds with the broad commitment given by key players in global politics following the First World War to the idea of self-determination. Britain would make no attempt to consult indigenous Palestinians, Balfour stated, adding:

> The four great powers are committed to Zionism. And Zionism, be it right or wrong, good or bad, is rooted in age-long traditions, in present needs, in future hopes, of far profounder import than the desires and prejudices of the 700,000 Arabs who now inhabit that ancient land.[24]

The idea that the 'national home' would be nurtured under joint Anglo-French stewardship – what some called a condominium – was briefly entertained. It was swiftly rejected by the British government. Lloyd George, in particular, was eager to keep France out of Palestine. Following the loss of a 1917 battle in Gaza, he approved plans for a large-scale operation to capture Palestine. 'The French will have to accept our protectorate; we shall be there by conquest and shall remain,' he stated. Instructed by Lloyd George, Mark Sykes told his French interlocutor François Georges-Picot that British suzerainty in Palestine was the only stable option. To bolster his case, Sykes pointed to Britain's 'preponderant military effort', its 'rights' to Haifa port and to railways in the country and to the preference which leading Zionists had expressed towards Britain being in charge.[25]

Weizmann constantly tried to present control of Palestine and support for Zionist colonisation as being in Britain's own interest. Sometimes, he exploited rumours about Jewish power while doing so. Making friends with 'the Jews of the world', he claimed would be something that 'matters a great deal, even for a mighty empire like the British.'[26] On other occasions he resorted to flattery – like when he told Robert Cecil that 'Jews all over the world trust Great Britain and look to this country as a liberator of Palestine.'[27] A consistency can be discerned, nonetheless. His case rested on the assumption that Palestine would be a loyal dominion for Britain provided that large-scale Zionist settlement could occur there. 'England does not seek Palestine,' he stated in 1917, either ignoring or oblivious to how Lloyd George did indeed have his eyes on the country. 'It is of value to her only if we are strong there.'[28] The following year, he wrote to William Ormsby-Gore, an MP who later became colonial secretary, that 'we consider a British Palestine and a Jewish Palestine practically identical.'[29]

Understanding how Britain wished to have an obsequious population in Palestine is not difficult if the broader historical context is taken into account. One year before the Balfour Declaration was issued, Britain had suppressed a rebellion in its nearest colony, Ireland. Balfour was among the many British politicians to have been directly involved in both the questions of Ireland and Palestine. So the prospect of having a 'little loyal Jewish Ulster in a sea of potentially hostile Arabism' – to use the words of Ronald Storrs, a governor of Jerusalem – undoubtedly appealed to them.[30] Zionists were perceived as being similar to the Scottish Presbyterians who took part in the 'plantation' of Ireland's north-eastern counties during the seventeenth century. Visiting Tel Aviv and Jaffa in 1918, William Ormsby-Gore claimed that 'the Zionists are the one sound firmly pro-British, constructive element in the whole show.'[31]

The Balfour Declaration, then, was really a product of both wartime expediency and imperial machinations. Well before it was drafted, Britain and France had been planning how the Middle East could be carved up between them. Allies in public, each of those powers plotted how to outmanoeuvre the other in private.

Herbert Samuel, a Zionist stalwart, was among those pushing to ensure that Britain was the boss in Palestine. As a cabinet minister in 1915, he advocated that Britain should endorse the establishment of a Jewish colony near Suez as part of a strategy to prevent the canal falling into French hands. Britain should not assume that 'our present happy relations with France will continue always,' he stated. Letting France assume responsibility for Syria or Lebanon, he suggested, would be 'a far smaller risk to the vital interests of the British Empire' than allowing France to gain a foothold in Palestine and Egypt.[32] Samuel wrote a number of memos for the government in support of Zionism. One of them, dating from January 1915, was sympathetic to the idea of a Jewish state but warned against rapidly placing the Palestinian majority under Jewish minority rule. Doing so might result in the 'dream of a Jewish state' vanishing 'in a series of squalid conflicts,' he wrote. As an alternative, he recommended that Palestine be annexed to the British Empire and that Britain sponsor its colonisation by Jews with a view to establishing a Jewish majority 'in course of time'.[33] Ultimately, Britain 'might plant three or four million European Jews' in Palestine, he argued.[34]

Samuel's recommendation resembled what soon was adopted as Britain's official war aims. As well as being involved in drafting the Balfour Declaration, the Conservative politician Leo Amery submitted proposals in early 1917 for what Britain should expect when hostilities ceased. The proposals were endorsed by the war cabinet; they stated that it was essential for the British Empire to secure 'continuity of territory or of control' between Egypt and India.[35] A few months later, the war cabinet resolved that the 1916 Sykes–Picot accord with France be amended so that Britain would be guaranteed 'definite and exclusive control over Palestine'.[36]

If the terms of Sykes–Picot were implemented, then an international administration would be established in Palestine, albeit with Britain put in charge of the ports at Haifa and Acre and allowed to 'own' a railway between Haifa and Baghdad. Free passage of French goods on British-controlled ports and railways was to be arranged. While the accord could be interpreted as giving France a stake in the political and business affairs of Palestine, the British were soon eager to dispel any such notions. Herbert Samuel went so far as to contend in 1917 that 'the French had no claims whatsoever in Palestine.'[37]

Cousins divided

Zionism, then as now, was a divisive ideology. Not only did its adherents and their political allies inflict injustice on Palestinians, they created rifts among Jews. While Weizmann and a few other Zionists did their utmost to give the impression that they spoke on behalf of the world's Jews, many of their co-religionists were not enamoured by their ideology and in some cases rejected it outright. It is highly significant that Edwin Montagu, Britain's only Jewish cabinet minister in 1917, was opposed to Zionism.

Montagu, the secretary of state for India, was a cousin of Herbert Samuel's yet the two men had divergent views on the idea of establishing a Jewish state in Palestine. In August 1917, Montagu lodged a complaint with his cabinet colleagues about the lobbying being undertaken by prominent Zionists. The memo argued that by supporting Zionism, British policy would 'prove a rallying ground for anti-Semites in every country in the world.' Once Jews are told that Palestine is their national home, 'every country will immediately desire to get rid of its Jewish citizens.'[38]

Zionism, according to Montagu, was a 'mischievous political creed, untenable by any patriotic citizen of the United Kingdom.' An English Jew longing to 'shake British soil from his shoes and go back to agricultural pursuits in Palestine' had 'acknowledged aims inconsistent with British citizenship.' As he regarded Judaism as purely a religion, Montagu spurned the concept that he belonged to the same nationality as Jews living in other countries. Displaying remarkable prescience, he wrote:

> I have always understood that those who indulged in this creed [Zionism] were largely animated by the restrictions upon and refusal of liberty to Jews in Russia. But at the very time when these Jews have been acknowledged as Jewish Russians and given all liberties, it seems to be inconceivable that Zionism should be officially recognised by the British government, and that Mr Balfour should be authorised to say that Palestine was to be reconstituted as the 'national home of the Jewish people'. I do not know what this involves but I assume that it means that Mohammedans and Christians are to make way for the Jews and that the Jews should be put in all positions of preference and should be peculiarly associated with Palestine in the same way that England is with the English or France with the French, that Turks and other Mohammedans in Palestine will be regarded as foreigners, just in the same way as Jews will hereafter be treated as foreigners in every country but Palestine. Perhaps also citizenship must be granted only as a result of a religious test.[39]

Another memo written by Montagu argued that Zionism was opposed by every British Jew 'who is prominent in public life, with the exception of the present Lord [Walter] Rothschild, Mr Herbert Samuel and a few others'.[40] That opposition did not perturb Balfour. Egged on by a coterie of Zionists, he was more willing to heed rumours about the political leanings of Russian and American Jews than the perceptive analysis of his only Jewish colleague in the cabinet.

Once they had captured Jerusalem, the British set up the Occupied Enemy Territory Administration South. An official serving with that inelegantly named body put his thoughts about the prevailing mood on paper in 1919:

> At the moment Palestine is in a turmoil owing to the Zionist menace. All elements of the population, Christian and Musalman [Muslim] alike, are organising themselves together to resist what they regard as the greatest injustice ever known under British rule, namely the discrimination in favour of the hated Jewish minority that is involved

in Mr Balfour's declaration regarding Zionism, and the overruling of the vaunted 'rights of small nations'. We shall have difficulty in keeping the peace.[41]

The official had pinpointed how the Balfour Declaration was perceived as an existential threat by Palestinians. The antipathy towards Jews to which he referred was not, as many Zionists would claim, the result of an innate prejudice. Palestine had a Jewish minority for centuries before the Balfour Declaration was conceived. While it would be naive to think there was never any tension between people of different faiths, the relations between Jews, Christians and Muslims was generally cordial. It was not unusual, by some accounts, for Muslims and Christians to take part in the celebrations of Jewish holidays.[42]

Those cordial relations were ruptured as a result of the waves of settlement by European Jews from the 1880s on, later under the direction of the Zionist movement and with direct support from the British government.

2

Bringing in the Black and Tans

Chaim Weizmann acted swiftly to exploit the opportunities afforded by the Balfour Declaration.

The Zionist Commission was formed in March 1918, at a time when northern Palestine was still in Turkish hands. Led by Weizmann, it was formally tasked by the British government with taking 'any steps required' to realize the promise of establishing a 'national home for the Jewish people'. Instructions to foster friendly relations with indigenous Palestinians – an unrealistic goal given the inherent bias of British policy – were brushed aside as the commission accelerated the pace of Jewish colonisation. Along with forming ministries for settlement and farming, it set about training an armed force.[1]

Soon the commission became a rival to the British military administration in Jerusalem. Louis Bols, a general in charge of that administration, complained that the commission's activities made 'good government impossible'. Not only did Jewish settlers treat the commission with more respect than the British administration, 'the Moslems and Christians can only see that privileges and liberties are allowed to the Jews which are denied to them,' Bols argued.[2] An official US government investigation into the partitioning of the Ottoman Empire reached a similar conclusion in 1919. The probe, conducted by the theologian Henry Churchill King and the entrepreneur Charles Crane, found that none of the British officers consulted in Palestine believed the Zionist programme could be implemented without force of arms.[3]

Weizmann did not have to worry too much about the misgivings of the military administration. Soon it would be replaced by a civilian administration that was dedicated to advancing the Zionist project. The Zionist movement aimed to set the agenda which the civil administration would follow. In a detailed paper submitted to the 1919 Paris conference of allied victors, the Zionist Organization recommended that Britain should govern Palestine under a League of Nations mandate. Britain's task would, according to the paper, be to stimulate the conditions required for developing a 'Jewish national home'.[4]

Herbert Samuel remained an especially valuable ally to Weizmann. The two men were in regular contact, accompanying each other, for example, to the Paris conference. Although Samuel lost his parliamentary seat in the 1918 election, his advice was still sought after by the government. In 1919, Samuel was asked by the Foreign Office how the British military authorities should deal with Palestinian antipathy towards Zionism. Samuel responded by deploring what he perceived as the insufficient level of support for Zionism among the British administration. Its officers, he complained, did not always behave as if the Balfour Declaration 'embodies the settled lines of policy'.[5]

In March 1920, Samuel wrote of visiting eleven 'Jewish agricultural colonies' in Palestine and how he found them 'full of promise for the future'. According to Samuel, the settlements 'constitute the most energetic and the most significant factor in the Palestine of today'. He predicted that Palestine could 'become a thriving country' and 'could offer, in a comparatively short period, a comfortable livelihood to several times its population' if it had 'a progressive government' and adequate investment. In the following month, news reached Palestine that Samuel was to become Britain's first high commissioner there. The announcement was, Bols noted, met with 'consternation, despondency and exasperation' among Muslims and Christians, who were convinced that Samuel would be 'a partisan Zionist and that he represents a Jewish and not a British government'.[6]

Samuel promptly issued a number of decrees to underpin the colonisation process. A 'land transfer ordinance' enabled the acquisition of farms and property by Zionists. Ottoman laws permitting Arab peasants to cultivate 'waste' land were repealed. And Zionist representatives were granted special authority to oversee immigration.[7] In consultation with the Zionist movement, Britain agreed that 16,500 Jewish settlers would be admitted to Palestine per year. The figure was just 500 less than what the Zionist leadership had demanded. Beginning the establishment of a 'Jewish national home' was 'essential', according to one of Samuel's memos.[8]

Norman Bentwich, the legal officer who drafted many of the ordinances introduced by the British administration in Jerusalem, has acknowledged that a system of 'economic apartheid' was established during this period. Bentwich, himself a Zionist, was correct to identify the Histadrut, a labour union that put pressure on employers to hire Jews exclusively, as being of critical importance to the system.[9] Yet the system was nurtured by Britain.

Samuel's appointment as high commissioner preceded the 1920 conference of allied powers in San Remo. There, on the Italian Riviera, Britain was formally tasked with administering Palestine under a League of Nations mandate.

Weizmann lobbied vigorously to ensure that the Balfour Declaration was enshrined in that agreement. He insisted that Palestine be treated differently to all other territories within the former Ottoman Empire. Syria and Iraq were to be run 'in the national interests of the present inhabitants', he wrote in one letter to Britain's Foreign Office. Palestine, by contrast, was to host 'the Jewish national home, the rights of the present inhabitants, of course, being adequately safeguarded'.[10]

Not for the first time, the profession of concern for the indigenous Palestinians was hollow. As advocated by Weizmann, the League of Nations' mandate stated that Britain was responsible for placing Palestine under conditions conducive towards setting up a 'Jewish national home'. To guide this process along, a 'Jewish agency' would be formally recognised by the British. Though it would work under the British administration's control, the agency would offer advice and assistance on making the national home a reality. Working in tandem with the agency, the British administration would encourage the 'close settlement by Jews on the land'. Ronald Storrs, governor of Jerusalem in this period, summed up the resentment that the partnership and its objective caused. The 'thinking Arabs,' he stated, regarded this colonisation 'as Englishmen would regard instructions from a German conqueror for the settlement and development of the Duchy of Cornwall, of our Downs, commons and golf courses, not by Germans, but by Italians, "returning" as Roman legionaries.' Storrs, incidentally, was broadly sympathetic to Zionism; in his memoirs, he argued that though the ideology was riddled with 'gratuitous errors', it was 'one of the most remarkable and original conceptions in history'.[11]

Copper-fastened by Churchill

In effect, then, the mandate allowed a Zionist quasi-government to be formed. The agency would enjoy both privileged access to the British administration and a considerable degree of autonomy. No equivalent body was envisaged for the Palestinians. The most Samuel was prepared to offer them was representation on a legislative council. It never came into being. Palestinian leaders wisely rejected the proposals for a council; they had been drawn up with the intention of making sure that the Palestinian majority did not hold a majority of its seats. Moreover, the planned council would have been forbidden from taking any decisions that ran counter to the objectives of the British mandate.[12]

Winston Churchill also used his brief stint as colonial secretary to affirm that Britain's support for Zionism was irreversible. Visiting Palestine shortly after assuming that post in 1921, Churchill displayed a condescending attitude when faced with complaints from Musa al-Husseini, whom the British had previously dismissed as mayor of Jerusalem. Churchill told al-Husseini:

> Our position in this country is based upon the events of the war ratified, as they have been, by the treaties signed by the victorious powers. I thought, when listening to your statements, that it seemed the Arabs of Palestine had overthrown the Turkish government. That is the reverse of the true facts. It has been the armies of Britain which have liberated these regions.[13]

Referring to a cemetery for more than 2,000 British troops that al-Husseini and others in his delegation would have seen on their way to the meeting, Churchill said:

> The position of Great Britain in Palestine is one of trust but it is also one of right. For the discharge of that trust and for the high purposes we have in view, supreme sacrifices were made by all these soldiers of the British Empire, who gave up their lives and their blood.[14]

Churchill would not brook any criticism of Zionism. He went so far as to recycle one of the Zionist movement's main talking points, the claim that the living standards of all Palestine's residents would improve as a result of Jewish colonisation:

> It is manifestly right that the Jews, who are scattered all over the world should have a national centre and a national home where some of them may be reunited. And where else could that be but in this land of Palestine, with which for more than 3,000 years they have been intimately and profoundly associated? We think that it will be good for the world, good for the Jews and good for the British Empire. But we also think it will be good for the Arabs who dwell in Palestine, and we intend that it shall be good for them, and that they shall not be sufferers or supplanted in the country in which they dwell or denied their share in all that makes for its progress and prosperity.[15]

Together, Churchill and Samuel discussed how they could persuade Arab leaders in the wider region to adopt a sympathetic – or at least not overly hostile – attitude towards both Britain and Zionism. Abdullah, the guardian – or *sharif* – of Mecca was central to their scheming. He had been eager to take military action against France in order to recapture the throne in Damascus, from which his brother Faisal had been ousted in 1920. Yet Churchill persuaded him not to do so. In March 1921, Churchill told Samuel that it was deemed important that Abdullah and his family be placed 'under an obligation' to Britain. Abdullah was given responsibility for running the protectorate of Transjordan, a territory adjoining Palestine, 'on the understanding that he used his influence to prevent anti-French and anti-Zionist propaganda' there, Churchill said. To 'guarantee there would be no anti-Zionist disturbances', Abdullah 'must be given support either in money or troops,' according to Churchill, who spoke about a package of agreements with Abdullah's family.[16] These measures would include placing one of the family on the throne in Iraq. Later that month, Churchill and Samuel had conversations with Abdullah directly. A record of the meeting states that Abdullah accepted 'there should be no anti-French or anti-Zionist agitation' in Transjordan. In return for a pledge of financial and military support from Britain, Abdullah 'only asked that he might be regarded as a British officer and trusted accordingly,' the minutes of the meeting add.[17]

Some of Churchill's remarks about Palestine were arguably racist. Whereas he rhapsodised about the 'smiling orchards' he saw in the Jewish settlement of Rishon Lezion, he depicted indigenous Palestinians as backward. It was significant, he later claimed, that an energy grid in Palestine was developed by a Zionist firm (with Britain's backing). 'Left to themselves, the Arabs of Palestine would not in a thousand years have taken electrification to Palestine,' he once told the House of Commons. 'They would be quite content to dwell – a handful of philosophic people – in the wasted sun-scorched plains, letting the waters of the Jordan continue to flow unbridled and unharnessed into the Dead Sea.'[18]

On 1 May 1921, two rival marches were held in Jaffa. One – by the Socialist Workers Party, a Jewish organisation nominally committed to cooperating with Palestinians in a common class-based struggle – had not been approved by the British administration. The other – by Labour Unity (Ahdut HaAvoda), which had a Hebrew-only policy – enjoyed the required authorisation. Clashes between the two demonstrations evolved into intercommunal fighting which lasted for a few days. A total of 48 Palestinians and 47 Jews were killed.

An official British investigation into the riots listed the 'unauthorised demonstration of Bolshevik Jews' as the initial cause. Headed by Thomas Haycraft, a British judge in Palestine, the investigation concluded, however, that 'there is no inherent anti-Semitism in the country, racial or religious.' Haycraft noted that Palestinian grievances had arisen from the way Zionists had put pressure on Jewish landowners to replace Palestinian labourers with Jews. He also pointed to 'the influence exercised or believed to be exercised' by the Zionist Commission over legislation and the appointment of officials in the British administration. Perceived or real, that clout had 'done nothing to lessen the distrust with which it [the Zionist Commission] is regarded by the Arabs, who have no similar body to exercise corresponding influence on their behalf.'[19]

CD Brunton, a captain in the British Army, was more forthright in identifying the riot's causes. In his opinion, 'the Arab population has come to regard the Zionists with hatred and the British with resentment.' Churchill's visit had 'put the final touch to the picture,' according to Brunton. The captain alleged that Churchill 'upheld the Zionist cause and treated the Arab demands like those of negligible opposition to be put off by a few political phrases and treated like children.'[20]

'A certain ruthlessness'

The response to these riots gave an indication of how resistance to British rule and to Zionism would be crushed. As well as declaring a state of emergency, Samuel ordered air strikes against Arab rioters.[21] A 'picked force of white gendarmerie' – the term used in a Colonial Office paper – was established on Churchill's recommendation. Churchill's idea was to bring in some of the auxiliary police that had been stationed in Ireland during its war of independence, which had just ended, and 'who might now be at liberty,' according to the Colonial Office. Henry Hugh Tudor, commander of the auxiliaries in Ireland, had advised Churchill that 'between 700 and 800 absolutely reliable men' were likely to be available, along with 'many of the best officers' from the Royal Irish Constabulary (RIC), the force they had supplemented. While the men sent to Palestine would be answerable to the civil administration, a committee of high-ranking soldiers and civil servants agreed that they could be used as a military force 'in the event of an emergency'.[22]

Churchill had also been instrumental, the previous year, in setting up the auxiliary division of the police serving in Ireland. Then secretary of state for war, Churchill had also urged that Tudor be hired as a police adviser to the British administration in Dublin.[23] Working alongside the Black and Tans – First World War veterans who joined the RIC – the temporary force gained a reputation for brutal behaviour. Their most infamous escapade was arguably the 'sack' of Balbriggan in north County Dublin. As revenge for the killing of a police officer by Irish republicans in September 1920, the auxiliaries burnt down an English-owned hosiery factory nearby.[24] Around 200 people were put out of work in the Balbriggan area as a result. Four pubs were also torched by the police and almost 50 houses were damaged or destroyed. The episode was widely covered in the British press and even debated in parliament.[25]

Nominally distinct, the Auxiliaries and the Black and Tans were often confused for each other. Often, the term 'Black and Tans' was used in reference to both these divisions. And the gendarmerie dispatched to Palestine included men from both. Norman Bentwich wrote that most of the gendarmerie 'had been in the celebrated Black and Tan Brigade in Ireland.' Tudor had, according to Bentwich, 'commented sourly that they had to leave Ireland because of the principle of self-determination and were sent to Palestine to resist the Arab attempt at self-determination.'[26] Briefing papers drafted in Whitehall noted, meanwhile, the strong similarities between the police forces Britain established in Ireland and Palestine. A Home Office paper, for example, drew attention to how the two forces were centralised and how the rules on disciplinary proceedings and on deploying extra police in 'disturbed or dangerous districts' in Palestine 'correspond with Irish practice'.[27] An overview of the gendarmerie, apparently written for the British Army, stated that its British element was:

> largely raised from ex-members of the Auxiliary Military Force, otherwise known as the Black and Tans, which was then being disbanded, and from ex-servicemen. This original composition gave the force a military efficiency, combined with a certain ruthlessness, which it appears to have maintained throughout its history.[28]

The demarcation lines between military and civilian policing were frequently blurred during British rule in Palestine. Churchill was partly to blame. Although he advocated that the gendarmerie should be under civilian administration, his initial 1921 proposal to create the force was tagged onto a series of suggestions about increasing both the manpower and the weapons available to British troops in Palestine. For a brief period, Tudor was put in charge of both police – including the new gendarmerie – and the soldiers. So was his successor, Arthur Mavrogordato. 'Together, these forces amounted to an armed force of brigade strength,' Edward Horne wrote in his book about policing Palestine, contending that the situation was 'rare' and 'anomalous' (presumably, he meant, in the wider context of the British Empire).[29]

Douglas Duff was among the first of the gendarmerie to arrive in Palestine, having previously worked as a police officer in Galway. Duff's book *Bailing With a Teaspoon* indicates that Churchill's racism was shared by members of the force which he helped establish. Describing how Palestinians in Haifa protested against Zionism and the British Mandate, he wrote: 'Most of us were so infected by the sense of our own superiority over "lesser breeds" that we scarcely regarded these people as human.' His prejudices were not restricted to people of one religion or ethnicity. The police, he wrote, 'arrogantly dubbed all Palestinians, whether they were Muslims, Christians or Jews' as 'wogs'.[30]

The connection between Churchill and the gendarmerie was so strong that its members were nicknamed 'Winston's own', according to Angus McNeil, the force's commander. In a 1926 letter to Churchill, McNeil stated:

> There were two serious disturbances soon after our arrival and we had to butt in and teach them a lesson. Luckily both Arabs and Jews had a taste of our methods, one riot being at Nablus and the other at Tel Aviv, so we early established a name for impartiality. We have had no serious trouble since.[31]

Duff's account of the 1922 Nablus riots – one of the 'disturbances' to which McNeil was presumably referring – was more dramatic. The trouble was sparked by a British-organised census, yet Duff blamed it on the 'innate fanaticism of the townsmen'. Claiming 'there are few Muslims in Palestine so treacherous, cruel and bigoted as the Nabulsis', he wrote:

> When the census-takers arrived they were met by abuse, and, when they persisted in their duties, cobble-stones began to fly. The age-old rallying call of Islam rang through the vaulted bazaars and the local police were driven out of the streets. The British governor of Samaria called out the gendarmerie, much as Pontius Pilate once loosed his legionaries on the Samaritans, and they waged a terrific fight in the night-filled rabbit-warren of lanes and side streets; against fanatics who honestly believed they were fighting for God and faith. The gendarmerie battled joyously with pick-shaft and rifle-butt, less than 100 men against close on 4,000, dodging tiles dropped from flat roofs, hurtling daggers and every kind of missile, including a few pistol bullets, until they had cleared the maze of cobbled lanes in the *suq* (the bazaar).[32]

One of Duff's fellow gendarmes produced a trophy from that 'joyous' battle in a canteen the next day. The trophy consisted of 'the brains of a man he had splintered with a rifle-butt' that the 'gloating, grog-blossomed' officer had stuffed into an old cigarette tin.[33]

The crude manner in which that violence was celebrated offers a very different view of the British Mandate than the nuanced one provided by the white paper which Churchill published in 1922. That document, widely believed to have been written by Herbert Samuel, sought to placate Palestinians, while simultaneously reassuring Zionists that the Balfour Declaration was 'not susceptible of change'. To honour Balfour's commitments, the number of Jews in Palestine would have to increase but 'immigration cannot be so great in volume as to exceed whatever may be the economic capacity of the country at the time to absorb new arrivals,' it stated. Denying that Britain wished to create 'a wholly Jewish Palestine', it applauded the assurances given by the Zionist Organization the previous year on 'the determination of the Jewish people to live with the Arab people on terms of unity and mutual respect'.[34]

As the term 'immigration' appears repeatedly in British documents, placing the term in its proper context is imperative. Jews moving to Palestine had, in very many cases, experienced persecution and, indisputably, there was a moral obligation on the authorities in Europe both to end that oppression and to protect its victims. However, the Zionist movement did not sponsor 'immigration' for humanitarian reasons. Nor did it wish all the Jews of Europe to arrive in Palestine at once. Britain's policy of keeping 'immigration' in line with Palestine's 'economic capacity' to absorb newcomers chimed with the Zionist movement's own wishes. During the early 1920s, Zionist representatives in Palestine argued that only Jews who would not be a 'burden' should be given visas. Young men willing to work in agriculture were favoured, provided that they were healthy. The Zionist Organization complained when boats landed in Palestine carrying Jews who were unwell.[35]

For these reasons, 'immigration' – when used by the British authorities and Zionists – was a euphemism for colonisation. Newcomers were, according to the Zionist movement's wishes, supposed to live apart from the indigenous population, preferably in Jewish-only towns or settlements. The farms or factories where they would work would, if both Zionist capitalists and trade unionists had their way, exclusively employ Jews. And the colonisation process was aided by the new land laws introduced by the British administration. By the time Herbert Samuel's five-year term as high commissioner had ended, the proportion of land owned by Zionists had increased by more than 60 per cent. Promises of compensation to Palestinian peasants evicted from their holdings were frequently broken. More than 8,700 Palestinians were expelled from 22 villages in Marj Ibn Amer, a region in the Galilee today known as the Jezreel Valley, in the first half of the 1920s.[36] Thanks to Samuel's policies, the dispossession of Palestinians had gained a momentum that has not yet stopped.

The Zionist movement displayed scant regard for the sensitivities of Palestinians. That was particularly so in relation to the status of Jerusalem and its holy places. Under both Ottoman and British Mandate laws, the Haram al-Sharif area of the Old City was considered Muslim public property. By tradition, however, Jews were allowed to pray in one section of the compound; it is known as the Western Wall to Jews and *al-Buraq* to Muslims.

Fears grew among Palestinians during the late 1920s that Zionists wished to build a synagogue in the area. The erection of a partition screen on the site exacerbated those fears. In August 1929, the British authorities ordered that Zionists must remove any permanent structures at the wall. Not only did the Zionist leadership refuse to take down the screen, it organised a rally in the Muslim quarter of the Old City. Palestinians responded by marching to the wall on a number of occasions. One of those marches resulted in a riot. According to Edward Keith-Roach, then governor of Jerusalem, it was sparked by a 'violent address' made by a preacher during Friday prayers, who warned that Jews wished to 'turn us Arabs out of our country'. Attacks on Jewish shops and Jewish passers-by ensued. Fighting also broke out in Hebron, Jaffa and Safed. As the British felt they did not have enough troops to suppress the uprising, they called for reinforcements from Egypt. A total of 135 Jews were killed over a one-week period. The Palestinian death toll reached 116. By Keith-Roach's own admission, 'many of these casualties were caused by the rifle fire of the military and the police in suppressing the rioters.'[37]

Teaching a lesson

Once the riots were over, British forces began a series of raids on Palestinian villages. 'It is hoped that the numerous arrests of suspects and undesirables will not only teach the villagers concerned a lesson – but will also remove out of harm's way, some of the persons who are likely to cause trouble,' declared a 1929 note from the headquarters of British troops in Jerusalem. Collective fines would be imposed on villages implicated in the riots, the note added, with the expectation that such measures 'should have a steadying effect'. And 'the leading men of the various villagers' would be warned 'that they will be held personally responsible for any recurrence of the disorders.' Those who failed to cooperate would face 'severe punishment' for themselves and for their villages.[38]

The collective fines amounted to £14,000 for the Hebron area and more than £3,000 for Jerusalem. Making villages pay often proved impossible for 'reasons of economic distress', the British administration found. Faced with the likelihood that the full amounts would never be handed over, the administration recommended in 1935 that the 'outstanding balance' be cancelled.[39]

A dossier compiled by the Palestine Arab Congress in October 1929 claimed that many of the Palestinians arrested around that time were 'beaten and kept under custody for long periods without being examined.' Applications for bail were refused 'in spite of the fact that such refusal is not within the law and although no similar treatment was extended to Jews,' the dossier stated. A request by the congress that Norman Bentwich be removed from his post as Britain's attorney general in Palestine because of his Zionist bias was rejected. John Chancellor, Britain's high commissioner for Palestine at the time, agreed to meet representatives of the congress. Yet the congress was told that Bentwich would continue overseeing prosecutions 'in respect of all offenders in the recent disturbances.'[40]

Michael McDonnell, the British chief justice in Palestine, was more receptive to Palestinian concerns. After receiving a telegram from Palestinian notables, he alerted Chancellor to the objections raised against Bentwich. According to Chancellor's account of that discussion, McDonnell felt that so long as Bentwich retained his position 'the Arab section of the population would view the government with suspicion and would feel that the scales of justice were tilted against them.' Writing to the Colonial Office, Chancellor complained that the chief justice's '*démarche* in the matter adds another to the enormous number of difficulties that confront me here and in the circumstances I hardly think it was justified.' Chancellor argued that McDonnell and his wife were 'devout Catholics and like all the Latins in Palestine are strongly anti-Semitic'. Although he reported on hearsay (referring, for example, to a conversation, he had 'three days ago' with a French diplomat), that 'the Latins' were 'strongly pro-Arab and against the government in the present crisis,' Chancellor did not present proof that McDonnell was motivated by a hatred of Jews.[41] Furthermore, the accusation smacked of hypocrisy; Chancellor sometimes resorted to anti-Semitic stereotyping. In a November 1929 letter to Sidney Webb, then the colonial secretary, Chancellor commented on his discussions with Judah Magnes, head of the Hebrew University in Jerusalem, who had contended that Jews should have a 'mediating influence' on Palestinians. Chancellor wrote:

> Throughout their long history, there was no record so far as I was aware of the Jews constituting a uniting and peace-making element in any community of which they formed a part. On the contrary, they had always been a disturbing and disruptive element, socially and politically. The evidence of that was overwhelming. Russia was the most recent instance and among the Jews in Palestine there was a considerable element of revolutionary communist and Bolsheviks.[42]

Walter Shaw, a jurist, was appointed by Sidney Webb to lead an official inquiry into the 1929 riots. The Shaw Commission, as his team was known, had a narrow remit. Webb issued instructions that the probe was 'limited to the immediate emergency and will not extend to considerations of major policy.' Anxious to scotch rumours that Britain was becoming less committed to Zionism, Webb stated:

> I have thought it well to make it quite clear that the government has no idea of reconsidering the British tenure of the mandate for Palestine and has no intention of departing from the policy laid down in the Balfour Declaration of 1917, and embodied in the mandate, of facilitating the establishment in Palestine of a national home for the

Jews. It is, indeed, not contemplated that the position of Palestine will be altered in any way.[43]

Webb sounded a similar note in discussions with Weizmann. Shortly before the Shaw Commission's report was published, Webb told Weizmann that the 'only grave question it had revealed' related to Palestinian landlessness. Speaking of the need to 'stabilise conditions' and 'avoid unrest', Webb concurred that expelling Palestinians to neighbouring Transjordan 'might be a way out'. Drummond Shiels, parliamentary under-secretary for the colonies, opined around the same time that mass expulsion was 'desirable', according to Weizmann's records.[44]

The Shaw Commission concluded in 1930 that the 'outbreak was not premeditated' and did not constitute a revolt against British rule in Palestine. Still, the commission accepted that Palestinians had genuine grievances. Noting that there were 'large sales of land in consequence of which numbers of Arabs were evicted' between 1921 and 1929, the commission warned that 'a landless and discontented class is being created' and 'such a class is a potential danger to the country.' Palestinians were afraid that 'by Jewish immigration and land purchases they may be deprived of their livelihood and in time pass under the political domination of the Jews,' the commission added. Despite claiming that the British authorities 'did discharge to the best of their ability the difficult task of maintaining a neutral and impartial attitude between two peoples,' it found that British land laws had failed to shield Palestinians from dispossession.[45]

Guns for the colonies

Privately, the British authorities conceded that their attitude and policies were far from impartial. Following the riots, Webb called on H.L. Dowbiggin, inspector-general of British police in Ceylon, to advise about what 'security' measures should be introduced in Palestine. Dowbiggin recommended that there should be 650 British police stationed in Palestine. Of that figure, more than 100 mounted on horses and 'motor transport' would be provided for more than 400. 'The British police will chiefly be employed in patrolling Jewish colonies,' he urged. Whenever 'serious riots, organised and simultaneous attacks on Jewish colonies' occurred, the military should assist police in offering protection to the colonies.[46]

Dowbiggin recommended, too, the greater deployment of mounted police and that weapons be supplied in greater quantities than they had been until then to Zionist colonies. The only alternative to doing so, Dowbiggin felt, would be stationing British police in each of the 120 Zionist colonies then in Palestine. While the latter step was deemed too expensive by the authorities, Chancellor agreed that there should be a permanent presence of police in more than half of the colonies or nearby. Acting on Dowbiggin's advice, Chancellor proposed that the colonies be equipped with 'Greener guns – a short-range weapon which is not suited for offensive action' that would be kept in sealed armouries, under British supervision. Chancellor told Webb:

> I recognise that there are obvious objections on general grounds to an arrangement which in effect involves the arming of one section of the population against another section but the conditions in Palestine are unique. A new population is being introduced into the country whose presence by reason of their different manners and customs is resented by the indigenous population.[47]

If taken at face value, Chancellor's comments indicate that the British authorities were in denial about the true causes of Palestinian resentment. Whereas the Shaw Commission accepted that the settler-colonial agenda being pursued had resulted in evictions and landlessness of Palestinian peasants, Chancellor attributed the unrest to the 'different manners and customs' of Jewish settlers. He also contended that Britain had a 'duty' to 'ensure the life and property of these newcomers and to create among them a feeling of confidence in the adequacy of the measures taken for their protection.'[48] It should be borne in mind that arming one community against another was part of a larger package of support for the Zionist enterprise. At around the same time, Chancellor approved the financing of roads to serve some of the colonies, particularly those in remote areas.[49]

Chancellor was adamant that some of the Palestinians who participated in the 1929 riots be executed. He ordered that three executions be carried out in Acre Prison during June 1930. The bodies of the men 'shall not be handed over to their relatives but shall be buried in the prison precincts at government expense,' he stated. In a letter to Webb, he wrote:

> I was of the opinion that if the people of Palestine received the impression that they could commit murders during racial riots without putting themselves in danger of the extreme penalty of the law, the probability of the renewal of the outbreaks would be increased, I realised that to carry out death sentences might cause trouble immediately but, on the long view, I felt that it would tend to diminish the chances of serious troubles in the future.[50]

The British authorities effectively banned protests against executions. Palestinian notables were told that 'customary pious acts' may be organised 40 days after an execution but 'no processions, no assemblies and no speeches having political character will be permitted.' Chancellor declined to meet lawyers seeking clemency for men who had been sentenced to death.[51] He also tried to obstruct court appeals in capital punishment cases 'because it is apprehended that there is a desire to draw out proceedings, so as to make it more difficult in the end to execute any death sentences.'[52]

The relationship between Britain and the Zionist movement became strained when two official papers were published in October 1930. John Hope-Simpson, a former Liberal MP, was asked by Webb to examine some of the issues raised by the Shaw Commission – particularly on land management. His report was critical of the Jewish National Fund, the Zionist body tasked with ensuring that as much land as possible came under Jewish ownership. The 'stringent provisions' of leases signed by the JNF meant that Palestinians were 'deprived for ever from employment on that land,' he found. So long as indigenous Palestinians were forbidden from working in Zionist colonies, 'it cannot be regarded as desirable that large areas of land should be transferred to the Jewish National Fund,' he added.[53]

Although that finding left no doubt that Zionist colonisation was inimical to Palestinians, it was the second of the two documents that caused greater consternation among the Zionist movement. Often called the Passfield White Paper – Sidney Webb's title was Lord Passfield – that document tried to absolve Britain of responsibility for the 1929 riots. Britain had the duty for administering Palestine 'imposed' on it by a League of Nations' mandate, the paper claimed disingenuously. 'Many of the misunderstandings which have unhappily arisen on both sides' were attributed to a failure in appreciating how Britain had that 'duty' apparently thrust upon it.

The paper reiterated Britain's commitment to establishing a 'Jewish national home' but contended that Palestine had reached a 'critical moment in its development'. Noting that the Histadrut was insisting that Jewish employers only hire Jews, it implied that such discrimination had caused high levels of unemployment among Palestinians. For the Zionist lobby, its most contentious passages related to immigration. If 'immigration of Jews results in preventing the Arab population from obtaining the work necessary for its maintenance,' then the British administration was obliged to reduce or suspend that immigration, according to the paper. Curbs on immigration had already been implemented earlier that year and were deemed to be 'fully justified'.[54]

The white paper may have echoed the idea originally put forward by the Zionist movement that immigration should be in line with Palestine's 'absorptive capacity'. Yet by scolding organisations like the Histadrut that were central to the Zionist enterprise, it predictably drew a hostile response from Zionists and their sympathisers. Leopold Amery, a drafter of the Balfour Declaration, signed a joint letter to *The Times* with two other eminent politicians, Stanley Baldwin and Austen Chamberlain; they wrote:

> It is only too evident that the effect of the white paper upon public opinion in American Jewry and elsewhere is to create a feeling of distrust in that British good faith which is the most precious asset of our foreign imperial policy.[55]

Speaking in the House of Commons, David Lloyd George called the white paper 'a practical revocation' of the British Mandate. Lloyd George feigned outrage at how a British Labour government had upbraided the Histadrut, a trade union. 'Could anti-Semitism go further than that?' he said. Herbert Samuel, at that time deputy leader of the Liberal Party, used the same debate to urge the relocation of Palestinians. Based on a comment in the Hope-Simpson report, Samuel claimed that Arabs 'do migrate easily' and that neighbouring Transjordan was 'underpopulated'. After effectively making the case for ethnic cleansing, he said that implementing the white paper's recommendations would be 'a grave discouragement to the whole Zionist movement'.[56]

Protesting that the white paper had negated the Zionist project, Chaim Weizmann stepped down as president of the Jewish Agency and the World Zionist Organization. After years of fawning towards the British establishment, Weizmann vowed that the Jews he purported to represent would not forgive Britain for having 'fooled' them.[57] According to Weizmann, the change in Britain's outlook had been 'fundamental' and the commitment contained in the Balfour Declaration 'by implication disappears'. Zionists in the USA vented their anger, too. The American Jewish Congress issued a statement which described the white paper as a 'repudiation of the solemn pledge given by the British government to the Jewish people.'[58]

The angry reaction from prominent Zionists prompted a reversal by the British government. Ramsay MacDonald, the prime minister, wrote to Weizmann assuring him that the idea Britain had made 'injurious allegations against the Jewish people and Jewish labour unions' was 'expressly disavowed'. On the contrary, Britain wanted to give 'every encouragement' to the Histadrut, according to MacDonald. While MacDonald stated that Britain 'feels itself under an obligation' to help Palestinian peasants who may have been uprooted after the land they farmed passed into Jewish ownership, he stressed that Britain was not halting the additional acquisition of land by Jews. Similarly, he emphasised that Jewish immigration was not being stopped. And though he contended that Britain must address any unemployment caused to Arabs by discriminatory hiring policies, he wrote that 'the principle of preferential and indeed exclusive, employment of Jewish labour by Jewish organisations is a principle which the Jewish Agency are entitled to affirm.'[59]

Sufficiently mollified by McDonald's letter, Weizmann returned to the World Zionist Organization's presidency (though he was not re-elected at a 1931 congress).[60] He continued to be courted and feared by the British government. In 1931, the Colonial Office learned that Weizmann had seen a 'private letter' that Hope-Simpson enclosed with his report on Palestine. In the letter, Hope-Simpson had 'expressed his views more freely than was possible in a report intended for publication,' noted Samuel Wilson, the under-secretary of state for the colonies. The leak of this document to Weizmann had caused a 'practical inconvenience', Wilson added as the government wished to appoint a 'development commissioner' in Palestine and 'it has always been our view that the best man for the post would be Sir John Hope-Simpson himself.'[61] In May 1931, Wilson told a fellow civil servant:

> You know how we are placed and how tender we have to be to Zionist susceptibilities in these matters. Until a few weeks ago it was believed that Hope-Simpson's appointment would be acceptable to Weizmann, or at least that he would acquiesce in it with a reasonably good grace. Since the contents of the private letter became known to him, he has taken up a position of violent opposition to the appointment, with the result that we shall probably have to look elsewhere for our commissioner and are very unlikely to get anyone so well-qualified as Hope-Simpson.[62]

The British administration proved receptive to Weizmann's lobbying, though it was sceptical towards some of his recommendations. In March 1931, he discussed economic development with John Chancellor. Weizmann displayed particular interest in a railway link between Haifa and Baghdad. Suggesting that the Jewish National Fund could contribute £500,000 to that project, he recounted a conversation with Sidney Webb, during which the colonial secretary indicated a willingness to invest a roughly equivalent sum. A note, apparently handwritten by Webb, in the margins of a report on the meeting with Chancellor stated: 'I have no recollection of having said anything of the sort!' Yet when Weizmann spoke of a number of wealthy American Jews wishing to 'bring their money to Palestine', Chancellor responded enthusiastically. In a letter to the Colonial Office, Chancellor wrote:

> I told him that such immigrants would in my opinion be of great value to Palestine. There were now far too many Russian and Eastern European Jews in the country. They were an unstable element. An influx of American Jews would make the country better balanced and would promote the development of the country. I reminded him that such immigrants – owners of capital – were now free to enter the country under the law without the control of the government.[63]

Those remarks reveal much about the mindset of the British administrators. Rich colonisers from America were welcome, poorer Jews
from Russia were regarded with suspicion. Chancellor referred to
Palestinians in even more derogatory terms. Writing to Webb in
March 1931, he complained that the 'local Jewish press' in Palestine
was frequently referring to further riots being planned. Predictions
of trouble tended 'to put foolish ideas in the heads of ignorant and
excitable Arabs,' Chancellor wrote.

About six weeks later, Chancellor was in Paris, where he met
Edmond de Rothschild, a French banker who had funded some of
the first Zionist colonies in Palestine. When de Rothschild urged that
Arabs be forced to leave Palestine for Transjordan, Chancellor replied
that such drastic measures were 'out of the question'. Chancellor's
rationale appeared to be based on concerns about instability, rather than
any moral objections. 'The Transjordanians regarded the Palestinian
Arabs as foreigners and would not welcome them,' he said.

When de Rothschild spoke against the idea of having a legislative
council in Palestine, he was assured that any such body would be
subject to gerrymandering. Under the terms of the mandate, Britain
was required to establish 'representative institutions', Chancellor
informed him, and the League of Nations had already 'taken His
Majesty's government to task for having done nothing in the matter
before now.'[64] Chancellor's record of the meeting reads:

> He [de Rothschild] said that it would ruin the country to hand over
> the country to the Arabs. I told him that was not what was proposed.
> The Jewish and government members combined would be in a
> majority over the Arabs.[65]

An official summary – prepared for the League of Nations – of
Britain's activities in Palestine during 1931 celebrated the 'striking
progress' that had been achieved towards building the 'Jewish national
home'. In little more than a decade, the Jewish population had risen by
nearly 170 per cent – from 65,500 to more than 175,000.[66]

In the autumn of 1931, Arthur Wauchope replaced Chancellor as
high commissioner. At one of his first functions, Wauchope declared
himself an 'entire stranger to Palestine', though recalling he had
fought in Mesopotamia during the First World War.[67] Before long this

'entire stranger' felt he had learned enough about the political situation in Palestine to make decisions that would prove hugely detrimental to its indigenous inhabitants. Corresponding with the Colonial Office in 1933, Wauchope conveyed the impression that he had no choice than to accept Zionist colonisation, notwithstanding its social costs:

> It is an essential principle of the Zionist policy not only to acquire ownership but to ensure that all the work required on the land shall be performed by Jews as far as possible and, in the case of the official land-purchasing agency of the Zionist Organisation, namely the Jewish National Fund, by Jews only, and it follows, as the result of this policy, that when the land is purchased by Jews not only is the landlord changed but the tenants and practically all the wage-earning class are compelled to move also. The right of the Zionists to follow this policy cannot be called into question but it obviously creates a difficult problem in relation to the displaced Arab cultivator.[68]

'Down with the English'

As Palestinian dispossession worsened, calls to halt cooperation with the British authorities grew. New ordinances enabling the censorship of the Palestinian press were introduced in an attempt to prevent articles demanding a freeze on Zionist colonisation from being published.[69] In October 1933, the British banned a number of protests. Jamal Husseini, a leading member of the Arab Executive Committee, the organisation calling protests in Jerusalem, was told not to proceed with an 'illegal demonstration when legitimate means of expression were open' to his colleagues, Wauchope noted. Husseini was informed that the British would hold him and fellow members of the committee 'morally responsible if any of their innocent followers suffered hurt in defying the law at their instigation.'[70]

Commenting on one protest, Wauchope described 'the prominent part taken by women of good family' as 'a new and disquieting feature'. He recognised that there was much anger among Palestinians towards Britain. In a letter to Philip Cunliffe-Lister, then the colonial secretary, Wauchope observed:

> It is also noteworthy and symptomatic of a new orientation of Arab nationalism in Palestine that the cries of the demonstrators

were 'Down with the English' and 'Down with the colonisers'. Arab feeling in Palestine is definitely becoming anti-British and anti-government. Without the British government, the Arabs think, they would have nothing to fear from the Jews.[71]

Some of the prohibited protests did go ahead; some became riotous. British forces responded to unrest by opening fire. Twelve Palestinians were killed on 13 October in Jaffa. Exactly two weeks later, British forces killed another 26 Palestinians, also in Jaffa.[72]

A six-year-old boy, Said Judeh, was among the victims on the latter occasion. A British inquiry found that he was killed by a stray bullet while playing with other children. On the following day, ten-year-old Deeb Saleem was shot through the hip by British forces during riots in Haifa. According to Wauchope, 'it may be fairly presumed, having regard to his age, that he was not taking part in an unlawful assembly or riot when he was wounded.' Wauchope recommended that the British government should give £100 to Said's parents and £25 to those of Deeb. Paying 'compensation' in these cases would not 'confuse the issue of responsibility for the disturbances', he contended (Wauchope pinned the blame for the riots on Palestinian agitators). Nor would it 'diminish the prestige' of the British administration. Said and Deeb were not the only children to be shot.[73] Following the riots, Wauchope met Haj Amin al-Husseini, a political leader who had been appointed grand mufti of Jerusalem, by Herbert Samuel. The mufti, according to British archives, asked that payments be made to families of all those killed in the riots. A report of the meeting states that Wauchope 'expressed regret that boys of 12 or 14 had received bullet wounds.' Yet he declined to give any pledges on paying compensation. Said and Deeb were treated as exceptions because they were so young. The treasury was willing to approve Wauchope's request that their families receive 'ex gratis payments' as it felt there were 'special circumstances'. It was as if the British authorities felt that they were doing the parents a favour, rather than being under an obligation towards them.[74]

In other correspondence with Whitehall, Wauchope heaped praised on British forces who had fired on the crowds in Jaffa. Raymond Cafferata, a former member of the Auxiliaries during Ireland's war of independence, was singled out. Heading a contingent of 40 British foot police, Cafferata called on the crowd to disperse. When they failed to do what they were told, a baton charge was ordered, with Cafferata as one of those leading it. 'The charge was magnificently executed and was completely successful,' Wauchope wrote to Cunliffe-Lister.[75]

Wauchope appointed Harry Herbert Trusted, a senior legal officer in Palestine, and J.W. Murison, a judge, to undertake an enquiry into the 1933 riots. Their findings were something of a whitewash. The police, they stated, acted 'with forbearance and restraint' and the 'loyalty, personal courage and discretion of all ranks were very commendable.' Force was only used, they maintained, after attempts had been made to convince protesters to disperse. Pandering to prejudice, the two men concluded:

> It is clear that an Arab crowd in Palestine is mercurial and excitable and when excited dangerous. These disturbances were aimed against the [British] government and not against the Jews but in mixed centres such as the Old City of Jerusalem and Haifa and in Jaffa, owing to its proximity to Tel Aviv, the fear of any disturbances becoming religious and racial, with the possibility of a repetition of the events of 1929, must always be present in the mind of every police officer. In these circumstances, the police of all ranks are placed in a particularly difficult situation when disturbances occur in Palestine.[76]

Following the Jaffa riots, Wauchope consulted the Colonial Office about whether all protests should be banned or whether some should be permitted. On a visit to Jerusalem, John Maffey, the under-secretary of state for the colonies, discussed the issue with Wauchope. 'I said that I did not see how the government could go on bottling up forever the expression of feeling on the part of Arabs,' Maffey stated in December 1933. Maffey was in favour of 'allowing specified demonstrations' yet suggested that Wauchope was better informed of local considerations than he was. In a telegram, Cunliffe-Lister informed Wauchope that he was 'absolutely free' to take whatever decision he wished, safe in the knowledge that he would enjoy full support from Whitehall. The colonial secretary wrote:

> I doubt if anyone here would criticise prohibition of demonstrations. If there were such criticism, I should have no difficulty in defending

prohibition. No comment has been excited in England by the prohibition of all public meetings in Malta, where the action could not be defended on ground of risk to public security. There would, however, be serious criticism if demonstrations led to further rioting and casualties. It would then be said that an error of judgment had been committed in permitting meetings, which might reasonably have been expected to lead to disorder.[77]

Instead of addressing allegations of brutality against British-led forces, the authorities seemed more fixated on issues relating to their private lives. Roy Spicer, an inspector of police and prisons in Palestine, was 'very emphatic' on having the power to prevent officers from marrying, according to a Colonial Office file. 'Palestine is full of undesirable women, many European and Jewesses, who try to get young British police to marry them,' according to the file. 'The man loses all standing and value as a policeman.' Spicer apparently gave several 'impressive illustrations' to bolster his case. His demands elicited a debate about whether or not the restrictions he coveted would be illegal. Yet the case he made was persuasive enough to have a new clause added in 1935 to a police ordinance dating from nine years earlier. Under the new provision, police had to ask the inspector-general's permission before they could get married.[78]

Spicer was less successful with activities of a promotional nature. In 1934, he wrote to New Scotland Yard enquiring if a show could be arranged at the London Olympia featuring the camel corps of the British-led police force in Palestine. 'We can make our camels jump in half section and they really do jump,' Spicer enthused. A 'mounting and dismounting' drill was 'rather fascinating', he added, including the camels' 'roar when their heads are pulled back'. Spicer's idea did not get very far. A telegram from the British administration in Jerusalem declared that the vets advising it were 'strongly opposed' to transporting the camels in winter. Either their voyages would prove fatal or 'impair the ability of camels to perform,' the telegram stated.[79]

The concern about the welfare of animals might be touching – were it not for how the animals in question were being made to do cruel tricks for entertainment. The people living under British rule often fared even worse.

3
'We must shoot to kill'

It was 3am when the police arrived. After waking up entire families, officers insulted women in front of their husbands. Furniture and food were destroyed. Copies of the Quran were thrown on the floor and trampled under foot.

The complaints of this nocturnal raid in the Bab al-Huta neighbourhood of Jerusalem's Old City were relayed to the British administration in June 1936. Arthur Wauchope, the high commissioner for Palestine, received a number of *ulema* – Muslim scholars and preachers – to hear their grievances. Wauchope tried to downplay the misconduct by saying that 'human beings were not perfect and some human beings are less perfect than others.'

Such excuses were often trotted out in the second half of the 1930s. A mass revolt had erupted against British policies. Force was needed to suppress it, according to Wauchope, and 'when force is used it is very difficult to avoid regrettable incidents.'[1]

Privately, the British recognised the events between 1936 and 1939 for what they were: a rebellion. An internal report drawn up by the British military in February 1938 admitted that the uprising was 'directed deliberately against the government and against British authority.' Palestinians had been 'profoundly disturbed' by the 'enormous increase' in Zionist colonisation during the previous few years.[2] John Maffey, the under-secretary of state for the colonies, argued in a June 1936 note that 'these disturbances are not a "stunt" organised by a few Arab leaders.' Instead, they were:

the expression of a deep-seated and widespread fear among the Arabs of Palestine, who are fighting, as they believe, for the preservation, if not of their own lives and livelihood, then for the preservation of the lives and livelihood of their sons and daughters.[3]

Richard Peirse, air officer commanding with British troops in Palestine, wrote later that year of how the rebels 'were fighting what they believed to be a patriotic war in defence of their country against injustice and the threat of Jewish domination.'[4]

The British were careful not to use the term 'rebellion' in public. When that word appeared in a draft statement, Whitehall mandarins instructed that it be replaced with 'disorders'.[5] Rather than recognising that they were encountering resistance of an inherently political nature, the British portrayed that resistance as criminal.

Ted Swedenburg, an American anthropologist, spent part of the 1980s interviewing men who had participated in the revolt. He was struck by how, almost 50 years later, the men remained incensed by what they called the 'barrels' incident. In October 1935, Palestinian dockers were unloading barrels at Jaffa port when one broke open to reveal that it contained ammunition and guns. The weapons, it was soon discovered, were destined for Zionist militants. Britain's failure to carry out any arrests fuelled the perception that it was facilitating a trade in illicit arms to the Zionist movement.[6] The perception resembled the truth. Towards the end of 1939, Chaim Weizmann praised successive high commissioners for tacitly accepting that settlers may smuggle arms (Weizmann was then expressing alarm – in correspondence and meetings with the Foreign Office – about an apparent reversal of that 'policy').[7]

An estimated 150,000 Jews immigrated to Palestine between 1933 and 1935, large numbers of whom had fled Nazi Germany. Palestinians knew little about Adolf Hitler's rise to power and cannot be held in any way responsible for it. What they discerned, however, was that a pattern of discrimination had been established within Palestine. In his pamphlet on the revolt, the novelist and activist Ghassan Kanafani cited census data showing that the average Jewish worker received 145 per cent higher wages than his or her Palestinian counterpart. One-third of all agricultural land had been expropriated in the years leading to the revolt. With around 20,000 peasant families evicted because of Zionist colonisation by 1931, 'the Palestinian Arab rural society was being destroyed', Kanafani wrote.[8]

The British administration in Palestine institutionalised racism. Palestinians employed on public roadworks were paid little more than half what Jews got 'for equal output', Arthur Wauchope informed the

Colonial Office. He tried to explain the discrimination by claiming that 'the Jewish standard of living demands' higher payment, whereas Palestinians were 'thankful' for their lower wages.[9]

Historians generally concur that the revolt began with the attack on a convoy of trucks on the Nablus–Tulkarem road in April 1936. Two Jews died in that attack; two Palestinians were killed in reprisal soon afterwards. The attackers of the convoy may, according to some historians, have been followers of Sheikh Izz al-Din al-Qassam, who had tried to call an insurrection the previous November.[10] Al-Qassam died in a battle with British forces amid the forest of Yabad, near Jenin. By speaking out against Zionism and denouncing Arabs who sold land to Jewish settlers, he became deeply popular among aggrieved peasants and workers, as was demonstrated by the huge turnout at his funeral.[11]

As soon as the revolt began in 1936, Britain tried to blame a coterie of Palestinian notables for its outbreak. Haj Amin al-Husseini, the grand mufti of Jerusalem, soon became the focus of their ire, with one government telegram claiming he 'appears to be [the] evil genius of Palestine Arabs throughout recent troubles.'[12] That overlooked how the uprising was a grass-roots one. Wauchope admitted as much in private correspondence. Briefing the Colonial Office, he stressed 'how perturbed the Arabs are at present', adding: 'When people are thoroughly discontented, any such incidents increase their effects 100 fold.'[13]

Wauchope was hostile to al-Husseini, yet had a somewhat more nuanced view of the mufti than others in the British administration. Writing to Maffey in October 1936, Wauchope indicated there was a difference of opinion between him and John Dill, the newly appointed commander of British troops in Palestine, on whether the mufti should be deported. 'Children, savages and RAF intelligence officers love creating bogies,' Wauchope stated.

> They are now getting Dill and others to believe that the mufti created, organised and was solely responsible for keeping going the strike and disorders. The defects of the mufti's characters are alone sufficient to render this view absurd.[14]

The general strike to which Wauchope referred was formalised on 21 April 1936 by the Arab Higher Committee, headed by the mufti. Yet it had actually kicked off a few days earlier. In a message addressed to Wauchope, the committee stated that the strike was called in protest 'against the partiality shown by government from time to time in order to strengthen the Jewish elements in this country and to annihilate the Arab national existence.' The committee's three demands were: a halt to Jewish immigration; immediate legislation to prevent remaining Palestinian lands being acquired by Zionists; and 'the formation of a national and parliamentary government'.[15]

Wauchope refused to accept the demands unless the strike was halted. The archives nonetheless prove that he understood the grievances. 'I have admitted far more Jewish immigrants during the past four years than ever admitted before,' he stated in a 1936 telegram.[16] In a letter to William Ormsby-Gore, then colonial secretary, he stated:

> the subject that fills the minds of all Arabs today is the problem of immigration, the dread that in time to come they will become a subject race living on sufferance in Palestine, with the Jews dominant in every sphere, land, trade and political life.[17]

Wauchope authorised brutal measures against Palestinians, while expressing misgivings about those measures. Repression 'will not lessen, but will increase, Arab discontent and apprehension, which are at the root of the trouble,' he informed Ormsby-Gore in May 1936.[18] That same month, Wauchope invited a delegation of British businessmen living in Jerusalem to meet him. Managers of Barclays Bank, Ottoman Bank and the president of the city's chamber of commerce signed an appeal for 'immediate drastic action against the ringleaders, including several of the youths, whose present conduct we consider to be a danger to the future unless an example is made of them now.' If deportation was deemed 'too drastic', the businessmen recommended 'protective custody', a euphemism for detention without charge or trial.[19]

Their wishes came true. Wauchope received a telegram from the Colonial Office in June, informing him that questions would soon be asked in the House of Commons about 'what steps are being taken' to ensure 'reasonable conditions at Sarafand concentration camp'. Wauchope replied by calling Sarafand a 'healthy locality, where many British troops are stationed.'[20] That was something of an understatement: the village of Sarafand al-Amar hosted Britain's largest military base in the Middle East.

Noting that plans for the camp had been approved by an unnamed director of medical services, he wrote that 'electric light and adequate water supply have been installed.' Wauchope stated:

Internees receive free rations on the scale approved by the medical authorities but supplement rations at their own expense by cooked food from outside. Rations are cooked by convict labour. Permission has been granted to establish a canteen within the camp to meet any further needs and a tradesman calls daily to take orders. Use of tobacco is unrestricted and alcohol is allowed on prescription of a medical officer.[21]

He added:

Scavenging and cleaning of huts is carried out by convict labour and internees need do no work except keep their huts tidy. They have been allowed a radio and may send or receive letters subject to censorship. Introduction of newspapers and books has now been allowed and at least one visit a week from a friend or relative will be permitted to each internee subject to the presence of a police officer; among themselves they enjoy full freedom of intercourse, subject to orderly conduct; and facilities are given for daily exercise within the camp.[22]

The words 'concentration camp' appear repeatedly in British documents from that era. While those words have become synonymous with the Holocaust perpetrated by the Nazis, the British Empire had been resorting to the practice of 'concentrating' detainees in particular sites for quite a few decades before then. Indeed, the British founded the twentieth century's first concentration camps – during the Anglo-Boer War in South Africa.

Not all briefing material supplied to diplomats or government ministers was sugar-coated in the manner of Wauchope's reply. A 1937 paper drawn up for British representatives in Geneva informed its readers that in June 1936 the emergency regulations for Palestine had been altered. 'More severe penalties' had thereby been introduced for shooting at British soldiers or members of the police force or for illicit possession of arms. One result was that '466 agitators were confined for months in the concentration camp at Sarafand without trial.' Among them were the Arab Higher Committee's secretary, Auni Bey Abdel Hadi, and his successor Izzat Darwaza.[23]

The camp consisted of two sections. The 'original intention', according to Wauchope, was that one should be reserved for the 'urban and *effendi* [noble] class of inmates', the other 'for the villager and *fellah* [peasant] class.' That was 'abandoned', however, because 'all the internees disliked this idea.' Claiming that 'I myself was inclined to sympathise with this Arab feeling', Wauchope wrote that 'no distinction on social grounds is now recognised'. His comments were contained in a July 1936 letter to the Colonial Office, in which he enclosed a message of protest from George Mansour, a trade unionist who organised a hunger strike while he was detained in Sarafand. Wauchope admitted 'there are no water closets and bathrooms' in the second section of the camp but stated 'there are running water taps and earth latrines.'[24]

Large-scale detention of peasants and urban workers occurred throughout the revolt. In May 1939, Malcolm MacDonald, colonial secretary at the time, was asked a parliamentary question about 'how many concentration camps are established in Palestine.' MacDonald said 'there are 13 detention camps at present in existence in Palestine.' He was then asked for details about 'the number of people interned in concentration camps in Palestine, and how many of them are *fellaheen*.' MacDonald's reply was terse: 'The total number of persons at present under detention in Palestine is 4,816, of whom about 2,690 are *fellaheen*.'[25] The quashing of the revolt that year did not lead to any swift release of detainees. Harold MacMichael, Wauchope's successor as high commissioner, reported to the Colonial Office that on 9 December 1939, '1,154 Arabs and 63 Jews were detained in concentration camp.' It is not clear whether his use of the singular was deliberate.[26]

More comprehensive details of detention facilities can be found in a 1938 paper signed by Alan Saunders, then inspector-general of police and prisons in Palestine. Saunders reported that there were 'three jail labour companies' in the country. Prisoners at one of these camps – Nur Shams near the town of Tulkarem – were 'accommodated in corrugated iron huts surrounded by a double barbed wire fence' and 'employed on quarrying operations under the direction of technical experts of the Palestine Railways.'[27]

Another labour camp had been founded near Acre 'to separate adolescents and first offenders from other prisoners,' according to Saunders. Designed for 250 detainees, it had been 'enlarged considerably' to hold people arrested because of the revolt.[28] Located on the Mediterranean coast, Acre also hosted Palestine's central prison. At one point during the revolt, Ormsby-Gore told British officials in Jerusalem that 'I feel concerned at the serious overcrowding' in that prison. He was responding to a March 1937 note stating that 47 prisoners were being held in a single cell at Acre. When Ormsby-Gore enquired if 'it is not possible, by any means, to effect an immediate improvement in the situation', he was assured that the particular cell was '47 feet long, 25 feet wide and 18 feet high'. By May that year, the number confined to a single cell had been reduced to 43. Ormsby-Gore's query may not have been motivated by altruism; as one MP was showing an interest in conditions at Acre around the time, the Colonial Office seemed anxious to avoid negative publicity.[29]

More than 130 detainees at the Acre camp took part in what British administrators called 'a hunger strike and other acts of indiscipline' in 1938. When the authorities tried to move the hunger strike's reported instigator, Arab Bank manager Abdul Hamid Shuman, to Acre prison, he refused to be transferred. Following allegations that he was ill-treated, the British administration in Jerusalem admitted that 'a certain amount of violence was undoubtedly used'.[30]

Discretion to destroy

Britain's elite decided at an early stage in the revolt that Palestinians should be targeted *en masse*. On 7 May 1936, Wauchope sought 'general covering approval' from the Colonial Office for imposing collective punishment on cities and towns where acts of disobedience occurred. He promptly received the go-ahead and chose Nazareth, Safed and Beisan as the first three areas to be penalised.[31] Further 'emergency regulations' were issued in the following month. They allowed death sentences to be imposed for shooting at British forces, throwing bombs and 'in certain circumstances for interfering with communications, or with any aircraft, locomotive, vehicle, ship etc.'[32]

Much leeway was granted to the military. Troops were instructed of a 1,000-yard 'safety zone' to be observed when using 20-pound bombs in the vicinity of towns and villages. Yet the air ministry in London stated that the zone was 'merely intended as a guide to the policy to be adopted and not as a hard and fast limit which should be strictly adhered to.'[33] The ministry believed that 'the military authorities on the spot should be given a wide discretion and, if in their view, the best course would be to bomb the houses of criminals or their sympathisers, they should be at liberty to do so.'[34]

In a 1936 report, Richard Peirse stated that it was 'quickly evident' that measures should be taken 'against the villages from which the rebels and saboteurs came.' The rebels were forming themselves into armed bands, the size of which rapidly grew from between 15 and 20 men to 'large parties of 50–70,' he added. Discussions between Wauchope and the Colonial Office on the tactic of 'punitive demolitions' – destroying communities from which rebels hailed – caused 'some delay' in responding to the revolt, according to Peirse. But during June, the 'urgency now was of another order' because a number of property owners were seeking court orders to halt demolitions. Because Peirse was expecting that the judges would rule against the British administration, he decided to 'push on with the final phase' of a major wrecking operation 'as soon as possible'.[35]

The operation was conducted in Jaffa during June. Peirse's fears materialised: the destruction of several hundred houses was swiftly denounced by the judiciary. Richard Manning, a judge at the high court of Palestine, ruled on 3 July that the inhabitants of Jaffa's Old City had been 'grossly misled'. Rather than stating that the demolitions had been carried out for military reasons, the British administration tried to 'sugar the pill', Manning said, by claiming that its real objective was to improve the city.[36] Michael McDonnell, the chief justice of Palestine, similarly accused the administration of displaying a lack of moral courage. Those comments were resented by Wauchope, who told Ormsby-Gore they would be 'construed by Arabs as a direct encouragement to continue their struggle against a weak government and anyone with any knowledge of the Arab mind must realise that this will be the inevitable result of such an accusation.' Rebutting claims of deceit, Wauchope insisted that the building of new roads through the areas that had been cleared would 'prove of great value' to Jaffa.[37] The roads were constructed with the aid of convict labour.[38]

More than 6,000 people lived in the Old City at the time. The British administration's department of health was asked to find shelter for 417 people – or 66 families – left homeless by the demolition. The department arranged that they would live in schools.[39]

The dispossession had lasting effects. Later that year, Wauchope sent Ormsby-Gore some data on the demolitions. Around 280 houses or 473 units, 'say 500 families' had been affected, the paper stated. Of the roughly 6,000 residents, 1,000 had returned, while others had gone to Lydda. When the weather deteriorated towards the end of 1936, Wauchope ordered that 'sufficient huts to house 20 families' be moved from the concentration camp at Sarafand and erected on the outskirts of Jaffa. 'Unfortunately, however, the refugees declined to move into the new accommodation which had been provided for them,' Wauchope wrote. To his apparent surprise, the refugees 'preferred to remain in their semi-demolished rooms or crowd into undamaged houses, rather than move their effects to more comfortable quarters.'[40]

In September 1936, Wauchope noted the 'unweakened determination of the Arabs of Palestine during the past four months of resistance to our troops despite loss of 1,000 killed and wounded and economic distress.' That determination signalled 'what we must expect if we start on ruthless measures when necessarily the innocent cannot be separated from the guilty.'[41] Wauchope was slightly disingenuous in implying that the measures already employed had not been ruthless. He was nonetheless correct in foreseeing that they were about to become more extreme. Later that month, he warned a grouping of Arab political leaders that John Dill was about to arrive in Palestine, where the commander would 'undertake his task of repressing lawlessness and restoring order.' Wauchope said:

Whatever troops and whatever measures are necessary to suppress disorder, they will be used by General Dill, backed by the resources of the British Empire. I shall have no influence on his actions and you must be sure that His Majesty's government will continue military action till all resistance is ended.[42]

At the end of that month, Wauchope signed an order, which effectively provided for the imposition of martial law. The order was not put into effect at that time: following appeals to Palestinians by British-anointed royals in Iraq, Egypt, Transjordan and Saudi Arabia, the strike was called off in October.[43] The official response from London to the strike was typical: a commission was formed to investigate its causes; William Peel, the commission's chairman, had previously served as secretary of state for India. On Christmas Eve 1936, Wauchope wrote a letter to Ormsby-Gore that described the 'whole atmosphere' in Palestine as 'highly charged'. Wauchope predicted 'another outbreak of rebellion' if Peel's conclusions did not satisfy Palestinians, adding: 'Should rebellion occur, rebellion will be suppressed, if need be by severe measures such as will prevent any further rising for some years to come.'[44]

Published the following summer, the Peel recommendations were manifestly unjust. Peel backed the idea of partitioning Palestine into separate Jewish and Arab states. He put at 225,000 the number of Palestinians then living in the area designated for a Jewish state. Arguing that the existence of such minorities 'clearly constitutes the most serious hindrance to the successful operation of partition', Peel urged a transfer of population 'voluntary or otherwise'.[45] The proposed Jewish state included the Galilee, where 92 per cent of the population had been Arab in the early 1930s.[46]

Not surprisingly, the call for mass expulsion outraged Palestinians. As the revolt resumed, Britain declared the Arab Higher Committee and similar groups illegal. British forces were instructed to arrest Haj Amin al-Husseini but he managed to hide in the Haram al-Sharif compound of Jerusalem's Old City; later he fled for Beirut – by some accounts, disguised in women's clothing.[47]

Some of Wauchope's proposals for crushing the revolt were harsher than Whitehall was prepared to countenance. He recommended, for example, that forced labour should be introduced for 'all able-bodied male inhabitants between the ages of 16 and 60' in towns or villages that defaulted on collective fines levied by Britain. Cosmo Parkinson, who became under-secretary of state for the colonies in 1937, replied by assuring Wauchope he appreciated the difficulty of dealing with 'recalcitrant villages' but pointing out it 'would be too strong a measure to treat the International Labour Convention as a "scrap of paper".' As a compromise, the administration in Jerusalem suggested that a 'system of compulsory day and night patrols by elders or notables of a township or village would, in certain circumstances, yield useful results.'[48]

Wauchope and his successor MacMichael were not prevented, however, from running a police state. The strength of the British-led police force in Palestine rose from 2,500 officers in 1935 to 5,400 in 1939.[49] Two infantry divisions of the British Army – around 25,000 troops in total – were also deployed.[50] Distinctions between police and military were blurred during the revolt. With the authorities deeming the police to be overstretched because of urban riots, soldiers assumed such tasks as the staffing of rural police stations and patrolling busy streets in Jaffa and Jerusalem.[51]

Supposedly sacrosanct principles of British 'justice' such as the right to a fair trial were discarded, too. Ormsby-Gore informed members of Parliament in November 1937 that the 'notorious gang-leader' Farhan Essaid and three others had been arrested as troops surrounded a village near Jenin. 'These men will be tried by a military court,' Ormsby-Gore said, though he had – to all intents and purposes – already found them guilty.[52]

Malcolm MacDonald wrote to Harold MacMichael in 1938 that 'we must set our faces absolutely against the development of "Black and Tan" methods in Palestine.' Yet the British authorities were more interested in preserving what he called 'the good name' of police serving in Palestine than in preventing the kind of atrocities that the Black and Tans committed during Ireland's war of independence. When a plan was hatched to dismiss British police officers who had killed three men in a village near Tulkarem, Harold MacMichael backed it; his expressed desire was that the plan should be implemented 'without exciting comment'.[53]

The Royal Navy provided back-up to the infantry. In 1938, the *HMS Repulse* anchored at the port of Haifa. Its logbook recorded:

A small number of rounds are fired by day and night at registered points in the close vicinity of villages whose occupants are credited with pro-bandit tendencies. This is said to act as a deterrent to evil doers and causes despondency among the villagers who now realise that at any time during the day or night they can be subject to accurate fire if they are naughty.[54]

The logbook betrays how British troops came to view an entire people as criminal. It notes that the military called Palestinians 'oozlebarts'. That epithet derived from the word for gang, *ursabi*.[55] In preparation for the 'surprise withdrawal' of the *Repulse* from Haifa in August 1938, a brigadier decided on 'an extensive round-up of "oozlebarts",' the logbook states. Between 300 and 400 Arabs were 'collected from the villages near the northern frontier' and 'incarcerated in cages at Iqrit and Malikiya.' The purpose of the action was 'to tranquilize the country and to give the brigands something to think about for a few days.'[56]

To distinguish residents of Deir al-Quasi village from those living in Sumata, the former had red paint daubed on their necks. 'This caused considerable amusement among the onlookers and the other villagers but was not so well received by the men themselves,' according to the logbook. The British forces, meanwhile, alleged that around 40 per cent of all members belonging to one gang were held in a cage 'but so far, in spite of some rather brutal interrogation by the police we have not been able to find out who they are.'[57]

Bad villages

'Brutal interrogation' – torture, to be more precise – was approved at a high level. Edward Keith-Roach has admitted that 'Arab investigation centres' were set up. Their purpose was to train police officers 'in the gentle art of "third degree", for use on Arabs until they "spilled the beans",' Keith-Roach recalled in his memoirs.[58] The idea for those centres came from Charles Tegart, a Derry man who had headed the British police in India. Tegart was tasked with providing advice on how the revolt in Palestine should be handled. His best-known recommendations were that a large network of reinforced concrete police stations should be built across Palestine and a massive fence erected along the northern border.[59] While British firms were eager to benefit from the fence project, a key contract for its construction was awarded to the Zionist company Solel Boneh and arrangements were made to import barbed wire from Belgium. Harold MacMichael defended the decision to bypass normal tendering procedures by arguing that the project needed to be completed speedily and that it had 'few, if any, parallels in the modern history of colonial administration.'[60] Around

£2 million – a colossal sum for the 1930s – was spent on what became known as Tegart's fence.[61]

Tegart was something of an innovator when it came to surveillance and pacification. He recommended that the fence should include an electrified 'detector' system. He urged, too, that registers be compiled of 'villages with bad reputations'. Details of all male residents aged 17 to 50 would be collected for each 'bad village'. By contrast, rewards such as tax remissions would be granted to those villages that supplied useful information to the police. Replying to those recommendations, the British administration in Palestine stressed it was putting some of them into practice. Arthur Wauchope stated: 'Orders have already been issued for the compilation of village registers in villages known to be definitely hostile to government.'[62]

According to the British Army, Halhul, which is located north of Hebron was 'well known' as a 'bad village'. On 6 May 1939, troops invaded the village, rounding up 116 of its male inhabitants, while searching for weapons. Eight men died from heat exhaustion after being detained in an open-air pen. The army's official account of the incident attributed their deaths to 'a concatenation of unfortunate circumstances and errors of judgement'. The 'abnormally hot weather' was listed as the first cause of their deaths. The second cause listed was that the amount of food and water provided to the men was 'insufficient' for the several days during which they were held. The army's explanation then became slightly surreal. It claimed that a group of elderly men, who had been held in a house, were transferred to an enclosure reserved for 'bad' younger men on 11 May. The younger men had requested consultations with their elders about whether or not rifles should be surrendered. Most of the victims were elderly and were, in the army's words, 'unable to stand the strain which young fighting men could resist.'[63]

Based on military briefings, Harold MacMichael decided that 'these fatalities were not in any way due to deliberate ill-treatment nor can they be classified under the category of atrocities.'[64] By that time, MacMichael had formed a habit of exonerating British forces. When troops killed two children in Nablus during October 1938, MacMichael claimed a single bullet had been fired at a suspect, who was evading arrest. 'The bullet struck some iron railings and ricocheted in fragments which unfortunately struck and killed two children in the vicinity,' he told the Colonial Office. One month later, a British police constable shot dead Musa Shuman, a resident of Jerusalem's Beit Hanina neighbourhood. The Arab National League in New York protested that Shuman was a non-combatant; MacMichael alleged that the constable opened fire as Shuman was 'climbing out of a corn bin armed with a shotgun'. When five women complained that same month about atrocities committed by British forces in Jerusalem's Old City, MacMichael stated that 'a number of innocent persons, including four persons, were accidentally killed' during the operation in question. He then argued that 'there was an imperative need to reduce superfluous correspondence to the minimum' and most complaints of this nature 'merit no detailed reply'.[65]

Even Palestinians who had previously been on good terms with the authorities vented their fury at the conduct of British forces. Fuad Dajani, director of a hospital in Jaffa, had received an MBE from King George V for his services to medicine. In June 1939, he requested that his name be deleted from the award as a protest at how the police burst into his hospital and shot dead one of his patients, Khalil Ibrahim Abu Ikheil. William James Fitzgerald, then the attorney-general in Palestine, carried out an investigation into the incident. The police hierarchy told him 'the fact that the deceased tried to escape' was 'a good enough reason' to open fire. For his part, Fitzgerald accepted that it was all a 'deplorable mistake'.[66]

Less official documents indicate that extrajudicial executions became almost routine. 'Any Johnny Arab who is caught by us in suspicious circumstances is shot out of hand,' Sydney Burr, a police officer, wrote to his parents.[67] Other Palestinians were used as what the British called minesweepers.[68] Taken hostage by troops, these men were placed in vehicles leading convoys so that they would take the full impact of any roadside bombs planted by rebels. The minesweeper was ejected from the vehicle once a journey had been completed. The 'lucky' ones got away with a broken leg, the 'unlucky' ones would be hit by the next truck, with nobody bothering 'to go and pick the bits up,' Arthur Lane, who served in Palestine with the Manchester Regiment, has stated.[69]

One consequence of the revolt was that it copper-fastened the alliance between British imperialism and Zionism. Jewish colonists were recruited to the British police in significant numbers. The costs of increasing the force were shared between the British government and the Jewish Agency, as the Zionist administration in Palestine was known.[70] Among the tasks allocated to the Jewish police was to provide security at the huts and stores of the Sarafand concentration camp.[71]

The recruitment occurred despite how the authorities predicted it could bequeath a toxic legacy. In January 1937, Arthur Wauchope warned the Colonial Office: 'If Jewish units [of the police] are allowed to act offensively against Arabs in Palestine, I fear that the chances of the two people ever living together will vanish for generations.'[72]

Dirty war

Wauchope's advice that Jewish police should be restricted to work of a defensive nature was endorsed by the British government. The term 'defensive' was interpreted flexibly. His successor, Harold MacMichael, wrote in July 1938 that 250 armed Jews were protecting co-religionists involved in erecting 'Tegart's fence'. MacMichael informed the Colonial Office that he had also sanctioned a 'small column of Jews and British troops' to undertake 'ambush work' when it was deemed necessary.

That autumn, MacMichael noted that there were 745 Jews in the 'regular' British-led police force in Palestine and that a 'supernumerary police establishment' was being reorganised. Once that process was completed, there would be an additional 1,900 Jewish 'temporary additional police' paid by the British authorities, 350 supernumeraries ('paid by private concerns', according to MacMichael) and 3,000 unpaid 'special constables'. All of the roughly 6,000 Jewish police 'are provided with rifles by [the British] government,' MacMichael stated.

'Practically all' of the supernumerary police were drawn from the Haganah, which MacMichael called an 'extralegal, semi-secret "army" of the Jews.' Acknowledging that its leading figures included representatives of the Jewish Agency, the Haganah 'could probably muster some 50,000 trained men' and had thousands of guns 'concealed in all towns and colonies'. While much of its arsenal had been illegally acquired, the Haganah was conducting nightly patrols overseen by men with licensed weapons.[73]

Many of the Haganah's commanders were either mentored or influenced by the doctrine of a particular British soldier, Orde Wingate. A committed Christian Zionist, Wingate was tasked by the

British Army with training Jewish supernumeraries for ambush work and for patrolling the Iraq Petroleum Company's pipeline. Bringing oil from Iraq to a terminal in Haifa, this economically vital resource was frequently targeted by Palestinian rebels.[74]

Officially, Wingate was put in charge of 'special night squads', which, as their name suggested, worked under the cover of darkness. In his book *The Making of Israel's Army*, Yigal Allon wrote that these squads – which combined British and Zionist forces – were too small and too lightly armed to protect the pipeline:

> Wingate therefore cooperated illegally with similar Haganah units already in operation, often borrowing weapons from the Haganah arsenal to carry out raids and ambushes, mostly at night, over wide areas of the Galilee on both sides of the pipeline. In the morning the illegal unit generally disappeared, while the legal unit returned to its base.[75]

According to Allon, Wingate saw himself 'in practice as a member of the Haganah'. He liaised closely with Yitzhak Sadeh, a leading figure in the Haganah, who trained many of the commanders in the Zionist militia and, later, Israel's army. Together, they 'significantly modified' the Haganah's tactics, Allon has written. By teaching how to conduct raids against 'enemy bases' – code, it would appear, for Palestinian villages – 'they effectively pulled the Haganah out of its trenches and barbed wire into the open field, making it adopt a more active type of defence.'[76]

Wingate ordered acts of immense cruelty. After attacks against the pipeline occurred, his special night squads invaded nearby villages at dawn, rounding up all the male inhabitants. Forcing them to stand against the wall, the squads then whipped the men's bare backs. At times, Wingate would humiliate the villagers; at other times, he shot them dead.[77] Hugh Foot, who served as a British official in 1930s Palestine, has accused Wingate of wiping out 'opposition gangs by killing them all' and of getting involved in 'a dirty war of assassination and counter-assassination'.[78]

Yet despite having maverick traits, Wingate's tactics were applauded by the top brass. In one report, Robert Haining, then the commander of British troops, stated that Wingate – 'from my staff' – had 'shown great resource, enterprise and courage in leading and controlling' the special night squads. Haining added:

> These squads have been supplemented by Jewish supernumeraries who have done excellent work in combination with the British personnel. The story of the inception and gradual development of this form of activity, and its significant results, provide a great tribute to the initiative and ingenuity of all concerned.[79]

Wingate's brutality has been whitewashed by establishment figures. Norman Bentwich, a legal officer who drafted some of the most important laws introduced by the British administration in Palestine, included a eulogy to Wingate in his memoirs. Wingate inspired so much 'daring and devotion' among Jewish settlers that they referred to him 'by the Hebrew name, the Dear One,' Bentwich wrote.[80] *Britain's Moment in the Middle East*, a 1963 book by the civil servant-turned-historian Elizabeth Monroe, contains just one sentence about Wingate. Echoing state propaganda, she claims that 'life was rendered so insecure [during the revolt] that Orde Wingate and other British soldiers were detailed to train Jewish settlements in methods of self-defence.'[81]

The British public was kept in the dark about the revolt. Rather than holding the powerful to account, the BBC facilitated censorship of its content. At an early stage in the revolt, it informed the government of a planned radio programme that would feature interviews with a 'man in the street' from Palestine. At first the BBC offered to allow the Colonial Office vet the programme's script. Yet when one mandarin contended that the broadcast would definitely prove controversial, the corporation agreed to scrap the idea.[82]

The censorship became more stringent as the revolt continued. In 1939, the Foreign Office was perturbed at how newsreel depicting demolitions in Palestine was being shown in German and Italian cinemas, thereby 'creating an unfavourable impression'. Diplomats in Palestine were more relaxed; after examining the footage, they concluded it was probably shot a few years earlier. Because regulations had since been tightened, it would now be 'exceedingly difficult' for unauthorised filming of military actions to occur, noted William Battershill, chief secretary with the British administration in Jerusalem.[83]

The most famous British soldier to have taken part in quelling the revolt was almost certainly Bernard Montgomery; he would subsequently play what many strategists considered to be a decisive role in the Second World War. Montgomery took charge of the Eighth Infantry Division in Haifa towards the end of 1938. He promptly formed the opinion that Britain was 'at war with a rebel army which is 100 percent Arab.' His orders for confronting the enemy were unequivocal:

> They must be hunted down relentlessly; when engaged in battle with them we must shoot to kill. We must not be on the defensive and act only when attacked; we must take the offensive and impose our will on the rebels. The next few weeks, before the winter rains set in, is an opportunity and during them we may well smash the rebel movement given a little luck. We must put forward our maximum effort now and concentrate on killing armed rebels in battle; this is the surest way to end the war.[84]

Considering that the rebels drew their support largely from the peasantry, Montgomery had a curious recipe for getting the bulk of the Palestinian population 'on our side'. While he advocated that troops be 'scrupulously fair' towards peasants and town-dwellers, he wrote that 'if they assist the rebels in any way they must expect to be treated as rebels; and anyone who takes up arms against us will certainly lose his life.'[85]

Montgomery returned to England on sick leave in 1939. He availed of that period to jot down his thoughts on the revolt, sending handwritten notes to army chiefs. By July that year, he had concluded that 'the rebellion is now definitely and finally smashed; we have such a strong hold on the country that it is not possible for the rebellion to raise its head again on the scale we previously experienced.'[86]

The revolt was 'smashed' at an enormous human cost. About 5,000 Palestinians were killed, thousands more wounded. As Mazin Qumsiyeh points out in his book, *Popular Resistance in Palestine*, the casualties were higher on a per capita basis than those inflicted by Israel during the intifadas which erupted in 1987 and 2000.[87]

British representatives continued to excuse the tactics deployed during the revolt for years afterwards. Alan Cunningham, the final

British high commissioner in Palestine, wrote a memo about those tactics in 1947. Admitting that reliable data on the damage caused by Britain was hard to come by, Cunningham noted:

> It is commonly said that some 2,000 Arab buildings were demolished for punitive reasons between 1936 and 1940. These were for the most part small village dwellings of mud or rough stone of comparatively little pecuniary value.[88]

That crude reasoning did not impress all of the memo's recipients. One Cairo-based diplomat told the Foreign Office it would be best to keep the document 'among ourselves', rather than make it public in Arab countries. Many people would not appreciate the inference that 'it was justifiable to destroy the humble dwellings of the Arab peasants because they were of little value,' the diplomat stated.[89]

The diplomat need not have worried. Britain's elite kept mum about its atrocities in 1930s Palestine and how little value it placed on Palestinian property or lives. The silence was set to continue, at least in the West. While today's Palestinians are acutely aware of Britain's brutality during the 1930s, the same cannot be said of the British population. In his book *The Blood Never Dried*, John Newsinger describes the British response to the revolt as 'one of the most shameful episodes in the history of the empire'. It is 'astonishing', he adds, 'how little it figures in British history books'.[90]

Britain's conduct was indeed shameful. But is the omission from the official narrative astonishing? The ignorance surrounding the revolt seems to be a logical consequence of state policies. Using concepts like 'collective punishment', Britain was able to criminalise an entire people and their struggle for survival. By doing so, it could conceal how the era's worst crimes were committed by Britain itself.

4

Sowing the seeds of
ethnic cleansing

Chaim Weizmann's attempts to cajole the British authorities lasted for several decades.

From Rehovot, a settlement in Palestine that became his home, he contacted William Ormsby-Gore early in 1938. Long a Zionist sympathiser, Ormsby-Gore had by then become colonial secretary. With that pedigree, he knew more of the relationship between Britain and the Zionist movement than 'any other living British statesman,' according to Weizmann.

The 'Jew knows what the friendship of Great Britain means' and 'would like an opportunity of showing his gratitude and attachment to the only free and fair country in this terrible world,' Weizmann wrote. A 'viable Jewish state would offer opportunity for valuable cooperation between the two peoples.'[1]

Not all British diplomats were impressed by his appeals. A note scrawled in a Foreign Office document from a few months later claimed that 'Dr Weizmann is becoming apocalyptic'. The observation had been prompted by a letter, in which Weizmann urged the 'speedy establishment' of a Jewish state. Addressed to Edward Wood, the foreign secretary who held the title Viscount Halifax, Weizmann's letter argued:

So soon as a state is set up, I am confident that there will be peace with the Arabs, and with the surrounding Arab countries, all of whom are heartily sick of the present state of affairs, and many of whom know their best interests to be bound up with the interests of Britain. The interests of such a Jewish state will be in every way identical to those of the British Empire.[2]

Weizmann asserted that 'the Jews have never given up the thought of the return to Palestine'. Hopes of a return had 'survived the destruction' of two temples, he argued. 'Under British aegis, we have engaged in building the third.'[3]

Most British officials dealing with Palestine were more focused on policy than prophecy. They were striving to achieve an uneasy balance. While resorting to great force in suppressing the Palestinian revolt between 1936 and 1939, they nonetheless felt compelled to address some of the grievances behind that insurrection. To achieve a modicum of stability, they felt, it was necessary to be less accommodating towards Zionist demands and more understanding of Palestinian fears than they had been so far.

As part of those efforts, the British government called a conference in St James' Palace, London, in 1939. The Zionist delegation to the event included both Weizmann and David Ben-Gurion; the Palestinian grouping included Jamal Husseini, a prominent figure in the Arab Higher Committee. The delegations did not formally negotiate with each other and, not surprisingly, the conference ended without an agreement. Following that fiasco, the British issued yet another white paper. It sought to clarify some matters which the government, perhaps dishonestly, presented as misunderstandings. For example, it declared that Britain had never planned to transform Palestine into a Jewish state. Rather, it proposed that an independent state would be formed within a decade, in which 'Arabs and Jews share government in such a way as to ensure that the essential interests of each community are safeguarded'. The paper nonetheless rejected Palestinian demands that Zionist colonisation should stop. It set the objective of having Jews comprise one-third of Palestine's population in five years' time. To reach that goal, 75,000 settlers would be admitted within that period.[4]

Leading Zionists reacted with fury to the paper. Breaking his habit of flattering the British government, Weizmann accused it of imposing a 'death sentence on the Jewish people'. Ben-Gurion described its contents as 'the greatest betrayal perpetrated by the government of a civilized people in our generation'.[5]

Soon, Ben-Gurion was to side with the nation he depicted as treacherous. A few months after the white paper was published, the Second World War broke out. Ben-Gurion tried to offer clarity about how Zionists should respond. 'We will fight with the British against

Hitler as if there were no white paper,' he said. 'We will fight the white paper as if there were no war.'[6]

The British authorities displayed some determination to implement the white paper. That stance caused much friction between them and the Zionist movement. Palestine was portrayed by leading Zionists as the only possible sanctuary for Europe's Jews, even though Chaim Weizmann admitted in private correspondence that many Holocaust victims did not aspire to live in Palestine.[7] Zionist propaganda was boosted by Britain's refusal to allow boats carrying Holocaust refugees from docking in Palestine. One ship, the *Exodus*, would assume an iconic status.

The Holocaust must never be trivialised; its victims must never be traduced. The response of the world's then most powerful nations to it was callous. Six million Jews were killed by the Nazis; hundreds of thousands were in need of protection by the time the war was over. Yet only 25,000 Jews were admitted into the USA between 1945 and 1947.[8]

Against that traumatic backdrop, the Zionist movement proposed that the best way to rescue Europe's Jews was to provide them with a safe haven in Palestine. Some supporters of that goal felt it should be attained through the removal of indigenous Palestinians. One of Britain's largest political parties endorsed the Zionist blueprint. At its 1944 annual conference, Labour approved a statement declaring that there was 'an irresistible case now, after the unspeakable atrocities of the cold and calculated German Nazi plan to kill all the Jews in Europe' to enable Jews enter Palestine in 'such numbers as to become a majority' if they wished. 'Let the Arabs be encouraged to move out as the Jews move in,' the statement added.[9]

Edward Norman, a New York-based financier, raised Labour's call with US President Harry Truman in 1945. Ensuring that the Labour plan had 'tangible value' depended on naming the country to where Palestinians could be moved, according to Norman. He favoured Iraq for that purpose, writing there would be 'no practical (as distinguished from political) difficulties' in the 'resettling of some 750,000 Palestinian Arab peasants' there.[10]

A strained alliance

Britain's alliance with Zionism became strained in the 1940s. Frustrated that the state they coveted had not yet come into being, many Zionists started to perceive Britain as the enemy. Two groupings, the Irgun and Lehi, decided to try and drive the British out of Palestine.

Their tactics were denounced by some of Zionism's most ardent backers. In November 1944, Walter Guinness, a minister of state in the Middle East, was assassinated by the Lehi in Cairo. Winston Churchill, then prime minister, expressed a sense of both revulsion and disappointment at the killing of Guinness, part of the famous brewing dynasty. Churchill said:

> If our dreams of Zionism are to end in the smoke of assassins' pistols and produce a new set of gangsters, many will have to reconsider the position we have maintained. These wicked activities must cease and those responsible rooted out.[11]

Following the Second World War, Britain broached the idea of assuming joint responsibility for Palestine with the USA. The Anglo-American committee of inquiry that resulted tried to appear even-handed and compassionate. In truth, it tried to relieve the world's most powerful nations of responsibility for providing shelter and succour to Holocaust victims. Published in April 1946, its report recommended that 100,000 survivors of Nazi and Fascist persecution should be allowed into Palestine 'as rapidly as conditions will permit'. Palestine was described as the only country to which the great majority of Jews languishing in Austrian or German refugee camps could go. 'Most of them have cogent reasons for wishing to leave Europe,' it stated. 'Many are the sole survivors of their families and few have any ties binding them to the countries in which they used to live.'[12]

The report echoed the claims previously made by the British authorities that a 'Jewish national home' was not a euphemism for a Jewish state. The 'Jewish national home', it contended, was 'today a reality established under international guarantee' and had a 'right to continued existence, protection and development'. Yet it warned that Palestine must not become either a Jewish or Arab state, in which a majority would 'control' a minority. To avoid civil strife, the committee urged that Palestine be placed under a UN trusteeship. The mandate system would, however, be preserved until the implementation of a trusteeship agreement.[13]

Clement Attlee, who succeeded Churchill as prime minister when Labour won the 1945 election, stipulated that two conditions would have to be fulfilled for 100,000 more Jews to enter Palestine. First, the Zionist 'private armies' there would have to be disbanded. Second, the USA would have to provide both financial and military assistance towards implementing the report's recommendations. Neither of the conditions were fulfilled and the 1939 white paper continued to form the basis of British policy.[14]

Zionist violence worsened. In July 1946, the Irgun bombed offices used by the British administration in Jerusalem's King David Hotel. A total of 91 people were killed.

Two days later, the British cabinet endorsed a plan that openly advocated putting the most fertile parts of Palestine under Zionist control. Drafted by Herbert Morrison, Britain's deputy prime minister and a Labour grandee, and the US diplomat Henry Grady, the blueprint urged that separate Jewish and Arab cantons should be demarcated.

Morrison and Grady acknowledged that some degree of 'compulsion' would probably be required to implement the plan. That was an understatement. The proposed Jewish canton would have an overall population of about 750,000. Of that number, 300,000 would be Arabs. Paying lip service to respect for the rights of that sizeable minority, the report was fuzzy on how Arabs in the canton could enjoy proper protection. It was more open, however, about how the Jewish area – comprising the Eastern Galilee, Haifa, the Jezreel Valley and Beisan – would have 'superior' land to the Arab canton. The plan was ultimately shelved.[15]

By 1946, Bernard Montgomery had risen in the British Army's hierarchy to become chief of imperial general staff. Late that year, he complained that the 'policy of appeasement' which Britain had recently adopted towards the Zionist movement had failed. He asked that the government in London order the administration in Palestine to use large-scale force against the Zionist private armies. Though the authorities were receptive to similar advice made by Montgomery when suppressing the Palestinian revolt a decade earlier, they overruled him on this occasion. Alan Cunningham – the latest, and as it turned out, final in a series of high commissioners to Palestine – felt that the retaliatory measures sought by Montgomery amounted to collective punishment. Although it was widely believed that the Jewish

Agency had directed and approved acts of violence against Britain, Cunningham resisted pressure from the British Army to declare war on the agency.

Cunningham described Palestinian complaints of Britain's lax attitude towards Zionist aggression as 'specious'. The character of the unrest Britain faced at that time was 'quite different' to that of the 1930s. In the earlier decade, Britain's opponents were 'rural guerillas'. Now it was dealing with 'a few thousand well-trained saboteurs, buried in the heart of a highly civilised urban population.' In a 1947 telegram to the Colonial Office, he wrote that 'methods to be used in one case will not always suit in the other, quite apart from the ethics of the question.' Making plain his sympathy for Zionism, he added: 'I must again stress that, through the mandate, His Majesty's government have an obligation to Jews, and this problem cannot be viewed solely through Arab eyes, certainly not by me.'[16]

The British authorities continued to treat Palestinians in a paternalistic manner. Another conference ostensibly aimed at finding a solution to Palestine's problems was held in London during 1947. Faced with objections to British support for Zionism, Arthur Creech-Jones, then the colonial secretary, effectively told Palestinian participants to ignore the dispossession and displacement of their people. Instead, he asked them to:

> recognise that as a result of the influx of Jewish capital, the whole economic outlook of Palestine has changed, with the result that communication had been developed, marshes had been drained and the field of employment for Arabs had been extended and their standard of living raised.[17]

Creech-Jones dismissed calls to disarm the Zionist private armies. Doing so would necessitate a major military operation and the government 'could not tolerate the indefinite employment of British forces on such a task,' he stated.[18]

'Corpse city'

Britain's grip over Palestine became untenable as the 1940s wore on. Although it still wished to preserve military bases in the region, the

British elite had to face some hard facts. An empire that had straddled several continents was unravelling.

In 1947, Britain asked the United Nations for guidance. According to Creech-Jones, Britain was not seeking to surrender its mandate for Palestine but was willing to discuss amending the mandate's terms.

Matters came to a head in September that year. On the recommendation of a 'special committee' formed to study options for Palestine's future, the United Nations general assembly voted that the country should be broken up. Separate Jewish and Arab states would be established, with Jerusalem declared as an international city. Britain responded by announcing that it would leave Palestine the following May.[19]

By the time they had decided to quit, the British had already created the conditions necessary for the ethnic cleansing of Palestine. As they prepared to leave, the British authorities displayed a nonchalant attitude towards the continued acquisition of arms by Zionist forces. When a question was asked in Parliament during February 1948 about how a fund had been opened by a 'Jewish welfare committee' in Shoreditch to buy weapons for use in Palestine, the government tried to dodge the issue. The government replied that it had 'no power, under the law as it stands, to prevent the remittance of money through normal banking channels to Palestine or any other scheduled territory'. That was despite how dossiers relating to Zionist forces were filed under the heading 'terrorist activity' by the Foreign Office.[20]

The following month, a note marked 'top secret' was drawn up by the British Army's headquarters in Palestine. Military commanders, it stated, faced a 'difficult problem striking a balance' between the need to take action when disorder occurred and 'the need to refrain from any action that is likely to create increased anti-British hostility among either community.' Action should only be taken in situations that involved a 'direct embarrassment to British security or communications.'[21]

Also in March, Cunningham told British diplomats that 'Jewish attacks on Arabs after our withdrawal are unlikely except as reprisals for attacks on Jews or Jewish property by Arabs.'[22] As it happened, unprovoked Zionist attacks started before Britain's departure. In April 1948, Zionist forces carried out a massacre in Deir Yassin, a village neighbouring Jerusalem. By some estimates, around 250 people were killed. Many of the victims were raped and mutilated. Although the Irgun and Lehi committed the atrocities, the attack had the backing of the Haganah.[23]

Briefing the Colonial Office a few days after the attack, Cunningham noted that the British authorities had not yet been able to visit Deir Yassin. A police officer sent there had been blocked by the Haganah. Cunningham had nonetheless heard that a Red Cross representative had been in the village and in 'one cave he saw the heaped bodies of some 150 Arab men, women and children, whilst in a well a further 50 bodies were found.'[24]

He added:

Arab allegations of Jewish atrocities such as the lining up and shooting with automatic weapons of unarmed men, women and children now seem to contain some truth. [The] Jewish Agency has claimed that [the] attack was organised and perpetrated by members of dissident groups and has issued the usual notices of condemnation, which, however, deceive nobody, especially as dissidents themselves claim that [the] Haganah let them pass through to the attack.[25]

Despite acknowledging that a 'deliberate mass murder of innocent inhabitants' had occurred, Cunningham sought to defend Britain's unwillingness to protect civilians. The British forces were 'not in a position to take action in the matter owing to their falling strength and increasing commitments.'[26]

Though not the largest massacre that Zionist forces carried out during that period, Deir Yassin is remembered as a pivotal event in the ethnic cleansing that led to Israel's formation. Palestinians refer to that ethnic cleansing as the *Nakba*, the Arabic word for catastrophe.

The inference that Britain was too weak to thwart massacres is disputable. Britain had 100,000 troops in Palestine, as well as a police force, when the *Nakba* began.[27] The Haganah, in contrast, had about 50,000 members; yet the actual number of active Zionist fighters may have been half that figure.[28] While Britain had planned to evacuate its troops from Palestine during 1948, it still had a considerable military presence in the country at the time of the Deir Yassin atrocities.

Ilan Pappe, the Israeli historian, has accused Britain of playing a 'truly diabolical role' while the *Nakba* was underway. Britain was capable of frustrating Zionist plans when it wished to. Later in April 1948, British troops stepped in to save much of Sheikh Jarrah, a neighbourhood near Jerusalem's Old City where some of the wealthier Palestinian families lived, from destruction by the Haganah. That intervention was an exception.[29] More than likely, it was prompted by an assessment from the British Army that the area's proximity to the main road to the north made it a vital exit route for troops.[30]

Focused on leaving Palestine, the British reneged on their obligation to protect civilians. On 20 April 1948, Cyril Marriott, the British consul-general in Haifa, informed Whitehall that a Zionist attack on the city was expected 'in the next day or so'. Based on intelligence received from Hugh Stockwell, a military commander, Marriott proposed that Britain's objective should be 'to safeguard the route and installations which will be essential for the safe evacuation of our forces and let Jews and Arabs fight it out in other parts of the town.'[31]

Marriott advised against stepping in to prevent bloodshed. Doing so would 'certainly embitter and possibly provoke both sides against us.' Bitterness would then 'spread throughout the country and seriously endanger the final withdrawal from all parts.' Marriott predicted that 'we are not likely to suffer any serious loss of prestige in the world' by sitting back 'and that any loss of prestige we may suffer is insignificant compared with strong feeling that will be aroused in the United Kingdom if heavy British casualties are caused by our armed intervention between Jews and Arabs.'[32]

Haifa had around 65,000 Palestinian inhabitants – and a similar number of Jews – before the attack. Stockwell was nonetheless conscious that the UN's 'special committee' had proposed including Haifa within a Jewish state. The general had, according to Israeli historian Benny Morris, intimated that he wanted Haifa to come under Zionist jurisdiction as a 'clean city' – a euphemism for a city purged of Palestinians.[33]

Yet Stockwell was equally aware that Britain had obligations to discharge until the moment its rule in Palestine ended. In March 1948, he sent a memo titled 'evacuation from Palestine' to the British Army's headquarters in the country. 'I consider the maintenance of law and order in the Haifa enclave to be of paramount importance, to enable the final evacuation to be completed without hindrance, and to uphold British prestige,' he wrote. He proceeded to list the tasks he had given British troops 'in order of priority'. First was keeping the Haifa port 'open and working'. Next came the tasks of keeping the railway working, protecting the oil pipeline and ensuring that 'Jewish and Arab labour' continued servicing the area's military and economic infrastructure. The task of 'keeping the peace between Jew and Arab throughout this area' came last on his list of priorities.[34]

The message that Zionists and Arab forces should be left to 'fight it out' overlooked the disparity in their capabilities. Walid Khalidi has cited estimates that the Arab garrison then in Haifa consisted of around 450 volunteers. The Haganah, by contrast, had set up the 2,000-strong Carmeli Brigade in Haifa. Whereas the Arab volunteers were armed with rifles dating from the First World War, the Carmeli Brigade had a copious supply of machine guns, grenades, mortars and tanks. The Haganah also dropped converted oil barrels filled with explosives on the neighbourhoods where Palestinians lived.[35]

Stockwell and Marriott held discussions with representatives of the Histadrut and Jewish Agency during April 1948. By Stockwell's own admission, the representatives told him they felt it was necessary for the Haganah to 'mount a major offensive' in the port area of Haifa. Stockwell subsequently told both Zionist and Palestinian representatives that 'clashes' should cease in order to maintain peace in Haifa. 'It was not my intention to estrange either community by getting involved in these clashes,' he stated. That message was conveyed on 21 April; the 'major offensive' of which he was warned occurred in the early hours of the following day. By dawn, Zionist forces were in control of 'a large portion' of Haifa, Stockwell reported.[36] He refused to allow Arab reinforcements to advance towards the town, claiming that he wished to avoid incidents in which many non-combatants would be killed and maimed.

A British Army assessment of the situation in Haifa undertaken a few days later described the attack as the first 'really large-scale Haganah offensive'. The 'predominant emotion' among Zionists was 'astonishment at the sudden withdrawal of British forces,' the note added.[37] Britain had limited itself to 'firing at the mortars' coming from Zionist forces on Mount Carmel and 'controlling the panicky crowds,' a separate army report noted. The 'panicky crowds' were Palestinians who had gathered at the gate of Haifa port and had come under mortar and machine gun fire.[38]

Stockwell instructed Palestinian notables to accept the Haganah's conditions for a ceasefire. They included the full handover of all Arab weapons, the imposition of a curfew on Arab quarters and the assembly of 'all foreign Arab males' at a place designated by the Haganah, followed by their expulsion 'under military control'. Arab weapons would initially be collected by the British Army but would be handed over to the Haganah when the British Mandate expired on 15 May that year.[39]

The Haifa-based Arab National Committee first protested that the terms of the truce offer were unfair. Running out of options, they then requested the evacuation of the Palestinian community in Haifa. The committee's letter to the British authorities emphasised that the request was prompted by Stockwell's 'refusal to take any action to protect the lives and properties of those residents.' Even as the evacuation took place, the Haganah fired on ambulances, ransacked a hospital and looted Palestinian homes. No action was taken by British troops. Writing another letter to Stockwell, the Arab National Committee complained that many families had been 'deprived of all their belongings save the clothes which they now wear.'[40]

The British authorities contended that Haifa's Palestinians caused their own suffering. Military commanders told the defence ministry in London that Arabs had been 'generally provocative' in Haifa. 'Armed men, including Iraqis' had infiltrated the city; Arabs had 'also attempted to interfere with the communications into and out of Haifa.' The same report alleged that the Arab forces were 'concerned with driving or starving the Jews out of as much land and property as possible, whereas the Jews have a defensive object, to keep as much as possible of what they already hold.'[41] The civil administration displayed a comparable bias. Cunningham alleged that Syrians who had sent 'armed bands into Palestine deliberately in defiance of our advice' had 'done their best to prevent any semblance of law and order' and 'in Haifa, they have now succeeded to their own considerable embarrassment and ours.'[42] A markedly different tone was struck when British representatives discussed Zionist conduct. Marriott praised Zionist forces in Haifa for the 'moderation of their truce terms' and 'their magnanimity in victory.'[43]

A few days before the British Mandate expired, the evacuation of Palestinians was raised in Westminster. Emmanuel Shinwell, the war secretary, said that 'no detailed orders were issued regarding the organisation and protection of refugees.' He added: 'All possible assistance was, however, given to the civil population by our troops while carrying out their normal duties in the maintenance of law and order.'[44]

His comments were jesuitical. Far from assisting Palestinian civilians, the British had reneged on their responsibilities. Cyril Marriott admitted as much in a 10 May dispatch to the Foreign Office. He wrote:

> I am now convinced that the civil administration has, for at least two months, been more interested in the liquidation of their own private affairs and with the detail of winding up their own offices than with the maintenance of law and order.[45]

Marriott was kinder in his assessment of the military. He praised Stockwell for keeping 'casualties to our forces to a minimum' and expressed understanding of how the general avoided measures that would jeopardise their evacuation. Put simply, this meant that protecting its troops was a higher priority for Britain than stopping crimes against humanity.[46]

David Ben-Gurion understood the significance of what happened in Haifa. Visiting it after the evacuation of its Palestinian residents, he described Haifa as a 'corpse city' and as 'a horrifying and fantastic sight'. Predicting 'great changes in the composition of the population' in Palestine, he wrote in his diary that 'what happened in Haifa can happen in other parts of the country if we hold out.'[47]

On 15 May, the final day of formal British rule in Palestine, Marriott noted that the number of Palestinians in Haifa had fallen to around 3,000. His telegram to the Foreign Office added:

> Jews control the town but their armed forces are little in evidence. They obviously want the Arab labour force to return and are doing their best to instil confidence. Life in town is almost normal, even last night, except of course for the absence of Arabs. I see no reason why Palestine Arab residents of Haifa and [the] neighbourhood should not return and my inclination, with which [the] army agree, is not to put the consulate general under strong guard in what amounts to

a fortress but to give the impression that things are and will remain normal by seeking permanent offices in the business quarter.[48]

Alan Cunningham gave a comparably sanguine assessment earlier that month. The high commissioner cited a higher estimate of 6,000 for the number of Palestinians still in Haifa and claimed 'many more are returning'. The safety of those wishing to come home would be assured and 'there is every reason to think that after 15 May they will be safe there,' he briefed Arthur Creech-Jones.[49]

Not every diplomat was so positive. The British embassy in Beirut reported that criticism of the army's conduct in Haifa by the Arab press had been 'bitter'. Britain was accused of breaking its promise to keep law and order, stopping Arab reinforcements from reaching Haifa and of not intervening to halt bloodshed. 'The British version of events and particularly [the] statement that Arabs themselves by provocation were responsible for the situation has been badly received,' wrote William Houstoun-Boswall, the British envoy to Lebanon.[50]

Henry Mack, the British ambassador in Baghdad, reported that the army's retreat from Palestine had caused 'astonishment' in Iraq. 'It was expected that the withdrawal would proceed from the interior to the coast, thus leaving Haifa the last place to be evacuated,' he noted. 'In fact, British forces withdrew from Haifa and thus made possible the painful events there.' Mack assured the Foreign Office that Arab rulers in the region had been 'frequently reminded' of how Britain would remain in charge of Palestine until 15 May. The rulers had been asked 'to refrain from any action that might cause embarrassment' to Britain before then. Iraq was among the governments willing to cooperate with that request, he added, but only on the assumption that Britain would actually protect Palestinians from Zionist aggression.[51]

Carving up Palestine

Feigning impartiality, the British were determined that Palestine would be carved up in a way that would allow them to retain a considerable degree of influence. To advance that goal, Britain turned to Abdullah, its royal client in Transjordan. Granted a notional independence following the Second World War, Transjordan was still in Britain's grip. Under the terms of a 1946 treaty, Britain was given 25 years in which it could use Transjordan as a military base.[52]

In October 1947, Alec Kirkbride, the top British diplomat in Amman, sent a telegram to Ernest Bevin, contending that:

> Transjordan should not be penalised for being an ally of Great Britain if, as may well be the case, there is a general scramble for Arab areas of Palestine as a result of our abandoning the mandate and marching out.[53]

Britain should stick by Abdullah, he added, even if the alliance drew criticism from other Arab states. Transjordan's occupation of what Kirkbride called the 'Arab areas' in Palestine would narrow the likelihood of conflict between an embryonic Jewish state and some of its neighbours.[54]

Soon after Kirkbride sent the aforementioned telegram, Abdullah met Golda Meyerson (later Golda Meir). Representing the Jewish Agency, Meyerson gave her tacit approval to Abdullah's suggestion that he should rule over an Arab state in a partitioned Palestine. While the precise boundaries of an Arab state were not agreed, Abdullah expressed an interest in the part of Palestine that has subsequently become known as the West Bank. An understanding was reached that the Zionists would not fight him over that area.[55]

Abdullah sent a delegation to London in early 1948. During secret discussions, Tawfiq Abu al-Huda, the prime minister of Transjordan, signalled that Abdullah would send troops into Palestine after the British had left on 15 May that year. Ernest Bevin, the foreign secretary, is said to have replied that it was 'the obvious thing to do', while insisting that areas earmarked for a Jewish state must not be targeted.[56]

It would be misleading to think that Transjordan enjoyed any military autonomy. The Transjordan-based army, known as the Arab Legion, was financed, armed and trained by Britain. It was headed by John Glubb, an officer from Lancashire. Glubb had written a memo in 1946 presenting partition as a 'solution to the Palestine problem'. He had predicted that many Palestinians would remain inside a Jewish state after its formation and 'the Jews would want to get rid of them'. Glubb added that it was not 'intended to move Arab displaced persons by force' but to 'arrange' that they could find 'well-paid jobs and good prospects' in an Arab state.[57]

Following the Deir Yassin massacre in April 1948, Alec Kirkbride, Britain's chief representative in Amman, reported there was 'a growing volume of pressure from both inside and outside Palestine for immediate intervention of the Arab Legion to contain the Jews.' Kirkbride assured the Foreign Office he was using 'the best arguments available against this pressure': the 'continued existence of a British Mandate, even if impotent and the fact that the military units of the Arab Legion are too small to afford any dispersal.' Kirkbride referred to the Deir Yassin massacre as an 'incident' and warned that further 'incidents' could render his calls for restraint ineffective. 'Arabs do not readily listen to reason when they are in the frenzy of indignation and apprehension, which is being created by present events,' he wrote.[58]

A few days before the British Mandate came to an end, Ernest Bevin appraised some cabinet colleagues of how an unnamed British officer in the Arab Legion had facilitated contacts between that force and the Haganah. 'It is understood that the object of these top secret negotiations is to define the areas of Palestine to be occupied by the two forces,' Bevin noted. He recommended that British officers should continue serving the Legion in order to avoid hostilities with Zionist forces. But if the Arab Legion was to fight in areas allotted to a Jewish state, then 'we shall, of course, have to order all regular British forces to withdraw from and remain outside Palestine.'[59]

The British were adamant that a future Jewish state must be defended even while Palestinians were being expelled. In May 1948, Kirkbride threatened Abu al-Huda with aid cuts if Transjordan 'went beyond the plan' agreed. Assuring that he and Abdullah 'adhered basically to their original intentions', the prime minister said it 'would be impossible for Transjordan to stop at the frontier of the Jewish state if the other Arab armies were sweeping all before them.' Kirkbride felt that such an eventuality was unlikely, according to his own account of the meeting. But if it did occur, Transjordan would 'spare us embarrassment by releasing the British officers concerned [from the Arab Legion] beforehand,' Kirkbride stated.[60]

Abdullah gave a similar pledge on 16 May – the day after the British Mandate for Palestine expired. In a letter to Kirkbride, Abdullah referred to 'my national duties and religious motives towards Palestine as a whole and Jerusalem in particular.' Yet he resolved to 'avoid, as far as possible, any action that might place Great Britain in a difficult position.' Kirkbride interpreted the message as an attempt to get a statement of 'support or at least acquiescence' from Britain should it be deemed necessary to fight in areas allocated to a Jewish state. Kirkbride recommended to the Foreign Office that Britain express 'gratitude for his anxiety to avoid making difficulties.' But he also felt that Abdullah should be reminded that 'any departure from the original scheme' would have repercussions. Ernest Bevin concurred. He instructed Kirkbride to underline that a 'full-scale Arab Legion attack on Jerusalem is exactly the kind of situation which would produce the greatest possible difficulty for us in our relations with Transjordan.'[61]

Complications did indeed arise. When the Arab Legion entered Palestine in mid-May, Abdullah felt that he could not stay aloof from the battle for Jerusalem. On 17 May, he told Glubb to send troops to Jerusalem from Ramallah. Glubb tried to stall but soon capitulated to Abdullah's pressure. Kirkbride's assessment was that Glubb acted 'wisely' to save the religious sites in the Old City and that he would win kudos from Arab states for doing so. A ten-day battle for Jerusalem ensued. It ended as Kirkbride had hoped – with the Old City controlled by the Arab Legion.

That did not stop Britain from punishing Transjordan. As the fighting split Jerusalem in two, Britain became increasingly anxious to see a truce. Britain convinced the UN Security Council to vote in favour of a four-week ceasefire. Britain suspended deliveries of small arms to Transjordan, Egypt and Iraq, all of whom had sent troops into Palestine. Britain also threatened to withhold an aid payment to Transjordan which was due to be transferred on 12 July and to withdraw British officers from the Arab Legion.[62]

Britain carried out its threat not to make the subsidy payment on 12 July. In Bevin's words, the situation in Palestine remained 'obscure' on that date. Twelve days later, however, he was satisfied that Abdullah's government had complied with the demand for a ceasefire. Bevin informed Kirkbride that Britain's financial assistance to Transjordan would be resumed. Abdullah and his henchmen were incensed by how Britain treated them. British 'stock has never stood lower in Transjordan than at present and we are for the first time in this country universally unpopular,' a diplomat in Amman reported.[63]

By deserting its Transjordanian ally at a crucial juncture, Britain arguably exacerbated the ethnic cleansing of Palestine. Despite its victory in Jerusalem's Old City, the Arab Legion was defeated by Zionist forces in the areas between Jerusalem and Tel Aviv. Thousands of Palestinians were expelled from Lydda and Ramleh by Zionist forces when Glubb pulled the Arab Legion out of those towns.[64] More than 400 Palestinians were massacred in and around the Dahamish Mosque in Lydda on 13 July. One day later, an estimated 50,000 Palestinians were marched out of Lydda by Zionist forces towards the West Bank. The downfall of Lydda and Ramleh meant that they would form part of Israel, even though they had been allotted to an Arab state by the UN's partition plan.[65]

A low-key ceremony marked the end of the British Mandate in Palestine. On 14 May, Alan Cunningham inspected a colour party from the Suffolk Regiment in Jerusalem. Richard Beaumont, a diplomat, recorded how a 'few bedraggled Arabs' at one of the entrances to the Old City 'raised a feeble cheer'. Beaumont was not sure if their reaction was motivated by gratitude or relief but concluded that it was a 'pathetic epilogue to nigh 30 years of toil and sacrifice.'[66]

Midwifing a miracle?

The State of Israel was formally established that same day. The new state was swiftly recognised by the USA and the Soviet Union. Britain, by contrast, waited a year before doing so. In an August 1948 note to various diplomats, Bevin acknowledged there was much speculation about Britain recognising Israel. He wrote:

> It is essential that we should not give the impression to either the Jews or the Arabs that we are about to modify our policy on this question. The Jews would immediately think that we were condoning the aggressive intentions of which they are at present giving too much evidence and that they had only to pursue this policy for a little longer to oblige us to grant them recognition. This is our only major political card with the Jews and it must be reserved for use at the appropriate moment when we may hope to get some worthwhile and lasting settlement in return. It is equally essential that the Arabs should not believe that we are about to take any such

step. In order to reach a settlement of any kind we shall almost certainly need to use all our influence once more with the Arabs at the appropriate moment. Our stock of influence is at present low and must be gradually built up over the next few weeks. If we take any step towards recognising the Jewish state, or even if the Arabs had good reason to believe that we were doing so, exactly the reverse would happen and we might find ourselves without any influence at all on Arab policy at a critical moment.[67]

No longer formally in charge of Palestine, the British were still trying to shape its future in the autumn of 1948. Incorporating those parts of Palestine designated as Arab into Transjordan continued to be the preference of the Foreign Office. Kirkbride, however, was nervous that the plan would not bear fruit now that Folke Bernadotte, a Swedish count, had been tasked by the UN with arranging a lasting truce. If annexing part of Palestine to Transjordan required approval from other Arab states, then it was likely to be blocked. In early September, Kirkbride wrote that 'no amount of political manoeuvring' would persuade Iraq and Syria to back such a scheme. 'One of the reasons for [the] instinctive reaction by the Arab world against [the] strengthening of Transjordan is the not unjustified belief that this would improve our own hold in the Middle East,' he stated.[68]

Bernadotte had put forward a plan to partition Palestine in June 1948. As it got a frosty reaction both from Zionists and from Arab governments, he went back to the drawing board. His modified plan, presented in September, dropped his earlier proposal for an economic union between an Arab state and a Jewish state. Bernadotte's revised blueprint argued that a new state called Israel 'exists and there are no sound reasons for assuming that it will not continue to do so.' The boundaries of this new state would have to be agreed either between what he called the 'parties concerned' or determined by the United Nations. He recommended that the Naqab (Negev) region should be part of an Arab state, that the Galilee should be part of Israel and that Jerusalem and its environs, including Bethlehem, should be an international zone. He urged that Palestinian refugees should be enabled to return home at the 'earliest possible date' or receive financial compensation if they chose not to.[69]

The revised Bernadotte plan was dated 16 September; on the following day, he was assassinated in Jerusalem by members of the Lehi. Britain's representatives differed on his proposals. 'It is unfortunate that Bernadotte in his last report said that the Arabs could decide the future of the Arab areas,' Glubb commented. 'If they did, an inter-Arab war might well result.' Glubb felt it was 'absolutely essential' that Britain should convince the UN to 'give a final decision' on partition. 'I am inclined to think that the best way would be for the Gaza and Beersheba districts to go to Egypt and Hebron, Ramleh, Ramallah and Nablus to Transjordan,' he told the Foreign Office.[70]

Speaking to an American diplomat, Bevin said that the British government 'liked' the Bernadotte proposals, though would not insist on their full implementation. Bevin said that he would 'help' Zionists over some of their settlements in the Naqab, hinting that he felt at least part of the region should be awarded to Israel.[71]

Bevin and his colleagues retained an imperial mindset as they oversaw the disintegration of the British Empire. Why was Transjordan, a small state established at the stroke of Churchill's pen, to assume a central role in the British game plan? One explanation is that Britain felt it could keep on being the boss of Transjordan, that Abdullah would continue being its vassal.

John Troutbeck, head of the British Middle East Office in Cairo, acknowledged as much in a 1948 memorandum. Following the Second World War, Abdullah 'for whatever motive has been more ready to follow the advice of HMG [His Majesty's government] and to accept a compromise on the Palestine question than any other Arab leader,' Troutbeck wrote.[72]

Troutbeck was aware of the pitfalls of relying on Abdullah. In a separate message to the Foreign Office, Troutbeck urged Britain to be reticent about its real intentions. 'If we advocate too openly the incorporation of Arab areas of Palestine into Transjordan and stimulate Abdullah to play his hand too forcefully, we shall risk exacerbating the resentment of other Arab states, both against Abdullah and against ourselves.'[73] All of Britain's planning, he observed, was 'based on the existence of a security base' in Egypt. Alienating Egypt by 'too obvious an advocated enlargement of a rival's territory' risked compromising that 'essential base'. He added:

So far as we ourselves are concerned, our ill-wishers have long been saying that the whole object of our policy since the end of the mandate has been to enlarge the territory of our satellite, Abdullah, so that we can continue to exercise a paramount influence in an area of strategical importance to ourselves. Such suspicions are likely to be fanned by too blatant an advocacy on our part of enlargement of Transjordan.[74]

In true colonial fashion, the British sought to dictate who should rule Palestine, rather than letting Palestinians have a say. An overriding concern was to neuter Haj Amin al-Husseini, the mufti of Jerusalem, and his supporters. Having fled Palestine during the 1930s revolt, al-Husseini had sided with Germany on the basis that he shared an enemy with the Nazi government – Britain. He famously met Adolf Hitler in Berlin and sought to enlist Bosnian Muslims into the Waffen-SS.[75]

Britain's real complaint about the mufti was not that he provided limited assistance to the Nazis. It was that he was a troublemaker. Al-Husseini's antipathy towards Zionism was considered inimical to British interests. Hugh Dow, who served as the British consul-general in Jerusalem, argued that allowing al-Husseini to have a 'large influence' in Palestine would be 'quite fatal to any hope of an enduring settlement'. In September 1948, Dow advised the Foreign Office to make the case that Britain was required to back Abdullah's encroachment into Palestine under its treaty with Transjordan. Britain, he felt, should tell Arab governments that Abdullah was preferable to the mufti, who would have 'an openly hostile attitude' to the new state of Israel. As the mufti would have no more than 'irregular and ill-armed forces' at his disposal, placing him in charge 'would result in a short time in a Jewish conquest of all Palestine and possibly the areas beyond its borders,' Dow warned.[76]

Al-Husseini was part of the 'all-Palestine government' set up in Gaza later that month. Intended as the launch pad of a Palestinian state, the 'government' lasted just a few weeks. Intense rivalry between Egypt and Transjordan was among the factors that made the experiment unviable.[77]

The partitioning of Palestine was formalised through a series of armistice agreements reached in 1949. The new arrangements turned out to be temporary, yet they broadly resembled the desires expressed by some British representatives. Britain did, however, oppose the idea of having an international enclave in Jerusalem. Its reservations were shared by the USA, which did not want an international force to be set up for the city, lest it may contain Russian soldiers.[78]

As a result of the armistice agreements, Jordan – as Transjordan was now known – was placed in charge of the West Bank, including East Jerusalem. Jabel Mukaber, the Jerusalem neighbourhood hosting Britain's Government House, was declared a demilitarised zone, supervised by the UN. Gaza fell under Egyptian military administration. Most of historic Palestine became known as Israel.

Chaim Weizmann became Israel's first president. He marvelled at the mass expulsion of Palestinians, describing it as a 'miraculous simplification of the problem'.[79] The comment reveals a great deal about the rulers of the new state. For them, the presence of an indigenous people was a 'problem' that had to be removed.

More than 750,000 Palestinians were uprooted in the *Nakba*. Generations of dispossessed would grow up in camps. Today, there are around 5 million registered Palestine refugees.[80] Britain was the midwife of that mass expulsion. For Palestinians, it was anything but miraculous.

5
Arming Israel (1953–1956)

Israel quickly won the respect of Britain's military elite.

As part of its intelligence gathering, the RAF regularly operated surveillance flights over the Sinai, many of which encroached into Palestine. In November 1948, a Mosquito spy-plane belonging to the force was shot down by an American pilot serving Israel. Despite the loss, the British were impressed by the new state's prowess. The top brass in the British Army recommended the development of friendly ties with Israel as it possessed the strongest armed force in the Middle East.[1]

Britain's government was more eager to appear balanced because of geopolitical considerations. In 1950, an agreement was signed between the USA, Britain and France, the West's three largest weapons exporters. Known as the Tripartite Declaration, it stated that all applications for arms from Israel and its Arab neighbours would be assessed according to the principle that each of these countries needed to defend themselves and the region. Israel and its neighbours had provided assurances that they would not behave aggressively, the declaration added.[2]

Israel did not share the declaration's apparent objective of avoiding an arms race in the Middle East. A 1953 Foreign Office memorandum referred to how an annual list was compiled of how much weaponry Israel wished to buy from Britain. The memo added:

This year Israel's demands reached alarming proportions and coincided with very substantial requests [from Israel] to the French and United States governments. The effects of meeting all these would be to increase Israel's armed forces and to upset the balance of power in the Middle East and to give the Israelis a marked superiority over the Arab states.[3]

Among the items that the Israelis had expressed an interest in buying were 60 Centurion tanks. The British government felt that authorising such a large order would violate the Tripartite Declaration. As a compromise, it signalled that it would instead give the go-ahead for Israel to get ten of the tanks. Yet when Britain held discussions with French and American representatives on the committee set up following the declaration, they were both 'firmly opposed to even the sale of 10 Centurion tanks', a separate Foreign Office paper stated. Britain wished to keep the existence of the consultative committee secret.[4]

Some mandarins felt that Britain should sell to Israel. The ministry of supply contacted the Foreign Office in 1953 to say 'we badly need orders' for Centurions, which were manufactured by the Cumbria-based firm Vickers. The ministry of supply was being badgered by an unnamed Israeli military attaché who had 'pressed us rather severely as to whether there is some political objection' to a deal being clinched. The ministry had tried to fob off the Israeli representative but felt it was running out of excuses. The ministry noted:

> It seems to us that the Israelis are inclined to place a great deal of importance on Centurions and it is not improbable that they regard this project as a kind of test case of the good intentions of Western powers and of the United Kingdom in particular.[5]

An assessment by Britain's Joint Intelligence Bureau for 1953 and 1954 stated that 'an arms race between the Arab states and Israel is now well under way.' The assessment concluded that efforts to keep the goal of arms limitation secret had not been effective. Israel and some of the Arab governments were aware that Britain, France and the USA had set up a committee tasked with controlling arms exports to the Middle East. It was 'plain that the Israelis are having the greater success' in buying weapons, the bureau noted. Total Arab purchases were 'undoubtedly larger but much is being bought piecemeal'. Israel, by contrast, had a 'coordinated procurement programme' that enabled it to buy both new arms and equipment needed for maintenance. The Arab states had double the number of tanks to Israel but 'almost all the Arab tanks are in poor condition because no regular imports of spares have been made.' Unlike the Arab states, the Israelis had 'consistently bought tank parts and their entire tank strength is operational.' Similar observations could be made about other ground weapons, with the result that 'the Israeli forces are thought to be both stronger and better equipped than any which the Arab states together could put into the field.'[6]

In January 1955, Ivone Kirkpatrick, the most senior civil servant dealing with foreign policy in Whitehall, noted that he had received 'unpalatable' advice from Britain's Middle East Office. The advice was that the most likely way to advance peace in the region was to keep Israel in a 'state of substantial military inferiority'. Britain, he told Foreign Office colleagues, could not 'publicly admit' that such an objective formed the basis of its policy on arms exports. 'The fewer arms of an offensive character we send to Israel the better,' Kirkpatrick argued. But, he added, that 'we shall be obliged to send something from time to time so long as Arab threats [to Israel] continue.'[7]

Israel kept trying to exert pressure on Britain. Licences were granted for the export of six Centurions from Britain to Israel. But their delivery was blocked because Israeli troops mounted an invasion of Gaza in February 1955. That offensive was denounced by the United Nations as it flouted Israel's armistice agreement with Egypt.

Instead of standing up to the Israeli diplomats who expressed disappointment in Britain's decision to suspend tank deliveries, the Foreign Office emphasised that its suspension was only temporary. The measure did not apply to Meteor fighter jets. Britain delivered five of those warplanes to Israel during the first three months of 1955; two of them were dispatched shortly after the attack on Gaza.[8]

Pressure from Peres

Britain was not sufficiently cooperative for Shimon Peres, then a top official in Israel's defence ministry. The British embassy in Tel Aviv alerted the Foreign Office to Peres' grievances during May 1955. His main complaint was that no export licenses were being granted for rockets and flares 'which were apparently obtainable elsewhere but were not of the same quality as the British product.' Peres had been trying to play Britain off against its old rival, France, the embassy suggested. He had hinted that if Britain could make a batch of Meteor night fighters available to Israel quickly, then Israel might order fewer warplanes from France.[9]

A hard-headed appraisal of the Tripartite Declaration and its effects was conducted by Britain's defence ministry in June 1955. It was 'still very much in our interests' to prevent a Middle East arms race and work with the USA and France towards that goal, the appraisal stated. Preserving a balance between Israel and its neighbours was, however, deemed unrealistic. Britain, the USA and France were not the only possible sources of weapons for the Middle East. Belgium, Turkey, Switzerland, Yugoslavia and Finland were also becoming important players in the arms industry. As a result, Israel and its neighbours had a fairly wide choice of where to buy weapons 'without coming to us'. Britain must be prepared to refuse sales for political reasons 'but if we do this too strictly, we shall divert the business to other suppliers,' the ministry argued.[10]

Peres kept lobbying. During a July 1955 trip to London, Reginald Maudling, the recently appointed minister of supply, said he was 'anxious' to help Peres in 'every way' he could as Israel was a 'long-standing customer'. Peres was nonetheless told it would be 'unwise' to expect fundamental changes in British policy. In subsequent discussions with British diplomats, Peres complained that Britain had provided Egypt with 30 Centurions. Those tanks, he claimed, could reach Tel Aviv within two hours if they set out from Gaza.[11] Nor did Britain appear too worried about the distinct possibility that Western arms would be used for internal repression. The new state of Israel had around 160,000 Palestinians inside it. Israel punished these people for managing to remain during the *Nakba* by placing them under a system of military rule between 1948 and 1966.[12] Britain was relaxed about weapons sales to an Israeli army that was enforcing a policy of racial discrimination against indigenous Palestinians. Within days of the February 1955 attack on Gaza, the Foreign Office stated it had no objection to France's plan of equipping the Israeli forces with 20,000 rifles.[13]

The British elite was not monolithic in its attitudes. In spite of the early admiration it had expressed for Israel, the British Army was opposed to giving Israel arms in 1955. Its chiefs of staff argued that if Britain provided Israel with heavy equipment such as tanks and aircraft, then it would be breaching its commitments. Jordan, in particular, would doubt whether Britain was willing to uphold promises that it would defend the kingdom if attacked by Israel.

Evelyn Shuckburgh, a leading figure in the Foreign Office, advocated a weakening of Britain's arms exports policy in July 1955. Britain, he felt, should 'give up' on trying to control the sale of weapons considered defensive rather than offensive. That broad category would include everything apart from tanks, aircraft and heavy guns. Efforts to maintain a balance should not be entirely abandoned, he argued, and Israel had to be given sufficient arms. Doing so was necessary in order to 'prevent a serious deterioration in our relations with Israel,' the Shuckburgh memo read. Shuckburgh also rejected the British Army's call for a ban on the sale of tanks and warplanes to Israel. The USA and France would not agree to introduce similar embargoes, he predicted, and Israel would cope with the effects of a unilateral British ban by shopping for arms elsewhere.[14]

Another Foreign Officer paper from the same month urged that Israel should be given the six Centurions that had been withheld from it because of the February attack on Gaza. British diplomats were now happy that Israel was behaving less stridently. Handing over the tanks would be a gesture of support towards David Ben-Gurion, Israel's supposedly 'moderate' prime minister, and strengthen his position against more extremist politicians, according to the Foreign Office. One passage in this document reveals much about Britain's perception of Israel:

It is true that we think the Israelis are more likely than the Arabs to commit aggression but we take the view that they would only be driven to a suicidal act of that kind if they had reached a point of despair and believed themselves to be abandoned by the West. Consequently, we advocate a more flexible policy which will at least have the appearance of being fair to Israel without sacrificing the major objectives of building up certain Arab states for defence against Russia.[15]

Israel's 1955 attack on Gaza accelerated the Middle East arms race. After 40 Egyptian soldiers were killed in an ambush overseen by Ariel Sharon, then a young commander in Israel's army, the Cairo government devoted much energy towards developing its military.

Tensions grew between the West and Egypt. Gamal Abdel Nasser, prime minister at the time, had been protesting against British colonialism since his youth. The 1952 revolution that he led – along with a few other members of the Free Officers – aimed to rid Egypt of British troops. Nasser was an opponent of the Baghdad Pact, the Cold War alliance between Britain, Turkey, Iraq, Pakistan and Iran. Set up in 1955, that alliance operated with America's blessing, though not its participation.

Nasser had signalled that he did not wish Egypt to take sides in the Cold War. Following Israel's attack on Gaza, however, Egypt turned increasingly towards the Soviet bloc – to the consternation of America and Britain. In the autumn of 1955, a major arms deal was signed between Egypt and Czechoslovakia.[16]

Ariel Sharon had led another assault on one of Israel's neighbours before 1955 was over. In December, a paratroop brigade under Sharon's command attacked Syria. The raid debunked the myth that David Ben-Gurion was a moderate; he was intimately involved in this flagrant violation of the 1949 armistice agreements. To try and justify the attack, his government cited Syrian restrictions on Israeli fishing vessels near the shore of Lake Tiberias (also known as the Sea of Galilee). The historian Avi Shlaim has challenged the official Israeli narrative by pointing out that Syria had not fired on the fishing vessels but on Israeli patrol boats that had come within 250 metres of the shore. The attack was condemned by the UN Security Council in January 1956. America responded by imposing a weapons ban on Israel.[17]

Britain banned exports of 'certain arms' – the term used by its defence ministry – to Israel. The list of weapons concerned came to ten items, mainly consisting of warplanes, fuses for bombs and equipment for tanks. There was little, if any, appetite for a broad or lasting ban. Selwyn Lloyd, the foreign secretary, informed Roger Matkins, Britain's ambassador to the USA, that Israel had been promised six Meteor night fighters the previous November. The export had not been formally rubber-stamped, though, and the procedure was interrupted because of the attack on Syria. The Foreign Office recommended that export licences for the plans now be issued 'to avoid an Israeli charge of bad faith'.[18]

Further delays were encountered. Britain and the USA decided that what diplomats called the 'trickle' of arms sales to the Middle East should not yet be resumed. Eliahu Elath, Israel's ambassador in London, made 'an impassioned appeal for a quick and satisfactory answer,' according to a Foreign Office record. According to that note, Elath told Ivone Kirkpatrick in March 1956 that Israel 'regarded us as under a moral obligation to give them what was necessary for defence and this included Centurion tanks, guns and a considerable quantity of equipment'.[19]

One idea discussed around this time was that Israel should be supplied with warplanes by Britain and France and with anti-aircraft guns and radars by the USA. Israel 'would then have something to frighten the Egyptians with,' a US State Department official told the British embassy in Washington. Back in London, Selwyn Lloyd remarked that 'the time has come' to give Israel more weapons – and not just half a dozen Meteors. Elath, meanwhile, threatened to sue Britain for breach of contract if it did not release a consignment of anti-aircraft cannons for installation in Israeli torpedo boats. 'This may be bluff,' the Foreign Office noted. Bluff or not, Elath's lobbying proved effective: in April, Evelyn Shuckburgh informed Elath that instructions had been made to enable the cannons' shipment.[20]

Anthony Eden, then Britain's prime minister, grew increasingly enthusiastic about arming Israel in 1956. On 12 April, he informed the defence ministry that 'we have got to continue our "trickle" to Israel'. Now that the Israelis had been provided with cannons and night fighters, 'I think we should give them some things which will strengthen their anti-tank defence and their anti-aircraft defences,' Eden remarked. He asked for advice within 24 hours about what items should be sold to Israel. Eight days later, Israel presented the British government with a list of coveted weapons. An accompanying letter from Elath read: 'In view of the considerable supplies of the most modern armaments now reaching Egypt and probably some other Arab states, it is imperative that Israel should have similar arms at her disposal.'[21]

Skullduggery over Suez

Across the Atlantic, Roger Matkins was privy to some American plans for the Middle East. One was code-named Operation Stockpile. In May 1956, the State Department briefed Matkins that the plan could be activated either if Israel was attacked or if it was the aggressor. In the former situation, the USA would draw F86 aircraft from its forces stationed in Europe and take them to Cyprus, where they would be handed over to Israeli pilots. If the latter situation arose, weapons could be made available to states attacked by Israel from a stockpile stored by the US naval fleet in the Mediterranean.[22]

Another plan, Operation Omega, concentrated on isolating Nasser by diplomatic and economic means, while leaving open the possibility that he could be wooed into the West's ambit. The desire to get tough with Nasser was shared by Britain and the USA. With America facing a presidential election towards the end of 1956, however, Dwight Eisenhower's administration felt it was not the right time for military action against Egypt. Matkins, whose stint in Washington was coming to an end, relayed that message to the British government.[23]

Undoubtedly, 1956 was the year when it was made plain that Britain's power had diminished. It was the year when America enforced a tacit rule that its allies were forbidden from embarking on military adventures that it frowned upon. Put more simply, 1956 was the year when America told Britain it was now the boss.

Yet there are nuances in this story. Eisenhower was kept in the dark about the collusion between Britain, Israel and France in October that year. American intelligence, however, was aware that collusion of that nature was being considered. When two CIA representatives visited London in April 1956, they discussed a range of potential interventions in the Middle East. Among the ideas floated by their MI6 counterparts was that of Britain and Israel undertaking a coordinated attack against Egypt; the goal of such an operation would be to 'topple' Nasser. 'Extreme possibilities' contemplated by Britain's secret service would include an 'outright Israeli attack [on] Gaza or other border areas,' the CIA noted.

John Foster Dulles, the US secretary of state, complained that Britain was making 'more drastic plans than we are' for dealing with Nasser.[24] America's anger towards Egypt nonetheless intensified. When Nasser granted recognition to China in May 1956, the Eisenhower administration decided to retaliate. The USA did so by halting all financial assistance it had earmarked to the Aswan High Dam, a project that had assumed pivotal importance in Egypt's economic development programme.

Nasser confronted the West more brazenly in July when he announced that the Suez Canal had been nationalised. There was a strong perception among the British political elite that its economic interests were under threat. Two-thirds of Britain's entire annual oil supply passed through the canal. Britain and France were also major shareholders in the Suez Canal Company, which, in their view, Nasser was putting out of business.[25] Labour, then in opposition, echoed Eden's outrage at the nationalisation. Hugh Gaitskell, the Labour leader, compared Nasser to Benito Mussolini.[26]

France ripped up the Tripartite Declaration in the summer of 1956. Angered by Nasser's support for Algeria's pro-independence National Liberation Front (FLN), France offered Israel a deal. In return for cooperation on intelligence and on striking FLN bases in Libya, Israel was promised $100 million in French weaponry. Ben-Gurion reacted to the conditions by describing them as 'slightly dangerous' – a massive understatement – but promptly accepted them.[27]

Britain's Foreign Office was not happy with the extent of Franco-Israeli cooperation. A paper prepared by the office for a visit by Christian Pineau, the French foreign minister, to London in late July, complained:

> For internal political reasons, the French want to supply large amounts of heavy [military] equipment to Israel. They realise the unfortunate effect this will have on their relations with the Arabs. They are therefore seeking to hide behind their other Western allies.[28]

The memo added that Britain was in 'an even more difficult position' than France and the USA as it had treaties with Jordan and Iraq.

The Foreign Office elaborated on its thinking a few weeks later. An internal report recalled that France had exploited Nasser's announcement on Suez to try and give Israel a consignment of Mystère warplanes. Britain had objected. It remained important to 'keep the Suez and Israel problems separate,' according to the Foreign Office. 'There would be no quicker way of alienating those Arab friends we still have than by making our quarrel with Egypt over Suez an occasion for such a substantial and conspicuous addition to Israel's armament.'[29]

Eden was more gung ho. He hinted of the collusion to come in a cryptic note to Selwyn Lloyd that August:

> I feel that Israel should have a trickle of useful arms on the condition they don't publicise them. Did they ever get the further delivery of

Mystères from the French? Even half a dozen more soon would help [the word 'soon' was underlined]. We may need Israel's help one day and it would be bad if they refused because they had no means of defence against Soviet bombers.[30]

Later in August, Eden was told by the Foreign Office that France may have 'quietly' shipped a number of warplanes to Israel. 'I hope so,' the prime minister replied.[31]

The military action that Eden wanted to take against Egypt lacked justification. That much had been acknowledged by his own cabinet colleagues during that summer. The cabinet conceded that from a legal standpoint, Nasser had done no more than decide to buy out the shareholders of the Suez Canal Company. He had not closed the canal to international traffic.

Gerald Fitzmaurice, legal adviser to the Foreign Office, had stressed that Nasser's actions did not provide Britain with any basis for military action. He had warned that an attack on Egypt would affect Britain's position in the UN 'extremely adversely'. On a war footing, Eden would not entertain such arguments. 'The lawyers are always against our doing anything,' Eden said. 'For God's sake, keep them out of it.'[32]

By seeking Israel's 'help' – to use his own term – Eden had to renege on or, at least, overlook some of Britain's commitments.

The West Bank town of Qalqilya was invaded by Israel in October 1956. The invasion amounted to an attack on Britain's staunch ally Jordan. It was one of a series of such raids conducted by Israel that autumn. Britain calculated that Israel killed 116 people, some of them non-combatants, in 'four largish military operations against Jordan' between 12 September and 11 October. Israel claimed the raids were in reprisal for violence by guerrilla fighters. The Foreign Office was not prepared to swallow that excuse; a memo stated that none of the incidents in which guerrilla fighters fired on Israeli targets were instigated by the Jordanian authorities.[33]

Israel's raids involved a 'deliberate flouting' of appeals by Britain to desist, another Foreign Office memo stated. 'The only effective way of showing the Israelis we mean business would be to hold up a decision on their requests for arms,' the memo added.[34]

Instead of 'showing the Israelis we mean business', Eden wanted to do business with them – in a deceptive and underhand manner. A few days after the Qalqilya attack, he welcomed Albert Gazier and Maurice Challe, a senior French politician and general respectively, to Chequers. There, at the country retreat, Eden schemed with his guests about launching an offensive against Egypt. The basic idea would be getting Israel to strike first, then using that strike as an excuse for France and Britain to occupy the canal.

The plan would have violated the Tripartite Declaration. Eden was reminded by his French guests that Nasser had publicly stated he did not wish for Egypt to be protected under that accord. Any statement by Nasser to that effect did not alter Britain's commitments. Egypt was not a party to the Tripartite Declaration; Britain, on the other hand, was. Yet Eden felt that Nasser's stance 'lets us off the hook'. He added: 'We have no obligation, it seems, to stop the Israelis attacking the Egyptians.'[35]

Without letting them know about his scheming, Eden ordered British diplomats to avoid upsetting Israel. On 19 October, the UN Security Council debated Israel's aggression towards Jordan. Pierson Dixon, Britain's ambassador to the UN, made some bland comments, during which he praised the 'great restraint' displayed by Jordan. 'Our Jordan ally has our sympathy and our commendation,' he said.

The following day Eden told Lloyd he was unhappy with the ambassador. 'I am really concerned about the effect of this on Israel,' Eden stated. 'The French warned us of how suspicious of us the Israelis are.' Lloyd duly cabled Dixon with this guidance:

> For a variety of reasons, I should like you to lie low during the next stages of the debate on the Jordan item and to work for delay. Your outspoken support of Jordan on the last occasion seems to me to be enough for the time being.[36]

The plan to attack Egypt was fleshed out at a secret meeting between Britain, France and Israel in the Parisian suburb of Sevres later that month. Moshe Dayan, the Israeli military chief who took part in the meeting, has written that the plan for action was presented as a British initiative. Taking place in the last few days of October, it would have three stages: Israel attacking Egypt; Britain and France issuing an ultimatum for the rapid withdrawal of Israeli and Egyptian troops from the canal area; and, finally, Britain and France bombing Egypt once the ultimatum had expired.

By Dayan's account, the British government encouraged Israel to act belligerently. Selwyn Lloyd 'urged that our military action not be a small-scale encounter but a "real act of war", otherwise there would be no justification for the British ultimatum and Britain would appear in the eyes of the world as an aggressor,' Dayan recorded in his memoirs. Lloyd's rationale was that Britain 'has friends, like the Scandinavian countries who would not view with favour Britain's starting a war'.[37]

After learning about the Israeli attack against Egypt on 29 October, Eisenhower called an emergency meeting in the White House. John Foster Dulles, the secretary of state, told Eisenhower that Britain and France appeared ready for a military strike and 'may in fact have concerted their action with Israel'. Eisenhower expressed a determination to flex his muscles with Britain and France, arguing that America was the only power to which they would listen. Though he favoured telling Britain that he understood its grievances over Suez, he insisted that 'nothing justifies double-crossing us'.[38]

A killing spree in Gaza

America's anger towards Britain and France rose as it tried repeatedly on the last two days of October to convince the UN Security Council that it should demand Israel's withdrawal from Sinai. Britain and France both applied their vetoes. The two countries went ahead with their attack. America exerted more pressure and eventually Britain and France agreed to a ceasefire on 6 December.[39]

Rather than admit any responsibility for endangering world peace, Britain tried to pin the blame on the Soviet Union. Pierson Dixon was anxious to avail of the opportunities afforded by the Soviet crushing of the 1956 revolt in Hungary. He proposed using a UN debate on Hungary to denounce the alliance between Nasser and the Kremlin.

Ahead of the debate, he notified the Foreign Office that he was thinking of 'making a decidedly anti-Russian speech, with the object of bringing out that the Russians are the real niggers in the wood pile in the Middle East and all round.' He would accuse the Soviet Union of pursuing a 'policy of repression in Europe and expansion in the Middle East' and of starting the Suez crisis by supporting Nasser diplomatically and with weapons. Dixon felt that hammering the Soviet Union 'might do some good' in 'rallying support for our position among European and Latin American delegations.' The Foreign Office replied that it would have 'no objection in principle to your speaking on these lines'.[40]

Israel did not only commit a 'real act of war', as Selwyn Lloyd had reportedly sought, it also perpetrated crimes against humanity. Israeli troops went on killing sprees in Gaza. UNRWA, the UN's agency for Palestine refugees, investigated these atrocities. The agency found that Israeli troops occupied the town of Khan Younis and the adjacent refugee camp on 3 November. On the pretext of searching for weapons, Israeli troops killed 'many unarmed civilians', the report stated. While the exact number of those killed was unknown, UNRWA noted it had been given the names of 275 dead. Of that number, 140 were refugees. This meant that Israeli forces were massacring the very people who had been uprooted at the time of Israel's foundation.

Another massacre took place in Rafah, close to Gaza's border with Egypt, on 12 November. UNRWA recalled that Israel had demanded that all men in Rafah's refugee camp of a certain age be screened, ostensibly to find guerrilla fighters. More than 32,000 refugees lived in the camp and many did not hear loudspeaker vans, which had called on men to gather at designated screening points. After learning that some were unaware of the announcements, UNRWA notified men in one section of the camp about the screening process. As time was running out for the men to reach the screening points before the designated hour, some began running. Israeli soldiers 'apparently panicked and opened fire on this running crowd,' the agency reported. Enquiries by the agency indicated that 111 people were killed by Israeli forces in Rafah that day, 103 of whom were refugees.

R.F. Bayard, an American lieutenant colonel chairing a team of UN observers, noted on 13 November it was 'quite evident' that Israel did not wish to have any monitoring of its activities in Gaza. Based on information furnished to him by UNRWA, he concluded that 'a good number of persons have been shot down in cold blood for no apparent reason.' Many of the Palestinians employed by UNRWA 'are missing from the camps and are believed to have been executed by the Israelis.'[41]

On 20 December 1956, Anthony Eden made a statement on the Suez crisis to the House of Commons. He insisted that there had been no collusion between France, Israel and Britain. He was equally adamant that Britain had no prior knowledge of Israel's plan to attack Egypt. To say that 'Her Majesty's government were engaged in some dishonourable conspiracy is completely untrue and I most emphatically deny it,' he added.[42]

Eden was telling lies. His dishonest speech turned out to be his last in parliament. On 9 January 1957, he resigned, citing ill health.

The British government's official website provides some historical information about the nation's prime ministers. The entry for Eden ends with an observation made by one of his biographers. The Suez crisis, it claims, has come to assume a 'disproportionate importance' in any assessment of Eden's career.[43]

Is that really the case? The skullduggery at Sevres has been thoroughly examined. Other aspects of the crisis have not been. Numerous books and articles on Suez omit any reference to Israel's massacres in Gaza. Those massacres cannot be brushed aside as unpleasant by-products of war. They were the direct results of an aggression that the British government endorsed.

6

Arming Israel (1957–1979)

Shimon Peres was prepared to acquire arms through clandestine routes. That is what the Foreign Office discovered when Peres, then director-general of Israel's defence ministry, visited London in December 1956.

Having colluded with Israel ahead of the Suez invasion, the British government now felt under pressure not to repeat that type of behaviour. For that reason, it decided to respect the terms of a resolution passed by the UN general assembly at the height of the Suez crisis. The resolution was somewhat vague: it called on governments around the world to 'refrain from introducing military goods in the area of hostilities' without defining the area in question. Perhaps erring on the side of caution, the British government revoked all export licences for weapons to Israel.

When Ivone Kirkpatrick at the Foreign Office informed Peres and an accompanying diplomat of that decision he was met by a stern protest. Peres predicted that Russia would disregard the UN resolution. Russia, according to Peres, had been sending arms to Syria and would soon begin replacing those weapons that Egypt had lost during the Suez crisis.

Kirkpatrick promised to relay Peres' remarks to cabinet ministers but argued it would be 'imprudent' for Britain to 'ask for further trouble' by violating a UN embargo, a record of the meeting states. Though he did not dispute the British reasoning, Peres 'kept harking back to Israel's need for arms' and suggested they could be delivered via Cyprus in an 'under the counter' manner. Kirkpatrick's reply was that he was 'much opposed to black market transactions'.[1]

It is unlikely that Kirkpatrick's opposition was based on matters of principle. He had, after all, engaged in deception during the Suez crisis. For example, he had advised diplomats in Baghdad to tell the Iraqi government that Britain was 'merely' engaged in a 'temporary fire brigade operation' in the canal zone.[2] Kirkpatrick was worried that Arab states would impose what he called an 'oil famine' on Britain and France unless the two governments distanced themselves from Israel's attack on Egypt.[3]

The embargo did not last long. Golda Meir, then Israel's foreign minister, successfully lobbied for the resumption of weapons exports when she visited London in August 1958. As a consequence of that trip, Britain agreed to sell Israel around £3 million worth of arms.[4]

That figure may not give a full picture of Britain's assistance to Israel. Some of the assistance was indirect. In September 1958, Britain's Atomic Energy Agency proposed that it sell back 25 tons of heavy water that it had bought from Norway. Heavy water is used in certain types of nuclear reactors but Britain's 'immediate demand' for it had declined, according to the agency. The agency wished to return the heavy water in the knowledge that Norway had found a new customer: Israel. The Atomic Energy Agency wanted to know if it should make its deal with Norway subject to any guarantees about the end-use of the heavy water by Israel. 'It would be overzealous to try and insist on any safeguards to cover this transaction,' the Foreign Office replied.[5] Through that cavalier attitude, Britain contributed to the development of Israel's nuclear programme.[6]

In October 1958, Peres attended a ceremony in Portsmouth Naval Yard as Israel took ownership of a 710-ton submarine. The 'sleek, black craft' had its name changed from *HMS Springer* to *Tannin* (the Hebrew word for whale), the Jewish Telegraphic Agency reported. It was the first of two submarines that Britain had sold Israel.[7]

The deal went ahead despite reservations from the British Army. An army paper from that year stated that Israel's navy, though small, was of superior quality to its enemies, Egypt and Syria. Giving Israel submarines would 'increase tension' in the Middle East, the paper added.[8]

In January 1959, the British ministry of supply signed a sales contract for 60 Centurion tanks with Israel. Sixteen of the tanks were from the Mark V range and were sold at £34,750 each; Britain agreed to deliver that batch by April that year. The remaining 44 were from the Mark VIII range and were sold at £49,000 each, on the understanding they would be delivered in 1960. Britain also agreed to help with training in using the vehicles and to provide ammunition.

British diplomats were instructed to keep the deal secret. The Israeli authorities promised that the tanks would arrive 'under censorship' but believed that 'sooner or later their presence will become known and will give rise to inflated stories in the Arab press,' a Foreign Office memo stated. The Israelis hoped that Britain would 'not be too apologetic' if news of the deal broke.[9]

The Foreign Office notified Britain's embassy in Tel Aviv during March 1959 that there had been a 'general relaxation' of the policy on exporting weapons to Israel. A 'fairly steady flow of military and quasi-military equipment' had already been established. Between November 1958 and February 1959, the value of that 'fairly steady flow' came to £760,000. A total of 18,000 Browning machine guns were supplied to the Israeli army in that period.[10]

Shopping for submarines

An Israeli 'shopping list' (the term used by British officials) drawn up around that time included a missile propellant. That made Britain's War Office nervous. The kind of ground-to-ground missile that Israel indicated it was developing would require a nuclear warhead to be 'effective', the War Office stated. Helping Israel to 'acquire such a weapon would draw down on the West bitter Arab antagonism,' a memo stated.[11]

Israel wanted one of its experts to visit Britain and inspect the missile propellant in question. An Israeli diplomat pressed the Foreign Office for a quick decision on the proposed visit. If permission to visit was refused, then Israel would find the material elsewhere, the diplomat reportedly said, yet he had surmised that Britain probably had the best propellant.

Britain refused the propellant request after seeking the opinion of the US State Department. The Foreign Office decided, however, not to consult France, even though it was the third signatory of the Tripartite Declaration. There was a risk that Israel would find out about any Anglo-French discussions, the Foreign Office stated in a March 1959 note. The Israelis, the note added, may then suspect 'us of ganging up on them'.[12]

During the 1960s, Britain teamed up with Germany in a secret project aimed at strengthening Israel's navy. Werner Knieper, an official in

Germany's defence ministry, told Britain's embassy in Bonn during May 1964 that a dossier relating to Israel had become 'very urgent'. Germany had 'in the quietest possible way' been implementing a military aid programme for Israel 'based on the policy of supplying not too offensive weapons,' the British embassy noted. As part of that cooperation, Israel had sought two submarines. While Germany was not willing to manufacture these weapons, it was prepared to finance Israel's acquisition of British submarines, Knieper stated.[13]

The two submarines were named *Turpin* and *Totem*. They were of Second World War design but in talks with Britain during January and February 1964, the Israelis had stressed they would only buy the vessels if they were modernised. Israeli commanders had been granted an opportunity to inspect the *Turpin* when it called on Haifa in April that year. The encounter proved 'extremely embarrassing', the vessel's captain Terry Thompson recorded. Thompson had not been informed about Israel's intentions and was caught off-guard when a naval commander asked him how he felt about the vessel being sold to Israel.

Shortly after the Haifa visit, the British government approved the sale of both submarines for a combined price of £2.2 million. A memo drawn up by Britain's defence ministry stated that: 'the Israelis could not find the money themselves so they have persuaded the Germans to pay for the submarines as part of their reparations to Israel.'[14] The 'reparations' referred to payments made by Germany to Israel as an act of atonement for the suffering caused to Jews by the Nazis. Entering into force in 1953, the reparations agreement between Germany and Israel was partly used to build up Israel's military capacity.

At the same time as it was eyeing up submarines, Israel sought to buy a large number of Centurion tanks. The British government gave a commitment in September 1964 to provide Israel with 250 Centurions. The deal was sealed through a subsequent exchange of letters between Denis Healey, Britain's defence secretary, and Levi Eshkol, Israel's prime minister (who also held the defence portfolio).[15]

Some details of the submarine sale were revealed by the British press in November 1964.[16] The Foreign Office complained to the defence ministry after its spokesperson was quoted in the *Daily Telegraph* confirming that the deal had been made. 'We regard it as particularly important to maintain as much secrecy as possible about our supplies of arms to Israel in order to avoid stirring up angry reactions from the

Arab countries and, by avoiding this, to retain our freedom to meet Israel's reasonable needs for defensive arms,' R.S. Crawford at the Foreign Office wrote.[17]

By spring 1965, the Foreign Office had judged Arab reaction to the submarine deal as 'mild'. And even if the Arab response was to get stronger Britain would fulfil contracts already agreed with Israel unless there were 'exceptional circumstances' such as an 'outbreak of war', a memo stated. The Foreign Office was worried, though, that details of its tank deal with Israel would find their way into the public domain. 'Compared with two submarines, 250 Centurions are of a different order of importance in the context of the Arab–Israel dispute,' the memo stated.[18]

Greasing the wheels of occupation

Arms cooperation figured prominently on the agenda when Levi Eshkol visited London in March 1965 for discussions with Harold Wilson, the British prime minister. Denis Healey met Eshkol, too. During their conversation, Eshkol enquired if Britain would be prepared to sell up to 300 Centurions to Israel. That would be in addition to the 250 already agreed. Healey had a novel argument about why he was inclined to approve arms exports to Israel. Maintaining the 'balance of power' in the Middle East would not be possible 'without modernising the Israeli army's equipment in due course,' he wrote to Eshkol, a day after they had dined together. Without making any firm commitments, he added: 'I see no reason to think that we shall not be able to meet your needs.'[19]

Britain also indicated a willingness to provide Israel with Chieftain tanks. Faster and more powerful than the Centurion, the Chieftain became Britain's main battle tank in the 1960s and remained so for the next couple of decades. In 1966, Britain loaned two Chieftains to Israel. The top tank specialist in its military, Israel Tal, was 'like a dog with two tails' when they arrived early the following year, according to the British embassy in Tel Aviv.[20] Typically, Britain was adamant that there should be no publicity around the loan. Israel did not refer to the loan in official comments until 1980, when its military published a potted history of the tanks in its arsenal.[21] Some British journalists were aware of the loan but decided to keep the public in the dark. Charles Douglas-Home, defence correspondent of *The Times*, learned about it in 1967 but promised the British government he would only write about it if he heard that another journalist planned to scoop him on the story.

Data compiled by Britain's defence ministry indicates that Israel was supplied with a total of 183 Centurion tanks by July 1965. A further 151 were delivered between then and May 1967. Sales of the Centurion meant that Britain was the main supplier of heavy tanks to Israel.[22] Israel owned a few hundred British tanks by June 1967 – when it once again went to war against its Arab neighbours.

Britain blamed Egypt's decision to block Israeli ships from passing through the Straits of Tiran for the outbreak of that war. Unsuccessfully, the British tried to form an international task force with the objective of lifting the blockade.[23] George Brown, the British foreign secretary, inferred that the strategic blunders of the Suez crisis would not be repeated. 'We are not setting out – to use the colloquialism – to topple Nasser,' he told the House of Commons, reminding his Conservative rivals they had 'once foolishly tried' to remove the Egyptian president. 'But neither are we prepared to accept that he has a right to topple another Middle Eastern nation at the risk of plunging us all into war.'[24]

Britain aided Israel considerably as it prepared the offensive. Eshkol's contacts with Wilson and Healey proved fruitful from Israel's perspective. They led to a series of secret arms deliveries. One shipment took place the weekend before the June 1967 war erupted. The *Miryam*, an Israeli cargo vessel, sailed from the port of Felixstowe, laden with armoured vehicles, tank shells and machine guns.

Britain's weapons were heavily used by Israel during the war. Centurion tanks featured prominently, for example, in the battle of Abu Aghelia. Israel's victory in that battle allowed it to seize control of the entire Sinai peninsula.[25] That did not go unnoticed by British diplomats in Tel Aviv. They observed how commanders, including the aforementioned Israel Tal, were 'particularly handsome in their praise' of the Centurion. The tank 'apparently did far more than was ever expected of it,' an embassy memo noted.[26]

Palestinians refer to the 1967 war as the *Naksa* (Arabic for 'setback'). The 'setback' made them refugees for the second time in two decades. Around 400,000 of Palestinians in the West Bank and Gaza were displaced because of the war. Half of those people had previously been uprooted by Zionist forces in 1948. The *Naksa* opened another chapter in the dispossession of Palestinians. Israel took control of almost 850 square kilometres of Palestinian land, beginning an occupation that continues to this day.[27]

While the war was underway, Denis Healey told cabinet colleagues that Britain should not hold up the supply of arms to Israel so long as the Soviet Union supplied weapons to Arab states.[28] The British government wished, however, to be perceived as even-handed and as committed to international law. As part of that effort, George Brown called on Israel not to remain in occupation of the territories it had invaded. Speaking to the UN general assembly on 21 June, Brown warned the Israelis that annexing Jerusalem's Old City 'will not only isolate them from world opinion but will also lose them the sympathy that they have.' Pointing to the UN Charter, he stressed that 'war should not lead to territorial aggrandisement'. Brown reportedly bumped into an Israeli delegation including Golda Meir shortly after his speech. Meir is said to have called him 'Judas'.[29]

Her outburst – if it occurred – did not reflect reality. Far from betraying Israel, Brown was minded to help it. In July 1967, Brown had a meeting with Aharon Remez, Israel's London envoy. When Remez informed him that Israel was thinking about the 'next generation' of weapons for its military, Brown said that Britain was committed to achieving an international arms limitation accord for the Middle East. But if an agreement could not be thrashed out, then Britain would be prepared to supply arms to Israel in any of the fields Remez had mentioned. The list of 'fields' was broad – it included equipment for the navy, armoured troops and the air force, as well as electronic weaponry.[30] Brown set out his thoughts on arming Israel in an August 1967 note to Wilson. Brown was not perturbed about how Britain's arms exports had contributed to ethnic cleansing and how fresh deliveries of weapons would almost certainly be used against Palestinians. Rather, his main concern was that 'tanks for Israel are hard to hide'. If Britain was seen to be supplying them to Israel alone, 'we shall without doubt intensify our difficulties' with such countries as Libya, Kuwait and Saudi Arabia, he noted. Brown felt that 'we might get away with Centurions for Israel' provided they were 'matched' with a delivery of warplanes to Jordan. 'But I am not too sure how rearming both sides in this way would look in political terms.'[31]

Britain maintained a steady flow of arms to Israel following the June 1967 war. The stance adopted by Harold Wilson and his ministers contrasted with that of Charles de Gaulle in France, whose government halted weapons supplies to Israel (in a clear departure from France's earlier policies). Soon after the June war, Israel's London envoy Aharon Remez informed the British government that 'we now urgently require' 150 Centurions, 'delivery of which should begin as soon as possible'. Remez pointed to the 'heavy wear and tear' on Israel's arsenal because of 'recent events' – a euphemism for war – and contended that 150 tanks would be the 'bare minimum' needed to 'retain our present level of effectiveness unimpaired'.[32] Remez was rewarded for his persistent lobbying. He was soon told that 50 tanks would be made available. Israel was also promised that Britain would supply it with a third submarine, the *Truncheon*.[33]

A total of 100 Centurion tanks were exported from Britain to Israel between August 1967 and January 1969.[34] Britain's arms exports policy to the Middle East became increasingly shaped by the Cold War. A Foreign Office memo from November 1967 cited estimates that Russia had 'already restored' around 80 per cent of armour that Egypt had lost in June. Maintaining a 'rough balance of forces' in the Middle East was necessary 'to avoid driving the Israelis into a situation where they felt compelled to rely on the development of a nuclear weapon for their defence,' the memo suggested.[35]

UN Security Council Resolution 242 was adopted that same month. That landmark decision listed two principles that should form the basis of a 'just and lasting peace' in the Middle East. The first one was that Israel should withdraw from all territories it occupied in June 1967. The second principle was that all belligerency should stop and the 'sovereignty, territorial integrity and political independence' of every state in the region must be respected, along with their right to live in peace.[36]

Michael Stewart – successor to George Brown as foreign secretary – wrote a paper in May 1968 about what Britain should do in the absence of a peace accord based on that resolution. His main recommendation was to sell Israel bigger and deadlier weapons. 'The survival of Israel as a separate state is a fundamental aspect of our Middle East policy,' he wrote. So long as there was a conflict between Israel and its Arab neighbours 'the requirements of survival dictate that Israel should maintain armed forces of sufficient strength and sophistication to deter any Arab attempt at her destruction.' Stewart advocated that Britain 'should be prepared to meet Israeli requests for arms' unless they infringed on three criteria. These were: that Britain should maintain 'an approximate balance of military strength' between Israel and its neighbours; that Britain should not sell weapons that were 'exclusively offensive'; and that Britain should not become Israel's main supplier of 'major new categories' of arms.[37]

His interpretation of these criteria was creative, to say the least. He was keen on clinching a deal to sell 1,000 pound high explosive bombs to Israel. Although he admitted that a 'strong case' could be made that such bombs were 'exclusively offensive', he argued that 'account should also be taken of the particular strategic circumstances of Israel.' Because Israel was 'a small country, closely hemmed in by her neighbours', the 'distinction between offensive and defensive use [of weapons] is, therefore, an unreal one in relation to Israel,' he wrote.[38]

'We cannot afford morality'

Civil servants working with him interpreted Britain's arms exports policy in a comparably loose way. Tony Moore, who handled discussion at the Foreign Office about what information relating to the Middle East should be made public, felt there was no problem with Britain remaining Israel's main supplier of tanks. By continuing to sell Centurions to Israel 'we should not be raising the level of sophistication of arms in the area,' he wrote in an internal paper. The 'main possible argument against supply is that it might provide a basis for propaganda against us should relations with the Arabs again deteriorate,' he noted. Moore described the possibility as an 'acceptable risk'. He noted that Britain's tank sales to Israel did not feature prominently in Arab criticisms of the West around the time of the June 1967 war.[39] (Much of those criticisms were based on Nasser's unfounded allegation – dubbed the 'big lie' by Western diplomats – that America and Britain were fighting against Egypt with warplanes. The truth about Britain's very real contribution of weapons to Israel's ground offensive received far less attention).[40]

The idea of stopping all weapons sales to Israel and her neighbours was briefly entertained in Whitehall. Geoffrey George Arthur at the

Foreign Office stated in 1968 that a comprehensive arms embargo for the Middle East would be 'the best moral position but I suppose we cannot afford morality nowadays.'[41] Many of his colleagues contended in less colourful terms that they viewed the potential growth of weapons exports as beneficial for British business. 'Economic – and, more particularly balance of payments – considerations are always in the forefront of our minds,' another Foreign Office paper stated.[42] The value of weapons exports was considerable: the British government calculated that selling 500 Centurion tanks to Israel between 1959 and 1968 was worth £7.6 million. Under a further deal signed in 1969, Britain undertook to ship 90 tanks to Israel. The value of that deal came to £1 million.

Having borrowed and tested two Chieftains, the Israeli military became increasingly interested in buying these tanks. Initially, the British cabinet agreed that it would be willing to sell Chieftains to Israel in 1968. But fears of an Arab backlash prompted a rethink. Government departments had different views. In spring 1969, the Foreign Office argued that the deteriorating situation in the Middle East meant that Britain should postpone work on the Chieftain dossier. It recommended that a scheduled visit of British tank specialists to Israel should be delayed indefinitely. Because the matter was deemed sensitive, the Israelis should not be informed why the postponement occurred. Denis Healey was not happy with that reasoning. He argued:

> If we are to stand the slightest chance of selling [to Israel] in future, I am sure that we have got to behave respectably towards the customer and not to make him think that we are willing to play ducks and drakes with his interests whenever it suits us.[43]

The Foreign Office was thinking beyond arms deals. It stressed that Britain had bigger commercial interests in Arab countries than in Israel. Angering Arab countries would leave Britain 'vulnerable' as they could reduce its oil supply, a Foreign Office paper stated, adding:

> Several of the Arab governments accept that we supply arms to Israel. The Chieftain deal has become an emotional issue and a symbol (if we go ahead) of support for Israel and hostility to the Arabs at a time when Israel still occupies Arab territory.[44]

Michael Stewart was at pains to underscore Britain's devotion to Israel when he met Aharon Remez in May 1969. The 'survival of Israel' was an 'essential consideration' for Britain, Stewart said. While Britain had large economic interests in Arab countries, it hoped that those interests would never come into conflict with its commitment to Israel. If a conflict did occur, protecting Israel would be 'paramount'. And 'if Israel's security was at stake, we would be prepared to set at risk our economic interests elsewhere,' an account of the meeting states.[45]

Golda Meir did not seem to bear grudges against Britain. In 1969, she became Israel's first and, to date, only female prime minister. When she and Yigal Allon, the deputy prime minister and former military leader, visited London that year, they emphasised that Israel needed friends, according to British government archives. Apart from Britain and the USA, Israel had nowhere it could turn to, they lamented.[46] Meir availed of the opportunity to tell ITN that Israel wanted a 'minimum proportion' of weapons 'so Israel can take care of itself'.[47]

Britain was happy to remain Israel's key tank supplier, provided it could avoid raising too many Arab hackles. A background note by Geoffrey George Arthur argued that Britain 'could get away with' selling Centurions to Israel 'almost indefinitely' by claiming it was simply fulfilling contracts. Goronwy Roberts, a Foreign Office minister, agreed with his observations, responding that Centurions had 'proved superior' to any Soviet tanks that had been exported to Arab countries. The Chieftains were another matter. Roberts believed that Israel was not pressing for Chieftain tanks purely for reasons of security. Another 'motive' lay behind the pressure, he wrote: 'to involve us on a major issue on their side and commensurately to detach us from the Arabs'.[48]

Eventually, the British government decided to reverse its decision to supply Israel with Chieftains. That news was formally conveyed in November 1969. Michael Stewart did not go into detail about the reasons for the refusal. In a letter to Abba Eban, his Israeli counterpart, Stewart simply stated that the surrounding issues had been studied 'in the light of the present situation in the Middle East'. Britain would continue 'the other things that we have been doing for you in the past few years,' Stewart wrote.[49]

Eban reacted by pointing out (accurately) that Britain was 'vulnerable to economic pressure' from Arab countries. Speaking to the press, he questioned whether Britain was fit to act as an 'umpire in diplomatic consultations' on the Middle East. 'You cannot be an arbiter, with someone else's hand on your throat,' he reportedly said. Although his written reply to Stewart was not quite so colourful, he warned that 'a point has been reached at which the British–Israel relationship is in danger of being seriously affected.'[50]

British representatives tried to put the Chieftain refusal behind them as quickly as possible. As part of efforts to mollify Israel, John Barnes, a newly appointed ambassador in Tel Aviv, suggested to Eban that Britain was selling ten Centurions for the price of one Chieftain. Some Israeli officials were 'rather surprised' by that claim, he told the Foreign Office, asking for clarification about some figures it had given him on the cost of weapons.[51] The Foreign Office told him it would be 'wrong presentationally' to offer the continued supply of Centurions and ammunition as 'compensation' for the Chieftains but that 'we would hope to demonstrate to the Israelis that it is business as before.'[52]

'Seize every order'

The 'business as before' approach had support from Britain's two largest political parties. One of the final decisions of the Wilson-led Labour government was to approve a contract for supplying 50 Centurions to Israel. Conservative ministers resolved that the contract should be renewed after their party won the 1970 general election. Alec Douglas-Home, the new foreign secretary, briefed Ted Heath, the new prime minister, that 'the arguments for agreeing to continue the supply of Centurions are very strong.' Douglas-Home was more concerned about potential Israeli hostility should a fresh batch of Centurions be refused than potential protests from Arab countries if Israel was supplied with more weapons. Arab countries 'may have become reconciled to the idea of a continuing flow' of tanks to Israel, Douglas-Home added.[53] Returning to the theme in November 1970, Douglas-Home stated in a matter-of-fact way that Britain was 'morally committed' to arming Israel. Heath concurred. Not only did Heath approve the ongoing delivery to Israel of ten Centurions per month, he asked 'when are we going to be able' to also supply 'both sides' with Chieftains?[54]

The flow helped Israel to develop its own weapons industry. Many of the Centurions exported from Britain were second hand. They were refurbished and, in the words of the Foreign Office, 'virtually rebuilt' by the Israelis. The rebuilding included installing new engines and fuel tanks; the Israelis were also making their own guns and ammunition in growing quantities.[55] It is no coincidence, therefore, that the prototype of the Merkava – Israel's own battle tank – was at least partly modelled on the Centurion.[56]

Furthermore, there is evidence that Britain provided the nascent Israeli arms industry with technical know-how. Foreign Office archives say that Britain agreed in 1967 to 'the disclosure of confidential information about our cluster bomb system to the Israelis.'[57] It seems highly unlikely that the Israeli authorities did not make some use of that confidential information in developing their own cluster bombs – weapons known to slice the limbs off their victims. By the late 1970s, Israel's capacity to manufacture cluster bombs had become so advanced that it was reportedly exporting them to Africa.[58] Subsequently, Israel has used the weapon in attacking Lebanon.[59]

Heath had a concise answer when asked his view on possible submarine sales to Israel a few months later: 'we must seize every order we can'.[60] The prime minister felt that one deal with Israel could lead to more orders as Israel was anxious not to rely too much on the USA as a source of weaponry.[61] That message was relayed when an Israeli military delegation visited Britain's defence ministry in November 1970. The delegation had stated that Israel's budget for foreign-made weapons came to $730 million that year, $600 million of which was being spent in the USA. Israel at the time bought between $20 million and $25 million worth of British weapons per year. If greater cooperation could be achieved, Israel would be in a position to buy a much greater quantity of British arms, the delegation suggested. Orders placed in Britain could be worth between $100 million and $200 million.[62]

The type of submarines coveted by Israel were made in France and Germany. As both those countries had halted weapons sales to Israel, its authorities approached Britain with a proposal. Israel wanted three 500-ton submarines (combined price: £18 million) built by Vickers in Cumbria, with a German firm cooperating on design and providing some components.[63] The submarines would be equipped with torpedoes. Once again, the Israelis portrayed these weapons as defensive in nature, though Douglas-Home acknowledged that they could be used offensively. Acquiring the submarines would give Israel 'the edge in underwater operations' over its Arab neighbours, he added, based on an assessment from the defence ministry.[64]

The submarine project was authorised by the British government in June 1971. An obstacle was soon encountered, however. Germany refused to allow the exportation of components required for the project. After learning about that snag, Douglas-Home enquired if substitute components could be found. The view from the Foreign Office was that Israel was so eager to have the submarines that it would source the components elsewhere, probably from the USA.[65] The prediction turned out to be correct. The submarines – named Gal after the Hebrew word for wave – were indeed assembled by Vickers during the 1970s. The first of the three arrived at Haifa port in 1976.[66]

Some details of the submarine deal were published by Egyptian and British newspapers in March 1972.[67] The British government immediately tried to tamp down the controversy. Anthony Parsons, a senior figure in the Foreign Office, acted to ensure that the government was not held to account. He did so by contacting Dennis Walters, a Conservative MP known to be sympathetic to the plight of Palestine's refugees. Walters was briefed about the submarine deal in confidence because 'it was clear that, if I had not, he and others would have raised PQs [parliamentary questions] by now,' Parsons noted. 'This we wanted to avoid.' Walters agreed to discourage like-minded MPs from raising the matter in public.[68]

Heath's government was also willing to facilitate cooperation with Israel's nuclear industry. In 1973, the UK Atomic Energy Authority sought permission to undertake joint research with Israel. Fearing a backlash from Arab states, the agency decided not to propose a formal arrangement but rather that it work with Israel in a discreet manner on such topics as seawater desalination. When asked its opinion, the Foreign Office stated it would have no difficulty with cooperation in a narrow range of activities. 'Desalination is a non-controversial subject and we could easily defend our cooperation with the Israelis in this field,' noted Patricia Long, a Middle East specialist at the Foreign Office.[69] Her comment was both revealing and deceptive. It was revealing because it showed Britain was more concerned about being able to project an image of propriety, than actually behaving properly. It was deceptive because it implied that Britain was only willing to cooperate on nuclear projects of a civilian nature. Yet the Israelis have never drawn a clear distinction between their military and civilian activities. Israel founded two nuclear research facilities, Dimona and Soreq, in the late 1950s.[70] Both have been used to develop nuclear weapons.[71]

The 'business as before' approach was interrupted by the October 1973 war between Israel and an alliance of Arab states led by Egypt. Britain responded by stopping the supply of weapons to Israel and a number of its Arab neighbours. US planes bringing weapons to Israel were also forbidden from landing on British military bases.[72] Douglas-Home said the measures were taken 'because we considered it inconsistent to call for an immediate end to the fighting and yet to continue to send arms to the conflict.'[73]

America was told that the decisions were taken because Britain did not want to upset the Arab oil providers on which it had become reliant. Rowland Baring, Britain's ambassador in Washington, stressed why no assistance could be provided to the USA as it prepared to replenish Israel's arsenal. 'Europe would not be content to go without Middle East oil because of American actions,' Baring said.[74] Britain's arms embargo was short-lived; it was lifted in January 1974.[75]

Harold Wilson tried to assert his pro-Israel credentials as leader of the opposition. In a 1972 speech, he effectively repudiated the policy to which he was committed as prime minister. It was 'utterly unreal,' he argued, to call for Israeli withdrawal from the territories it occupied in 1967. 'Israel's reaction is natural and proper in refusing to accept the Palestinians as a nation,' he added.[76] The following year, Wilson urged Heath to lift the weapon restrictions placed on Israel. Wilson imposed a three-line whip on Labour MPs when the issue was debated in the House of Commons. He is reported to have overruled objections by Roy Jenkins, a prominent Labour politician, by saying: 'Look, Roy, I've accommodated your fucking conscience for years. Now you're going to have to take account of mine. I feel as strongly about the Middle East as you do about the Common Market.'[77] Speaking in Parliament, Wilson alleged that 'the present government's refusal to meet our arms supplies is symptomatic of a wider general attitude to Middle Eastern affairs, a total change in Britain's position since 1967.' Britain had been in 'the inner circle' when UN Security Council resolution 242 was negotiated because it was perceived that it and the USA would take a broadly pro-Israel line, according to Wilson, whereas France would be more sympathetic towards Arab concerns. By ceasing to sell weapons, Britain was as likely to be 'disqualifying' itself from a seat at the mediators' table, he argued, as winning a seat.[78]

Labour formed a minority government after the February 1974 election, with Wilson becoming prime minister for the second time. Jim Callaghan, the new foreign secretary, soon set about making some adjustments to British policy on arms exports. He advocated a 'more liberal policy' towards Egypt, according to the report of a May 1974 discussion between him and Wilson. Nasser had died in 1970 and his successor Anwar Sadat was considered more anxious to buy weapons from the West than from the Soviet Union. Callaghan felt that Britain should try to persuade Israel it was better for Egypt to buy from Britain than from Russia or France.[79]

Britain's stated commitment to preventing a Middle East arms race had never been credible. The policy was, in effect, abandoned in the 1970s. A 1975 memo from the defence ministry concluded that it was 'even more pointless' to envisage major arms exporters restricting supplies to the Middle East than it was before the 1973 war. America's promise to give Israel a huge quantity of arms in return for signing a Sinai disengagement accord with Egypt was cited as evidence of how Britain's influence had waned.

The paper also hinted that an arms limitation accord would not be in Britain's financial interest. Between January 1974 and July 1975, Britain had received orders worth £200 million from the Middle East. Israel accounted for just £9 million of that sum. Although Israel was now turning almost exclusively to the US arms industry, the Middle East region was the destination for almost 40 per cent of annual British weapons exports.[80]

The trend whereby the USA is the top exporter of arms to Israel has persisted. Yet British arms sales also grew during the second half of the 1970s. The value of British military exports to Israel was placed at £18 million per annum in 1978 – double the figure for 1975. Israel's share of the global arms industry grew during the 1970s. By the end of the decade, it was estimated that Israel's arms exports exceeded $1 billion.

The British embassy in Tel Aviv rated Israel as being at fourth place in the 'western arms exporting league'.[81]

The rating revealed much about how Britain's diplomats – even those stationed in the Middle East – saw Israel as belonging to the West. A historical and psychological connection with the Zionist movement trumped geographical facts. Perhaps that explains why Britain shielded Israel's military activities from scrutiny.

Along with the USA and the Soviet Union, Britain was one of the three depository states to the nuclear Non-Proliferation Treaty. Britain, therefore, has an obligation – since the treaty came into force in 1970 – to avert the threat of nuclear war. Persuading Israel to sign the NPT and allow inspections of its nuclear facilities are among those duties. Yet Britain does not appear to have applied any serious pressure on Israel to come clean about its nuclear activities. An internal Foreign Office paper from 1978 stated that the issue was 'inauspicious' and predicted that any attempt to arm-twist the Israelis would fail.[82] Margaret Thatcher tiptoed around the question of Israel's nuclear capability in correspondence with Menachem Begin, her Israeli counterpart, the following year. Thatcher's choice of words was instructive; she asked Begin to 'consider very carefully the part which Israel herself has to play in avoiding the spread of nuclear weapons into the Middle East.' The officials who drafted Thatcher's letter were fully aware that Israel either had nuclear weapons at that point or the capacity to develop them; one official specialising in nuclear matters stated that Israel could 'quickly assemble about a dozen low-yield weapons'.

Britain helped to conceal the reality of Israel's activities. When the issue was raised at the 1979 UN general assembly, Britain refused to support Arab calls for a study on Israel's nuclear capability. Similarly, Britain was not willing to back a resolution criticising the nuclear cooperation between Israel and South Africa.[83]

The British stance was not surprising. Britain had helped found and arm the state of Israel. Now, Britain was protective of its *protégé*.

7
Sidelining the PLO

'We are careful not to be chummy with Palestinians here.' Those words
– written by a Beirut-based diplomat in 1973 – encapsulated Britain's
attitude to the victims of ethnic cleansing.[1] The Palestinians living in
Lebanon were survivors of the *Nakba*. By this time, they had been
repeatedly attacked by Israel. Abba Eban, Israel's foreign minister, had
defended the massacre of children in one aerial bombing of a refugee
camp as a 'strictly preventive measure', asking 'who can guarantee that
these children will not become terrorists when they grow up?'[2] Some
refugees were fighting back. The Palestine Liberation Organization
(PLO) had set up its headquarters in Lebanon after being expelled
from Jordan during the early 1970s.

The idea of setting an objective for British dealings with the PLO
was discussed around this time. What should that goal be? Foreign
Office documents from 1974 put it bluntly: 'splitting off the extremists
from the rest' or 'to separate the Arafatists from the wild boys'. That
was code for Britain's desire to convince Palestinians that they should
accept Israel's apartheid system. Yasser Arafat, the PLO's chairman,
was considered – by British officials – as someone who would be willing
to do just that. The 'extremists' were those deemed too stubborn to
embrace injustice.

The goal of encouraging divisions appears to have first been mooted
by Glen Balfour-Paul, then Britain's ambassador in Amman. It did not
immediately find favour in Whitehall. David Gore-Booth, a Middle
East specialist in the Foreign Office, felt the 'time was not yet ripe
for outsiders, by which I mean non-Arabs, to promote such a split.'
Gore-Booth argued that 'it is hardly for us to contemplate giving
Arafat a shove from behind, even discreetly, when there is no sign that
the Americans are yet contemplating doing so.' He added:

My assessment, in any case, is that Arafat needs no shoving. He is longing to have the appurtenances of power which a settlement will bring him. But he knows that the power will elude him if he moves too fast. He is trying to bring as many of the wild boys as possible along with him and thus to turn what Mr Balfour-Paul sees as handcuffs into cuff-links. But if he cannot do this and they remain handcuffs, he will try to slip them off as soon as he calculates that he safely can. Oddly enough, his interest in all this is parallel with that of the Israelis. There is no point in their negotiating with Arafat if he is only a small part of the PLO since any result of such a negotiation would not bind the rest of the PLO. This is a worry which the Israelis are constantly voicing.[3]

The bitter irony is that the British government's own policy on Palestine was inflexible. Anthony Parsons summed up the policy: 'We would obviously have no truck with the "multinational, secular state" idea of the Palestinian organisations. Such ideas are wholly incompatible with our attitude toward Israel.' One of his colleagues at the Foreign Office, J.P. Bannerman, similarly described the 'establishment of a multiracial Palestine' as an 'extremist objective'.[4] Those attitudes illustrate how Britain was determined to enable Israel to remain an apartheid state. The entirely reasonable demand that all of historic Palestine – including the state that had become Israel – be transformed into a democracy, guaranteeing equality to citizens irrespective of their ethnicity or faith was viewed as outlandish.

The PLO's aspirations were listed in its 1968 charter. It made clear that the organisation regarded 'Palestine, with the boundaries it had during the British Mandate, as an indivisible territorial unit.' It committed the PLO to strive for the 'elimination of Zionism in Palestine' and left no doubt that Palestinians regarded the Zionist movement as 'racist and fanatic in its nature, aggressive, expansionist and colonial in its aims and fascist in its methods.' The charter drew a distinction, however, between Zionism and Judaism, which it called (accurately) a religion, rather than a nationality. Jews who had lived in Palestine 'before the Zionist invasion will be considered Palestinians,' the charter stated. It also stated that the:

liberation of Palestine, from a spiritual point of view, will provide the Holy Land with an atmosphere of safety and tranquillity, which in turn will safeguard the country's religious sanctuaries and guarantee freedom of worship and of visit to all, without discrimination of race, colour, language or religion.[5]

Though mostly clear, some aspects of the charter were ambiguous. For example, it did not specify if Jews who had moved to Palestine (including present-day Israel) and, in very many cases, no longer had homes in Europe should be allowed to remain there once Zionism had been vanquished. Arafat provided clarity on that matter during his speech at the UN general assembly in November 1974. He said:

In my formal capacity as chairman of the PLO and leader of the Palestinian revolution, I proclaim before you that when we speak of our common hopes for the Palestine of tomorrow, we include in our perspective all Jews now living in Palestine who choose to live with us there in peace and without discrimination.[6]

The British held some discussions with the PLO ahead of Arafat's speech. James Craig, head of the Middle East department at the Foreign Office, told PLO representatives that Britain would find it difficult to accept calls for the right of Palestinians to self-determination. A UN resolution containing such a call 'might be used to cast doubt on the legal existence of Israel,' a British diplomatic cable stated.[7]

Kowtowing to Kissinger

Britain's policy in the 1970s was that meetings with the PLO should be conducted in an informal manner and outside government buildings. As leader of the opposition, Harold Wilson met PLO representatives on two occasions. When he became prime minister, however, Wilson was advised by the Foreign Office to turn down requests for dialogue from the PLO. Jim Callaghan, the foreign secretary, felt that any encounter between Wilson and the PLO would become public and would 'evoke considerable criticism in Israel, in Jordan and from many people in Britain,' a memo stated. The Foreign Office was also worried that Henry Kissinger, the US secretary of state, would regard high-level British contacts with the PLO as 'most untimely' given that he was leading a 'peace' initiative in the Middle East. Britain was not willing to confer any status on the PLO, without America's permission; Kissinger's line was that the USA would not speak with the PLO until it recognised Israel's 'right to exist'.[8]

'The accolade of respectability, if it is ever to be given to the PLO, will have to be given by Dr Kissinger,' James Craig had argued.[9] The likelihood of Kissinger granting that accolade was remote. He had strenuously opposed a 1974 Arab League decision – subsequently endorsed by the UN general assembly – that the PLO should be recognised as the sole legitimate representative body for the Palestinian people.[10]

Jim Callaghan, then Britain's foreign secretary, warned British diplomats that they should exercise caution if they had contacts with PLO members. He stated:

> It is extremely difficult for us to contemplate extending any form of recognition to the PLO so long as the PLO's official objective remains the merging of Israel into a secular state and so long as the PLO leadership endorses terrorist methods.[11]

The British government felt that the 'legitimate political rights of the Palestinian people should be taken account of in a settlement of the Arab–Israel dispute,' he stated, too.[12] Taking account of a people's rights is, of course, very different to ensuring that those rights are realized.

A Foreign Office discussion paper from April 1975 reveals how subservient Britain had become to the USA. The paper noted that Kissinger's initiative had not been fruitful and that the US government was conducting a review of its approach to Middle East affairs. It also referred to private comments by Kissinger that the USA would only undertake negotiations in future if there were 'prior guarantees' that an agreement would be reached. Various options for British policy on the Middle East were outlined. But the paper concluded by recommending that 'our best course would seem to be to maintain our unheroic but realistic posture of support for Dr Kissinger.'[13] In effect, this meant that Britain was allowing its policies to be dictated by the USA, a highly partisan superpower. Kissinger would make plain how far the

USA was prepared to go in supporting Israel later that year. He asked Congress to award Israel $2.2 billion in economic and military aid. 'The keystone of our policy in the Middle East has always rested on the ability of Israel to preserve its own defence,' Kissinger said.[14]

In November 1975, the UN general assembly passed a resolution declaring that Zionism was a form of racism and racial discrimination. Britain's response was one of 'natural repugnance', Goronwy Roberts, a Foreign Office minister, told the House of Lords. The resolution, he claimed, 'served no purpose than to bring the United Nations into disrepute' and 'may also make more difficult the already formidable task of finding a peaceful solution to the Middle East conflict.'[15]

The British government was prepared to argue that 'peace' required Palestinians, a people who had been colonised and uprooted, to make concessions, rather than Israel. That view was advanced by David Roberts, a British envoy to Damascus, in December 1975, when he wrote: 'It is a thousand pities that Arafat is neither strong nor shrewd enough to make some sort of gesture of compromise at a moment when his sagging stock is likely to enjoy a brief rise in the market.'[16]

Britain did not leave its historical baggage behind when it joined the European Economic Community in 1973. The first years of membership coincided with the bloc stepping up its activities on the Middle East. In 1975, Israel and the EEC signed a free trade agreement.[17] That marked the beginning of a process whereby Israel's exporters would be given preferential access to European markets. Five years later, the community made an attempt to influence the international debate about how 'peace' could be achieved in the Middle East.

At first glance, the 1980 Venice declaration looks progressive, although with cumbersome phrasing. It advocates a 'comprehensive peace settlement' based on two principles: 'the right to existence and security of all states in the region, including Israel, and justice for all the peoples, which implies the recognition of the legitimate rights of the Palestinians.' The Palestinian people, the declaration adds, 'must be placed in a position, by an appropriate process defined within the framework of a comprehensive peace settlement, to exercise fully its rights to self-determination.' The declaration also states that the PLO 'will have to be associated' with negotiations towards a peace agreement.[18] Although the idea of the PLO being 'associated' to talks was nebulous, the declaration appeared to be recommending a different approach to that taken during the US-brokered negotiations which led to the Camp David accords between Israel and Egypt. Those agreements ushered in an era of collaboration between Egypt and Israel, which ultimately led to the Cairo authorities helping to enforce Israel's twenty-first century siege of Gaza. Despite having a profound impact on Palestinians, the Camp David accords were written without any Palestinian input.

The language on Palestinian rights in the Venice declaration was arguably negated by the emphasis it placed on Israel's perceived entitlements. The declaration stated that Israel had a right to exist but did not acknowledge the fact that Israel had been founded as an apartheid state. The existence of an apartheid system in historic Palestine could hardly lead to the justice for Palestinians which the EEC ostensibly desired.

Speaking notes prepared for Margaret Thatcher, the prime minister, ahead of the summit indicate that Britain was more concerned with protecting Israel than rectifying the wrongs done to the Palestinians. The EEC, Thatcher was advised, 'must concentrate on [the] problem of how self-determination can be put into practice and reconciled with Israel's security needs.' She was also recommended to stress that the EEC's governments 'cannot aspire to play the dominant role in peace efforts', that 'US goodwill must be retained as far as possible' and 'great care [is] also needed to avoid alienating Israelis'. The diplomats who drafted these notes stated that the opinions of other EEC governments 'coincide in general with our own' but that the French 'remain inclined' to push the community towards 'as independent and far-reaching a role as possible'.[19]

Israel reacted to the Venice declaration in a hysterical manner – by accusing the EEC of appeasing the PLO in much the same way that Neville Chamberlain had appeased Hitler. An official government statement described the PLO as 'that Arab SS'. All 'men who revere liberty' would see the declaration as 'another Munich-like capitulation to totalitarian blackmail,' the statement added.[20] Peter Carrington, foreign secretary at the time, wrote to his Israeli counterpart Yitzhak Shamir shortly after the statement was issued. Carrington contended that the declaration was 'even-handed and constructive'.[21]

In a note to Thatcher from August that year, Carrington argued that Britain could not ignore 'Israeli intransigence'. But he was at pains to stress that he was not suggesting that Britain should 'turn away' from Israel. 'We are responsible in history for her creation and could not contemplate any betrayal,' he wrote.[22] Preparing for the EEC's follow-up discussions on the Venice declaration, Carrington advocated a role for the bloc that would complement that of the USA. European governments could 'tread where the Americans cannot,' he believed, according to a Foreign Office memo, referring to their contacts with the PLO. 'We have an opportunity here to shift the PLO along a more moderate path,' the memo stated.[23]

The Foreign Office drafted a detailed blueprint for the Middle East in the autumn of 1980. It began by identifying the 'Arab–Israel problem' as 'probably the single most dangerous threat to world peace'. Not only did the problem undermine 'the American position throughout the Arab and Islamic world', it 'effectively prevents the development of healthy relations between the EC [European Community] and the countries of the Middle East, with all the risks to trade and oil supplies which that implies.'[24]

Solving the problem, the paper indicated, required denying the Palestinian rights that were central to their struggle. Chief among them was the right of return for Palestine's refugees. The paper dismissed the Palestinian insistence on the full right of return to their homes or to compensation as 'unrealistic'. There was no 'practical possibility' for 'more than a small number of Palestinians' to return to present-day Israel, it claimed. 'Equally, Israel alone will not be in a position to pay anything more than token compensation,' the paper added.[25]

The Foreign Office also proposed the disenfranchisement of refugees. Its paper floated the idea of a referendum or some other form of public consultation on how the West Bank and Gaza should be administered once Israel had withdrawn from them. While the paper argued that it would be unrealistic to confine that referendum to Palestinians living in the West Bank and Gaza, it argued against giving every Palestinian in the diaspora a vote. A 'system of qualification for a vote designed to exclude or limit the role of a large proportion of the diaspora might be needed,' it added. 'Palestinians in Israel proper pose a special problem.'[26]

Moreover, the paper advocated a soft approach towards some of the territories Israel had seized in 1967. 'The position of East Jerusalem would have to be left at least theoretically open,' the paper added.

Pressure on Israel for an early commitment to withdraw from East Jerusalem would 'destroy the negotiations' towards a 'peace' accord, it claimed. The Foreign Office recommended that the status of Jerusalem be left to 'a late stage in any settlement process'.[27] It is hard to see that recommendation as anything other than a recipe for allowing Israel to continue colonising East Jerusalem indefinitely.

A patronising attitude

Despite nominally accepting that Palestinians had a right to self-determination, Margaret Thatcher's government was one of the most hostile in the world to the PLO. By 1980, more than 100 countries around the world had recognised the PLO as the Palestinians' only legitimate representatives. Britain had refused to; its policy of having no more than informal contacts with the organisation tended to give the impression that 'we are deliberately snubbing the PLO,' according to a Foreign Office memo.

The guidelines on British contacts with the PLO were relaxed in this period – but only slightly. PLO representatives were allowed to visit the Foreign Office and British embassies; they were still not received at a ministerial level. Carrington approved some meetings between British diplomats and the PLO. One such diplomat, John Graham, figured that the logistics of setting up an appointment with Yasser Arafat were 'a bit like meeting the Emperor of China and the Grand Master of the Ku Klux Klan.' As it happened, Arafat promptly agreed to Graham's request for a meeting in Beirut. That was one of several encounters during which British officials tried to persuade the PLO to recognise Israel. When Nabil Ramlawi, the PLO's London representative, made his first visit to the Foreign Office in 1980, he was told that the organisation should tone down its rhetoric. 'Every reference to "liquidation of the Zionist entity" and other such wild talk was a setback to our efforts to bring the PLO into the negotiation of a peace settlement,' Oliver Miles, a Middle East specialist at the Foreign Office, argued.[28]

Miles was among the officials who sifted through PLO tracts looking for clues that the organisation was moving towards abandoning key principles. In April 1981, he complained about comments from leading PLO figures against recognising Israel and in support of guerillas fighting the brutal regime in El Salvador. Miles branded those comments as 'horrors' but observed that they were omitted from the official documents emanating from a session of the Palestine National Council (which he called the Palestinian 'parliament') in Damascus. 'Perhaps the worst feature' of the session, he argued, was 'its strong anti-American tone'. Before the session kicked off, the Foreign Office asked diplomats in the Middle East to let the PLO know that Britain would be keeping an eye on its proceedings. The message that the Foreign Office wanted conveyed was patronising: 'The Palestinians have an opportunity to show the world that they are a responsible people capable of negotiating peace.'[29]

Britain held the EEC's rotating presidency during the second half of 1981. As it prepared to assume that role, Peter Carrington proposed a new initiative aimed at persuading the PLO to compromise. Thatcher's foreign policy adviser, Michael Alexander, gave her a briefing on what Carrington wished to achieve. 'We might now seek from the PLO the most explicit possible on the record statement of their willingness to accept in the context of a negotiated settlement Israel's right to exist within secure frontiers,' Alexander noted. A statement of that nature would be 'an implicit disavowal' of the PLO's 1968 charter, he added.[30]

The British government was unwilling to give the PLO anything tangible in return for the compromises being sought. A Foreign Office memo made clear that 'we cannot offer the PLO formal recognition'. The PLO, however, 'could be certain of a very different relationship not only with us but with other Western countries.' Friendship with a former imperial power was adequate recompense for sacrificing principles that were fundamental to the Palestinian struggle, the British inferred.[31]

A few weeks before Britain's EEC presidency kicked off, Israel bombed the Osirak nuclear reactor in Baghdad. Menachem Begin's government tried to justify the attack by alleging that the French-built reactor was capable of producing 'Hiroshima-size' weapons that presented 'a mortal danger' to Israel.[32] The attack took place during an Israeli general election campaign. John Robinson, Britain's ambassador in Tel Aviv, told Downing Street that 'in ordering this operation, Begin will have had electoral advantage uppermost in [his] mind.' Robinson added:

But the advantage will depend on there being no serious escalation or counter-attack against Israel, nor any serious American reaction. And this must be his [Begin's] calculation. There will be some embarrassment and criticism here if Europeans have been killed but no votes lost on that account. Extensive contamination could backfire on Begin electorally. But it is the Americans who are in a position to ensure that this operation fails in its electoral purpose. It is the Americans who aid and arm Israel and who have connived at and even encouraged use by Israel of US weapons for aggressive operations. Until the Americans put a stop to this, as they can, any Israeli prime minister will believe he can repeat such operations with impunity.[33]

Robinson's critique was incisive, albeit obvious. The lesson to be learned was obvious, too: halting Israeli aggression required exerting pressure on both Israel and the USA. Reverting to habit, Britain was not prepared to hold Israel accountable. When Iraq tabled a UN resolution seeking sanctions against Israel, Peter Carrington responded it would be 'extremely difficult' for Britain to back that call, according to a Foreign Office paper. Support for sanctions against Israel would lead to criticism from the USA and to allegations of double standards, given that Britain had opposed the imposition of sanctions on South Africa. Britain did not wish to be accused of valuing its economic links with South Africa more than those with Israel, the Foreign Office stated in a note to Thatcher's adviser Michael Alexander.[34]

When a resolution demanding sanctions against Israel went before the UN Security Council, Thatcher and her cabinet colleagues discussed vetoing it. The Foreign Office advised that Britain would feel obliged to follow the USA in applying its veto, even though Britain had not vetoed a resolution relating to the Middle East for more than 25 years.[35] In the end, America succeeded in having the clause on sanctions removed from the resolution. The final text of the resolution condemned Israel for violating the UN Charter and the 'norms of international conduct'. But it did not penalise Israel in any way.[36]

Humouring Israel

Britain's tendency to ride pillion on America's motorbike was reinforced by its willingness to oversee implementation of the Camp

David accords. The 'multinational force and observers' (MFO) that America assembled for the Sinai peninsula was founded in the early 1980s without a mandate from the United Nations.[37] Britain became one of the force's leading participants by providing a headquarters unit.[38] This meant that Britain was helping to reduce frictions between Israel and its neighbours without the massive injustices inflicted on the Palestinians being addressed. Douglas Hurd, Britain's minister for Europe, cited Britain's involvement in the MFO as 'evidence that our commitment to Israel's security is not just verbal.'[39]

Hurd was speaking to a delegation from Israel's parliament, the Knesset, when he made that comment in late 1981. He was at pains to present Britain as siding with Israel. 'No one blames Israel for refusing to negotiate until the PLO does so,' he said, according to Foreign Office notes. 'That is why most of our efforts have been devoted not to asking Israel to change her policy but to urging PLO to change theirs.'[40]

In January 1982, Hurd sent a grovelling letter to Conservative Friends of Israel (CFI), a lobby group within his party. Britain would be 'making a substantial effort' that year to 'reach a closer understanding with the Israel government and Israelis generally,' Hurd stated. 'I know we can rely on groups like the Conservative Friends of Israel to help us in this.' Hurd was adamant that CFI should not be rebuked for supporting Israel's theft of the West Bank. The group had just issued a statement about a trip it had undertaken to the Middle East, in which it contended that 'settlements are not a bar to Palestinian autonomy'. Peggy Fenner, an agriculture minister, had taken part in the visit and was named on the statement, even though it contradicted the official British policy that Israel's colonisation of the West Bank violated international law. Oliver Miles at the Foreign Office described the statement and Fenner's association with it as 'clearly not satisfactory' and advised that Hurd speak to Fenner about the matter. Hurd rejected the advice. A handwritten note by Hurd reads: 'I think we should leave Mrs Fenner alone and assume that her membership of the government overrides her membership of the visiting group. It is not worth reopening the issue unless the Israelis try to exploit it.' The CFI trip had been endorsed by Thatcher. 'I take pride in the fact I was one of the founder members of Conservative Friends of Israel,' she wrote, in a message to the trip's organisers.[41]

A key component of the 'substantial effort' to which Hurd referred was a visit by Peter Carrington to the Middle East in late March and early April 1982. A scene-setter for the visit noted there had 'been a blight on Anglo-Israeli relations since the Venice declaration of June 1980.' Israel had perceived EEC policy on the Middle East as 'directly inimical to her interests and strongly suspects Britain of playing a leading role in its formulation,' the document added. One purpose of Carrington's sojourn was 'to improve at least the atmospherics of our exchanges with the Israelis.'[42]

As the Foreign Office mulled over the purpose of and protocol for Carrington's visit, Israel intensified its repression of Palestinians living in the West Bank. Among the targets of that repression were local authorities that Israel viewed as sympathetic to the PLO. The mayors of Nablus, Ramallah and al-Bireh were sacked for refusing to cooperate with a military body – given the Orwellian name 'civilian administration' – overseeing the occupation. The administration was headed by Menachem Milson, an academic who had been appointed to that role by Ariel Sharon, then Israel's defence minister.[43]

Although Britain had criticised the mayors' dismissal, the Foreign Office did not want the issue to overshadow Carrington's trip. It recommended that Britain's displeasure be registered in a tepid manner. One member of Carrington's entourage, John Leahy, would visit the Palestinian mayors but only after Carrington had left the country. In that way, Carrington was distancing himself from anything that could be construed as a gesture of solidarity with the Palestinians. Not only did he accept the advice to keep the talks with mayors separate from his official programme, Carrington instructed diplomats to let Israel know Britain was taking that step. 'It will not do to be seen to back down under Israeli pressure,' Carrington wrote, in a telegram. 'On the other hand, I should prefer to take account of Israeli sensitivities and avoid a bruising row.' As well as trying to humour Israel, Carrington rejected a call by the PLO that he cancel his trip. Echoing arguments that Britain used to 'defend' its engagement with apartheid South Africa (where Leahy had been posted as an ambassador for the previous three years), the Foreign Office claimed that the troubles in the West Bank made it more necessary to maintain dialogue with Israel.[44]

In the end, Israel refused to allow Leahy to meet the mayors, whom it had put under house arrest. Leahy's response was nonchalant

– he merely said that the refusal was a matter of 'regret'. For his part, Carrington used his public comments during the visit to strike a stridently pro-Israel note. Asked about the PLO during a press conference, he said:

> It does not seem to me reasonable or possible to ask the Israelis to sit down and talk about a negotiated settlement about all the problems of the Middle East with an organisation which in its covenant is dedicated to the destruction of Israel.[45]

A Foreign Office assessment of the visit deemed it a success. Oliver Miles claimed that the 'reasonableness of the Israelis – even [Ariel] Sharon – was striking'. He wrote: 'It is perhaps too much to hope that our relations with Israel will now dramatically improve. But some warmth has been restored to our relations.'[46]

One day after Carrington returned to London, Argentina sent troops onto the Falkland Islands. Confessing that the military action had caught him unaware, Carrington promptly resigned. That was, by no means, the end of his political career: he went on to head NATO. For Thatcher, the Argentinian action was a boon. Unpopular among the British public, judging by the opinion polls, she sniffed an opportunity. By going to war over a colonial outpost, she was able to assert herself as a muscular leader. Once Argentina had been defeated, she set about implementing a plan to dramatically reconfigure Britain's economy and society, with ruinous consequences for very many ordinary people.[47]

British diplomats were stung by criticism of the war from certain quarters. When the PLO urged a meeting of the Non-Aligned Movement in Havana to oppose British militarism in robust terms, the Foreign Office's team on UN affairs recommended that the organisation be reprimanded. The Falklands issue was 'far removed' from the PLO's 'legitimate concerns', a Foreign Office memo argued.[48]

The message was both condescending and inaccurate. As Israel had established a lucrative arms trade with South America, events in that part of the world were hardly irrelevant to Palestinian concerns. Skyhawk jets that Israel sold to Argentina before the war were among the weapons used in the conflict. Margaret Thatcher's government was fully aware of that fact: in some cases British troops were killed with weapons from Israel.[49]

Worse, Foreign Office archives state that Israel was alone among Argentina's top weapons providers in maintaining the flow of arms during the Falklands War. 'We have firm but, for the most part undisclosable evidence, that the arms supply relationship [between Israel and Argentina] continues on a large scale, including military training,' stated a Foreign Office note from 1983.[50]

Britain did not punish Israel for arming its declared enemy. Diplomats went no further than soliciting clarifications. A Foreign Office note from 1982 stated that 'we are inclined to believe Israeli assurances' that it did not export armed helicopters to Argentina at the time of the Falklands War. That was despite how Britain's own intelligence reports indicated that Israel had made shipments of military helicopters and missiles to Argentina after the war began. British officials even expressed understanding for Israel. A Foreign Office memo read:

> They [the Israelis] have their own interests to protect as an arms supplier in Latin America. There is also a large Jewish community in Argentina. Some Israelis would argue that we can hardly expect favours when we refused to supply Israel with tank spares and ammunition during the 1973 Arab–Israel war.[51]

The Falklands War was still being fought when Israel invaded Lebanon in June 1982. Having mobilised troops to protect a remnant of the British Empire and recently authorised brutality against the Catholic community in Northern Ireland, Thatcher did not have the moral authority to chastise Israel. By urging the immediate withdrawal of Israeli troops, she was arguably inconsistent with her own bellicose policies. Then again, Thatcher was not renowned for having qualms or for absolute consistency.

Rallying behind Reagan

Thatcher contended that the offensive – which targeted Palestinian resistance fighters – should prompt Western governments to reflect on their relationship with Israel. In a letter to Ronald Reagan, the US president, she stressed that 'Israel's apparent intention of removing the

Palestinians and the PLO as an element in the Middle East equation just will not work.' She wrote:

> We must now try not only to deal with the present crisis but also to draw conclusions for future policy. The latest fighting has once again demonstrated the urgent need for a balanced policy towards the Arab–Israel conflict. Both the Israelis and the Palestinians have legitimate rights which must be taken into account in working for a lasting peace. Unlimited support for Israel can only lead to growing polarisation and despair in the Arab world. I have to tell you from our Arab contacts that Arab opinion is running violently against the United States since the impression has been given, rightly or wrongly, that you condone rather than condemn the recent Israeli action. The loss of life and destruction have been horrifying and I fear that the Arabs, including some of our friends in the Arabian Peninsula, will look increasingly to the Soviet Union unless they see some move in their direction. Attempts to limit the damage of the present conflict, although urgent, are not enough. We must tackle the Palestinian issue which lies at the heart of the dispute. Unless we do this we shall never achieve a lasting peace.[52]

Israel has long twisted the truth in order to excuse its invasion. A potted 'history' on the Israeli foreign ministry's website gives the impression that it was purely an act of retaliation to violence by Palestinians. It notes that the military operation began three days after the attempted assassination of Shlomo Argov, Israel's ambassador in London.[53] Conveniently, the account neglects to mention that Argov was not shot by the PLO, the target of Israel's invasion, but by its sworn enemy, the Abu Nidal faction.[54]

Despite the forthright nature of Thatcher's message to Reagan, British officials baulked at taking action that could cause offence to Israel. The – by now – perennial topic of a possible meeting between a government minister and the PLO was raised once again in the Foreign Office. John Leahy advised against such a step, maintaining it would be sufficient for civil servants to have contacts with PLO members. 'Although our ability to influence the Israelis is already limited,' a high-level discussion with the PLO would 'put ourselves even further out of court with them,' he argued. 'That is not in our interests.'

Some British officials were prepared to swallow the broad thrust of Israel's narrative. Twelve days after the invasion was launched, Issam Sartawi, a PLO representative, called to see John Moberly, a former ambassador to Jordan, then working at the Foreign Office. Moberly, by his own account, subjected Sartawi to something of a lecture. A 'clear and unambiguous statement of conditional acceptance of Israel' was needed from the PLO, Moberly argued. 'I pointed out that the Lebanese disaster might never have happened if the PLO had taken the step we had been pressing on them throughout the last year.'[55]

Thatcher had discussions with a number of Arab governments in 1982 and gave feedback on them to Reagan. In July, she talked with King Hussein of Jordan about the best way to encourage the PLO along a 'moderate' path – 'moderate' being code for a path acceptable to Israel. Both Hussein and Thatcher agreed that it would not be desirable for the PLO to base itself in Syria once it had been forced out of Lebanon. Hussein, according to Thatcher, claimed that the Syrian government had plans to 'change the PLO into a more extreme form'. The subtext of that warning appeared to be that the Damascus authorities should not be trusted because of their alliance with the Soviet Union. 'I have to say frankly that I do not believe sending the bulk of the PLO, including the leadership, to Syria will serve western interests by permitting a genuinely moderate leadership to emerge,' Thatcher told Reagan.[56]

At the beginning of September, Reagan announced details of something that has often been called a 'peace plan'. In reality, it was an initiative that treated Palestinians with contempt. Despite calling for a freeze on the construction of Israeli settlements in the West Bank and Gaza, Reagan effectively said that Israel could maintain its control over much of the territory seized in 1967. He said:

I have personally followed and supported Israel's heroic struggle for survival, ever since the founding of the state of Israel 34 years ago. In the pre-1967 borders Israel was barely 10 miles wide at its narrowest point. The bulk of Israel's population lived within artillery range of hostile Arab armies. I am not about to ask Israel to live that way again.[57]

Reagan ruled out supporting the establishment of a Palestinian state. All he was prepared to offer was a vague concept of 'self-government' by Palestinians in the West Bank and Gaza, in conjunction with Jordan. He said:

> When the border is negotiated between Israel and Jordan, our view on the extent to which Israel should be asked to give up territory will be heavily affected by the extent of true peace and normalisation and the security arrangements offered in return.[58]

Thatcher backed this manifestly unjust blueprint to the hilt. In personal correspondence with Reagan, she argued that the proposals offered 'the most realistic way forward'. Only the USA could 'restore confidence in the peace process', she added, 'but we shall try to support you to the best of our ability both nationally and through the European Community.'[59] She was, in effect, pledging allegiance to a US president who had dramatically increased military aid to Israel. The USA was financing 37 per cent of Israel's military expenditure in this period, making the idea that America was striving for peace absurd.[60]

Not everyone in Whitehall rushed to criticise the invasion of Lebanon. The defence ministry was eager that cooperation with Israel should continue. Barry Miller, a senior official in that ministry, contacted the Foreign Office during July to say that Israel had been 'sharing with us their latest battle experience'. Miller was impressed at how Israel had been sending high-ranking soldiers to attend training courses run by the British Army. His colleagues would 'certainly regret any decision to stop them coming in future years or to cut back significantly on other contacts where combat experience might be discussed,' Miller argued.[61] More than 100 Israeli soldiers received training in Britain in the fiscal year between 1981 and 1982. Declassified archives confirm, too, that Britain and Israel regularly exchanged intelligence in this period. The British authorities were particularly interested in receiving information about Soviet weaponry to which Israel had access.[62]

The most infamous crime committed following the invasion was the massacre of between 800 and 3,500 Palestinians in the refugee camps of Sabra and Shatila. The atrocity was committed by the Phalange, a Lebanese Christian force allied to Israel, during September 1982.

The Israeli military had surrounded these camps in South Beirut at the time. Israeli troops helped the Phalange make its way through the camps at night-time by firing flares into the sky.[63]

Thatcher condemned the massacre as an 'act of sheer barbarism'.[64] Soon, Britain was once again striving to please Israel, the state that enabled such barbarism. Francis Pym, who replaced Carrington after he resigned as foreign secretary in 1982, displayed some determination to defend Britain's pro-Zionist credentials. Pym's advisers at the Foreign Office prepared meticulously for a discussion he had with Israeli journalists in December that year. It was likely, they predicted, that Pym would face questions about whether or not Thatcher's opposition to the invasion of Lebanon meant Britain was anti-Israel. Pym was advised to respond that any allegations of that sort were 'nonsense' and to say: 'We are active in Israel's interests, in constantly urging the Arabs and the PLO to recognise Israel and to abandon the path of violence.' Pym's briefing notes recommended that he stick to the line that the invasion of Lebanon was an aggressive act but to also say that 'only Israel can decide what is in her own security interests.'[65] Because Israel had claimed that invading Lebanon was necessary to protect its security, the messages were somewhat muddled. There was nonetheless some underlying clarity: Britain was not going to take any strong action against Israel.

The double standards at the heart of Thatcher's approach were flagrant. Despite her professed outrage at the Sabra and Shatila atrocities, Thatcher did not rupture diplomatic relations with Israel; there is no hint that she entertained the thought of doing so. Yet she told the Arab League that its delegations could not include PLO representatives if they wished to visit her or her cabinet colleagues. That was despite the fact that the PLO was a full member of the Arab League and that Thatcher had actually shaken hands with Yasser Arafat at the funeral of Josip Broz Tito, the Yugoslavian president, in 1980 (her biographer Charles Moore has claimed that Thatcher had exchanged pleasantries with Arafat before realising who he was).[66]

Because of that stance, the Arab League called off a trip to Britain it had planned to make in late 1982. Thatcher had insisted that she would not welcome a delegation that included a PLO member to Downing Street. Her stance was at odds with that of François Mitterrand, the French president, who had personally held discussions with the PLO.

Thatcher indicated, however, that she might be willing to meet such a delegation if a statement could be made at the end of the meeting, stating that all its participants 'confirm their rejection of terrorism'.[67] While the Foreign Office defined terrorism as armed action against civilian targets and was satisfied that the PLO had renounced such tactics, Thatcher's definition of the term was considerably broader. She believed, according to a note written by Douglas Hurd, that terrorism included 'armed action against military targets of the occupying power'. If Hurd accurately represented Thatcher's views (and the available evidence indicates that he did), then Thatcher regarded resistance to the Israeli occupation as criminal.[68] Thatcher's advisers had previously informed the Foreign Office that she was not pleased with a short comment that Peter Carrington made in a 1980 House of Lords debate. Carrington had said: 'I do not think that the PLO, as such, is a terrorist organisation.'[69]

Writing to King Hussein of Jordan, Thatcher argued that the PLO would have to abandon some of its key principles if it wanted high-level dialogue with Britain. 'I believe it is your own view that the PLO must not be encouraged in the illusion that their maximum demands are negotiable,' she wrote. Britain's conditions proved unacceptable to Arab leaders.[70]

Ivor Lucas, Britain's ambassador in Damascus, wrote a pointed critique of the government's intransigence. In a message to Oliver Miles at the Foreign Office, he argued:

> I do not suppose you were any more surprised than I was by the PLO's flat rejection of our ploy on their inclusion in the Arab League's delegation. While understanding the imperatives operating in London, it seemed to me (and it must have seemed to them) that instead of imaginatively seizing an opportunity to forward the peace process, we have cynically attempted to exploit the situation by repeating our earlier conditions while offering the PLO little more in return than we had already given them. As a result we are not simply back to square one with the Arabs but further back than before.[71]

The atrocities at Sabra and Shatila did not seem to weigh on minds at the Foreign Office as it considered a number of dossiers relating to the trade in potential military items in 1983. During February that year, the nuclear energy department at the Foreign Office recommended that a licence for exporting a mass spectrometer to Israel should be granted. The machine – valued at more than £200,000 – was wanted by Beer Sheba University, an institution known to be undertaking nuclear research. A Foreign Office assessment fully acknowledged that the machine could be used in a process of uranium separation in which Israel's nuclear scientists were interested. As America had indicated that it would be prepared to allow an export of such technology to Israel, the Foreign Office felt there was 'little point in denying British industry' the order in question.

That was one of several incidents in which British officials advised that scruples yield to pragmatism. In March 1983, the Foreign Office confirmed that it would have no objection to the Royal Air Force buying weapons from Israel provided that the truth could be concealed. The RAF was running low on gun-pods and spare parts for its Phantom fighter aircraft. According to the defence ministry, the need for this equipment had become urgent since the Falklands War as Britain was bolstering its military base on the islands. United Scientific Holdings, a British broker, had been hired to find the equipment; the only way these items could be sourced at relatively short notice was through Israel's arms industry.[72] Asking the Israelis to sell the goods was not regarded as a viable option. Britain had imposed a weapons embargo on Israel because of the Lebanon invasion. So long as the embargo remained in place, the Israeli government 'would probably relish the opportunity of turning down our request,' the Foreign Office had surmised.[73]

Both the defence ministry and the Foreign Office connived to import the Israeli arms and components in an underhand way. The scheme to which both ministries gave their go-ahead involved United Scientific Holdings having the goods shipped to the USA. From there, they would be sold to a subsidiary of the firm and then on to the RAF. If any details of the transaction became public, the British government would lie that the equipment had been bought 'in good faith from a reputable UK company, who had in turn purchased them from a US company,' an internal Foreign Office paper stated.[74]

When an Arab League delegation visited London that spring, Thatcher's government sent out somewhat bizarre signals. Britain, it was promised, would cooperate with the USA in order to put pressure on Israel. 'Time is short,' stated a briefing note prepared for Thatcher.

It added that the Reagan initiative and 'the favourable mood in [the] US' presented 'an opportunity to be seized'. The 'expanding Israeli settlements programme otherwise threatens to make Israel's hold on [the] West Bank irreversible,' the paper warned, without analysing how the Reagan initiative was effectively facilitating a significant Israeli land grab in the West Bank and beyond. Thatcher had refused to receive the delegation if it included a PLO representative. In the end, a compromise was found. The British were willing to accept that the Palestinian academic Walid Khalidi would join the delegation as he was, according to the Foreign Office, not 'associated with any PLO bodies'.[75]

Douglas Hurd did, however, meet the PLO's Farouq Qaddumi in Tunis – where the organisation moved after Israel forced it to leave Lebanon – in April 1983. Foreign Office records indicate that Hurd's purpose in accepting the meeting was to try and persuade the PLO that it should not reject Reagan's proposals. The PLO had made a 'serious mistake', a Foreign Office memo claimed, by 'blocking King Hussein's efforts to enter negotiations on the basis of the Reagan initiative.' The meeting between Hurd and Qaddumi was intended as a one-off, not the beginning of high-level dialogue between the PLO and Britain.[76]

Hurd was more accommodating to Israel in this period. He authorised the relaxation of controls on arms exports to Israel. That followed complaints by the arms industry that Britain had a more restrictive approach to weapons sales than France or Germany. Hurd's decision meant that Britain allowed the exports of weapon components provided that they were not for equipment scheduled for 'immediate service' with the Israeli military, the Foreign Office noted. The arms industry adopted clever tactics in its bid to have arms exports resumed. First, it bemoaned how the embargo was so broad that mundane items such as soldiers' berets and trousers could not be exported. Once that hurdle was cleared, manufacturers were able to secure permission for the export of other military goods.[77]

The Reagan administration let it be known around this time that it wanted Israel and Britain to, in effect, forget the friction caused by the Lebanon invasion. Antony Acland, the head of Britain's diplomatic service, recorded how that message was relayed to him as he visited Washington. Lawrence Eagleburger, then America's under-secretary of state for political affairs, said 'he greatly hoped we could gradually improve our relations with Israel and increase our dialogue with them,' Acland noted. 'He believed that when the Israelis felt isolated they tended to act more dangerously and more erratically.' Oliver Miles commented that 'the facts point the other way' and that Israel had invaded Lebanon immediately after Peter Carrington had made a major effort to improve Anglo-Israeli relations. It is perhaps superfluous to add that Miles' comments were made within the confines of the Foreign Office. Eagleburger got the kind of answer he wanted from his British guest: 'it was our policy slowly to increase the dialogue with the Israeli government.'[78]

In keeping with that policy, Richard Luce, a Foreign Office minister, visited the Middle East in November 1983. The Israeli authorities behaved in a similar manner to how they had when Carrington had paid his visit in the previous year. Two mayors of West Bank cities and a Gaza-based representative of the Red Crescent humanitarian group were blocked from travelling to meet Luce in East Jerusalem.[79] The terms in which the Foreign Office complained about the matter were telling. 'We did not, of course, dispute Israel's right to put whatever security restrictions they saw fit on inhabitants of the occupied territories,' Edward Chaplin from the Foreign Office noted, after raising the issue with Israel's London embassy. 'But we found it difficult to understand why the Israelis had disrupted Mr Luce's programme at the last minute.'[80]

By suggesting that Israel had some right to dictate what Palestinians may do, the British government was conferring legitimacy on an occupation to which it was officially opposed. British diplomats were also anxious to prevent Luce and his entourage from seeing too much of that occupation. The idea that Luce's wife, Rose, would visit a women's project in the West Bank was entertained but rejected by the British consulate in Jerusalem. Calling to see the project it had identified would necessitate passing 'refugee camps notorious for unpleasant incidents' on 'the day following the anniversary of the Balfour Declaration,' the consulate noted.[81] Witnessing first-hand the 'unpleasant' consequences of imperialism should be avoided was the implicit message.

Richard Luce did not display any signs of being more sympathetic to Palestinians following his trip. Later in 1983, he instructed that British diplomats should be 'very chary of contacts with the PLO,' according to a Foreign Office memo. There was no point, he felt, in holding talks with the organisation 'until there is evidence that Arafat is prepared to start acting as a real leader and moves towards accepting the right of Israel to exist.'[82]

Britain's desire to placate Israel became more apparent during Thatcher's second term as prime minister. As he prepared for a Middle East trip in 1984, Geoffrey Howe, then foreign secretary, requested that diplomats 'avoid the sort of difficulty' that beset Luce's visit. Any Palestinians invited to meet him 'should be as uncontroversial and reliable as possible,' Howe argued, even though he accepted that 'the Palestinians who are least controversial in Israeli eyes may not be seen as representative by other Palestinians.'[83]

The Thatcher government, meanwhile, was not too exercised about how uranium found its way from Britain to Israel's nuclear industry. The depleted uranium came from Sellafield, a nuclear complex in Cumbria that gained notoriety for its radioactive discharges into the Irish Sea. Forty tons of the substance were exported from Britain to Luxembourg, a country without nuclear power, in 1984. The Luxembourg-firm International Metals then sold it to Israel.[84] British Nuclear Fuels, the state-owned operator of Sellafield, had previously been given permission from the Foreign Office to cooperate with Israel. BNFL wished to sell refel silicon carbide to Israel. The Foreign Office stated that it would have no objection to the export of that ceramic material provided that it was used for items with wide industrial applications. Refel silicon carbide was originally made to provide cladding for nuclear fuel in certain reactors. The Foreign Office also stated that it would have no objection to the export of depleted uranium to Israel on the condition that 'the arrangement be subject to adequate safeguards' and the quantity did not exceed one ton per annum.[85]

The implicit policy objective of driving a wedge between the PLO's perceived hawks and doves received something of an imprimatur from Thatcher in the mid-1980s. She went so far as inviting two PLO members to visit London. Elias Khoury, an Anglican bishop of Jerusalem, and Mohammed Milhem, formerly mayor of Halhul in the West Bank, were viewed as acceptable because they were 'trying to move the PLO into the path of peaceful negotiation and have called for a peaceful settlement,' a briefing note written by Charles Powell, Thatcher's foreign policy adviser, stated. Thatcher held discussions with Conservative Friends of Israel about the invitation. She explained that the men were to visit in their individual capacities, rather than as PLO representatives; they would be coming as part of a joint Jordanian-Palestinian group. The explanation was accepted; CFI declared itself 'convinced and assured that the prime minister's attitude towards the PLO remained unchanged.'[86] The visit did not go ahead, reportedly because Khoury and Milhem objected to a British demand that they sign a statement recognising Israel's 'right to exist'.[87]

In 1986, Thatcher undertook an official visit of Israel – the first by a British prime minister since that state's inception. The organisers of the trip were given strict instructions to make it a success. Because Shimon Peres, by now Israel's prime minister, had hosted a reception in Claridge's when he was in London, Thatcher's entourage felt compelled to do something similar in Jerusalem. Gathering 500 people at a reception in the King David Hotel was priced at £10,000. 'It is expensive but we should swallow hard and regard the money as well spent,' Charles Powell wrote to Thatcher. 'We shall look a bit feeble if we cannot at least match what Mr Peres did in London'. Thatcher concurred in a handwritten reply: 'If we can't afford to do the thing properly, there is no point in going.'[88]

Thatcher pandered to the Israeli government during her trip. At a press conference, she dodged a question about the status of Jerusalem by describing it as 'internal politics'. It is hard to believe that her evasion was accidental: more than likely, she was fully aware that Britain, like most of the world's countries, officially regarded Israel's annexation of East Jerusalem as illegitimate. Arrogantly, she also inferred that Israel and its Western allies could chose who would represent Palestinians, rather than the Palestinians themselves. She said:

Yes, we have been discussing representation other than the PLO, obviously; if not the PLO, who should represent the Palestinian people and obviously there have been a number of proposals put forward. But you must never stop trying and I think that there perhaps might be different views as to who should represent the Palestinian people, but we must consider an alternative because we simply must follow all routes. We know that you cannot simply have negotiations between King Hussein and Israel unless King Hussein is accompanied by people who are accepted as representing the Palestinian people.[89]

Soon after she arrived back in London, Thatcher expressed her gratitude to her Israeli hosts. In a message to the Knesset, she claimed 'there are few countries in the world where one actually feels democracy flourishing as strongly as in Israel.' Writing to Peres, she claimed to enjoy her visit 'more than any other I have made'.[90]

Thatcher had further contacts with Peres. The following year, Peres and King Hussein visited London (with Thatcher's encouragement) to discuss what is often called the Jordanian option. Favoured by Peres (then foreign minister), the idea was to give Jordan greater responsibility for managing Palestinian affairs, while Israel maintained effective control of the West Bank. A key objective was to sideline the PLO. Elements of the plan are still resurrected by Israeli politicians every so often in the twenty-first century. At that time, however, Peres' plan had to be shelved because the Palestinian *intifada* erupted later in 1987 and because it failed to win support from Yitzhak Shamir, who had succeeded Peres as Israel's prime minister.[91]

The PLO ultimately proved malleable in the way that British diplomats hoped. At a November 1988 conference in Algeria, the organisation approved a political programme which, in effect, accepted that the partition of historic Palestine was a *fait accompli*. Rather than striving for a democratic, multiracial state covering all of Palestine, the PLO limited itself to struggling for a state comprising of the West Bank (including East Jerusalem) and Gaza.[92] William Waldegrave, a Foreign Office minister, hailed the decision as a 'great step forward'. He held talks with Arafat in Tunisia early the following year.[93]

Reporting on Thatcher's death in 2013, the BBC misrepresented her legacy. Jeremy Bowen, its Middle East correspondent, wrote that under Thatcher, 'Britain was one of the first western countries to establish contacts with the Palestine Liberation Organisation'.[94]

It would be far more accurate to say that Britain kept the PLO at arm's length during the Thatcher era. When contacts were established, their purpose was to push the PLO towards a surrender of sorts. Britain was indeed careful not to be chummy with those Palestinians who insisted on the full restitution of their rights.

8

The loyal lieutenant

Israel's occupation of the West Bank and Gaza entered a new phase in the 1990s. Palestinians were theoretically given a degree of autonomy, while, in practice, Israel continued to exert control over their lives. A photograph of Yasser Arafat and Yitzhak Rabin, then Israel's prime minister, shaking hands on the White House lawn made the front pages of newspapers throughout the world. The handshake may have been effusive but it was not a harbinger of real change. Core issues – the fate of refugees, the status of Jerusalem – were placed in the freezer and Israel was in no hurry to take them out.

The Oslo accords – as the 1993 pact between Arafat and Rabin became known – were branded 'an instrument of Palestinian surrender, a Palestinian Versailles' by the intellectual Edward Said.[1] The PLO was required to recognise and cooperate with Israel, without that state's apartheid system being dismantled. The West Bank was cut up into zones. The newly established Palestinian Authority would nominally be in full control of its largest towns and cities. Yet 60 per cent of the land would be completely under Israel's yoke. Israel has taken advantage of this invidious situation by constantly expanding its settlements in Area C, as that 60 per cent zone is called. The promises to reach a broad solution by 1999 have been broken – by Israel. And the West has kept on claiming to support a 'peace process' while allowing Israel to act with impunity. The very idea of peace – not merely the absence of tension but the presence of justice, as Martin Luther King memorably defined it – has been redefined. Israeli politicians have bandied about terms like 'economic peace', knowing that powerful institutions in Europe and North America would not pose awkward questions.

The British government backed the Oslo accords enthusiastically. Douglas Hurd, by then promoted to foreign secretary, celebrated them as 'a blow against pessimism everywhere'. He said:

In recent years, Britain's role has deliberately been patient and supportive. We stood back once we were convinced that the Americans were serious about the peace process. Now that the deadlock has been broken, our involvement can go into a rather different gear. We are talking more visibly now to those involved in the negotiations and we are encouraging them towards a comprehensive settlement.[2]

As mentioned in Chapter 7, Britain relaxed its restrictions on arms sales to Israel relatively soon after the 1982 invasion of Lebanon. The restrictions were fully removed in 1994, even though part of Lebanon remained under Israeli occupation. John Major – successor to Thatcher as prime minister – said the removal meant 'the way is now open' for a 'responsible two-way trade' in weapons between Britain and Israel, adding that armaments was 'a sector in which both countries excel'.[3] Hurd announced that the step was taken 'in light of favourable developments in the Middle East peace process, in particular the Israeli withdrawal from Gaza and Jericho.'[4] His explanation was mealy-mouthed. Israel's 'withdrawal' from Gaza was partial. Soldiers stayed put around the 19 Israeli settlements that covered one-third of Gaza's surface area.[5] And those settlements would not be evacuated for more than another decade.

With the full support of the government, Britain's commercial relationship with Israel became stronger. Speaking to Conservative Friends of Israel in 1995, Major cited data indicating that Anglo-Israeli trade was worth more than £1.5 billion per year. He applauded new steps to foster cooperation in scientific research between Britain and Israel. He remarked, too, how the British firm Cable and Wireless had acquired a stake in the Israeli telecommunications operator Bezeq and how BT was investing in Israel.[6] Such deals would make British industrialists complicit in Israel's war crimes. Bezeq has provided services to all of the main Israeli settlements and military installations in the West Bank and Golan Heights.[7]

One consequence of the Oslo accords is that it turned the PLO leadership into enforcers of the Israeli occupation. Under the guise of 'security cooperation', Arafat's newly formed Palestinian Authority was required to liaise closely with Israel. The objective of such 'cooperation' was eliminating 'terrorism'. Israel and its supporters used 'terrorism' as a catch-all term for resistance, lumping together activities that targeted the military, with those affecting non-combatants.

Britain was an avid supporter of this neo-colonial project. It tried to keep the project alive after Rabin's assassination in 1995 and the election victory for his rival Benjamin Netanyahu in the next year. Netanyahu's intention to seize Palestinian land was made plain. In 1997, he announced the construction of a major new Israeli settlement, Har Homa, between East Jerusalem and Bethlehem. The plan was denounced in a resolution backed by 130 countries at the UN general assembly. America and Israel were the only two UN members to vote against the resolution.[8] Although Britain opposed the expansion of settlements, its two largest political parties, the Conservatives and Labour, displayed increasing sympathy towards Israel.

Support for Israel came to be regarded as almost obligatory for ambitious Labour politicians wishing to curry favour with their then leader Tony Blair. Siôn Simon, a corporate lobbyist and newspaper columnist who later became a Labour MP, claimed in 1997 that being pro-Zionist was 'an infallible admission test' for 'the sect of Labour modernisers'.[9] Blair himself had joined the pressure group Labour Friends of Israel when he first entered parliament in 1983.[10] Avowed Zionists played a prominent role in helping Blair to prepare for Downing Street. The role of the music business tycoon Michael Levy was particularly significant. He had previously been a fundraiser for the United Israel Appeal, a national institution responsible for financing Israel's activities.[11] After the two men met at an Israeli embassy function in 1994, Levy went on to become a top fundraiser for Blair. Levy reportedly collected £12 million ahead of the 1997 general election campaign.[12]

For the first half of 1998, Blair's government held the EU's rotating presidency. Preparing for Blair's visit to the Middle East in April that year, the British presidency asked fellow EU states to endorse proposals for fostering 'security cooperation' between Israel and the Palestinian Authority.

The proposals were that an EU 'security' specialist and the heads of 'preventive security' in the West Bank and Gaza would meet once a fortnight or 'at time of crisis'. The purpose of these discussions would be to allow the EU identify what 'practical assistance' it would provide the Palestinian Authority. The assistance would contribute towards fulfilling the PA's 'security obligations to combat terrorism', according to the EU document.[13]

Those 'obligations' were elaborated on in the so-called Wye River Memorandum that Arafat and Netanyahu signed in October 1998. A sequel to the Oslo accords, the memorandum – negotiated in Maryland – made the PA's police subservient to Israel. A 'zero tolerance' approach to 'terror and violence' would be taken by the PA, it stated. That approach would involve such steps as arresting all those suspected of violence, outlawing all 'terrorist' organisations and collecting all of their weapons. Israel would be furnished with details on all police officers working for the PA. All of this 'cooperation' would be supervised by the USA, working in tandem with Israel. While Israel made a vague commitment to preventing violence against Palestinians, its soldiers were not required to withdraw from the West Bank and Gaza, despite the numerous killings they had carried out and the injuries they had caused.[14]

A swift peace?

In May 1998, Arafat and Netanyahu visited London. The talks in which they took part were officially hosted by the British – yet they were actually chaired by Madeleine Albright, then US secretary of state. She was driven from one hotel to another for separate meetings with the Israeli and Palestinian leaders. Predictably, the exercise proved futile.[15]

Blair responded enthusiastically to Ehud Barak's appointment as Israeli prime minister in 1999. Blair said:

His victory offers the Middle East peace process a chance to move forward. And I know that that will be done on the basis of the Wye River Memorandum, which offers a tremendous opportunity for rebuilding the Middle East on the basis of security for Israel and justice for the Palestinian people.[16]

The lip-service to 'justice' was misleading: it was far more significant that Blair wanted Barak to be guided by the Wye River Memorandum.

Jonathan Freedland, a pro-Israel commentator with *The Guardian*, credited Blair with Barak's win. The tactics employed during campaigning copied those of New Labour in 1997 – even Barak's slogan 'Israel needs a change' smacked of Blairite spin. That was no accident: Barak had hired the same American advisers that Blair had availed of in 1997. According to Freedland, Blair had personally recommended the pollster Stan Greenberg to Barak, who had visited London in the previous year 'with the express purpose of learning the black arts of electioneering at the feet of [Blair] the 179-seat master,' Freedland wrote, referring to Labour's majority following its 1997 landslide. With apparent approval, Freedland observed:

> While Blair sought to reassure Britons that he was a new kind of Labour leader by posing with police officers and businessmen – so deflecting the charge that his party was soft on crime and weak on enterprise – so Barak ensured he was photographed with military brass at every stop, underlining his own record as Israel's most decorated soldier.[17]

Barak had 'earned' his decorations by taking part in a series of offensives aimed at subjugating Palestinians. He had been a reconnaissance group commander in the June 1967 war and a deputy commander of the military force that invaded Lebanon in 1982. Before becoming a full-time politician, he had been the army's overall chief. By definition, then, he was head of an army that was occupying the West Bank and Gaza, as well as parts of Syria and Lebanon.[18] During his election campaign, Barak pledged that the large settlement blocs in Gaza and the West Bank would be retained. He insisted, too, that Israel would stay in control of Jerusalem in its entirety.[19] To keep such promises, Barak would have to ensure that Israel was able to continue violating international law, no matter how many states in the UN would condemn it for doing so. Tony Blair was, therefore, propagating a myth by hailing Barak as 'a man of leadership and vision' when the Israeli prime minister visited London soon after his election victory. 'He has impressed people around the world with his desire to make peace as swiftly as possible,' Blair said.[20]

Another pervasive myth is that Barak made an offer of unprecedented generosity to Yasser Arafat and that Arafat turned it down because he had no real interest in peace. That myth is based on discussions that took place behind closed doors in Camp David, the country retreat of the US president. Details of the offer that have subsequently emerged indicate that it was anything but generous. In line with Barak's afore-mentioned election pledge, Israel wished to annex enough of the West Bank (including East Jerusalem) to retain its large settlement blocs and to allow 80 per cent of its settlers (the numbers of whom doubled during the 1990s) to stay put. Israel's military would also stay in control of an expansive 'security zone' along the Jordan Valley. And Barak wanted the PLO to recognise Israel as a 'Jewish state', thereby perpetuating the discrimination faced by Palestinians living within it.[21]

In September 2000, Ariel Sharon undertook a triumphalist visit to the Haram al-Sharif in East Jerusalem, accompanied by other members of the Likud party. The riots sparked off by that event are widely viewed as the beginning of the second Palestinian *intifada*, which lasted more than four years. Between 29 September 2000 and mid-January 2005, 3,189 Palestinians were killed by Israeli forces. A total of 950 Israelis were killed by Palestinians in the same period.[22] Therefore, more than three times as many Palestinians were killed by Israeli forces as Israelis killed by Palestinians. That should leave no doubt that the State of Israel was the main perpetrator of violence and that it behaved in an extremely provocative manner. More than one million bullets were fired by Israeli troops in the West Bank and Gaza during the first few days of the *intifada*.[23]

Sharon's belligerence boosted his career; in 2001, he was elected prime minister. His first year in that post saw him overseeing the kind of behaviour that the so-called international community purported to deplore. In April 2001, Israeli ground troops invaded Gaza.[24] In July, the Israeli cabinet gave the military *carte blanche* to carry out extra-judicial executions of suspected Palestinian fighters.[25] In September, Israel attacked Jenin, Jericho and Gaza.[26] And in October, Israel seized Abu Sneineh, a neighbourhood in Hebron nominally under the PA's control.[27]

Through authorising such actions, Sharon displayed his contempt for even the miniscule level of autonomy granted to parts of the West Bank under the Oslo accords. He did so with Britain's acquiescence. More than 90 arms export licences for Israel were approved by the British government in 2001. Some of the licences fell into categories like torpedoes, armoured vehicles, bombs and missiles; categories that nobody could honestly label as 'defensive'.[28] Blair voiced sympathy for

Sharon, implicitly endorsing such tactics as extrajudicial executions. Blair said in March 2002:

> I understand how difficult it is for a prime minister in situations where he knows that terrorist attacks are about to happen. Does he sit back and do nothing or does he take pre-emptive action? I understand the problems that Israel has.[29]

Under Blair, Britain sometimes behaved as a proxy for Israel. In 2002, the Israeli authorities agreed that six Palestinian resistance fighters would be incarcerated in Jericho under British and American guard. The detainees had been accused of involvement in the assassination of Rehavam Zeevi, Israel's tourism minister. One of them, Ahmad Saadat, general secretary of the Popular Front for the Liberation of Palestine, was not charged with any recognisable criminal offence. He remained imprisoned despite the fact that a Palestinian court in Gaza had ordered his release.[30] The provision of British and American prison guards followed the so-called Ramallah agreement aimed at ending Israel's siege of Arafat's presidential compound. According to Blair, Britain provided the guards so that the PA could 'take charge' of detaining the six men. Britain facilitated an Israeli raid on the Jericho jail in 2006 by giving the occupation authorities advance notification that the British guards were being withdrawn (nominally because the PA could not guarantee the guards' safety). Saadat – elected to the Palestinian Legislative Council while he was held under British guard – was taken into Israeli custody and is still imprisoned at the time of writing.[31]

'Get rid of Saddam'

The report of the Chilcot Inquiry into the Iraq War – published, after a lengthy delay, in 2016 – illustrated how obsequious Blair was towards George W. Bush. By starting a note on the possible consequences of military action with the words 'I will be with you, whatever', Blair committed Britain to taking part in the invasion eight months before it got underway.[32]

It would be wrong to claim that the USA and Britain attacked Iraq simply because Israel wanted them to. Almost certainly, other considerations came into play: American imperialism and a determination to topple an unfriendly regime, oil, Bush's alliance with the Saudi royal family, the power of the arms lobby. Yet it is beyond dispute that Ariel Sharon wanted Saddam Hussein removed from power. Sharon reportedly told Blair:

> He [Saddam] could wake up in the morning and decide to invade Israel. His army of one and a half million needs just an hour to reach our borders. In the Middle East, nothing is predictable. If you have a problem, deal with it. Get rid of Saddam.[33]

It is also true that pro-Israel politicians were overwhelmingly in favour of invading Iraq. Many of the 244 Labour MPs who voted for the invasion in March 2003 had joined Labour Friends of Israel or taken part in that group's activities.[34] They included Gordon Brown, Ben Bradshaw, Chris Bryant, David Cairns, Stephen Byers, Wayne David, Louise Ellman, Lorna Fitzsimons, Caroline Flint, Kim Howells, Eric Joyce, Anne McGuire, Denis MacShane, James Purnell, Siôn Simon, Jack Straw and Blair himself.[35]

Britain dropped Israeli bombs while fighting in Iraq. According to Human Rights Watch, the Iraq War marked the first time that Britain used M85 cluster bombs in combat operations.[36] More than 100,000 of these grenades were dropped by the British Army in Iraq during 2003, arms industry monitors have calculated, based on data released by the British government.[37] The M85 is designed by Israel Military Industries. That state-owned firm is the principal supplier of ammunition to Israel's army, which markets its products as 'battle proven'.[38]

Unnoticed by the mainstream media, the invasions of Afghanistan and Iraq may have ushered in a new era of cooperation between British and Israeli arms-makers. The cargo projectiles used in firing the M85 cluster bombs were manufactured by BAE Systems, Britain's top weapons company, under licence by Israel Military Industries.[39] Israel and Britain's weapons industries have forged even deeper ties since then, as will be demonstrated in Chapter 9. There is a high probability that such cooperation has directly led to large-scale civilian suffering; cluster bombs are an inherently indiscriminate weapon. The group Iraq Body Count has documented how two children were among 50 people killed during a March 2003 incident in which cluster bombs were the main cause of death.[40]

As part of his attempts to justify his involvement in the invasion of Iraq, Blair has pointed to how he won a commitment from Bush that the USA would 're-engage' with the 'Middle East peace process'.[41] The commitment was a tangible achievement, Blair implies in his memoirs, of his 2002 discussions with the US president in Crawford, Texas.[42] Blair's choice of language is confusing. America had never disengaged from issues relating to Palestine. Nor had it engaged on a genuine quest for peace; it kept on lavishing Israel (under Barak and Sharon alike) with military aid. All it had really done was to tell Anthony Zinni, its 'peace envoy' (an Orwellian title that the mainstream media later bestowed on Blair) that he should leave the Middle East. Zinni, an army general, had not succeeded in halting the *intifada*.[43]

Palestine's police state

The 're-engagement' led to a document with an unwieldy title, *A Performance-Based Roadmap to a Permanent Two-State Solution to the Israeli–Palestinian Conflict*. Endorsed by the so-called Middle East quartet – the European Union, USA, United Nations and Russia – and published in 2003, the 'roadmap' depicted violence by Palestinians as the cause of all the problems, rather than a symptom. Palestinians would be required to take the first steps towards reaching a solution by 2005. A Palestinian 'security apparatus' would be trained by the USA to confront 'all those engaged in terror'. With American supervision, 'security cooperation' between the PA and Israel would be intensified.[44]

The *Palestine Papers* – a trove of confidential documents made public by Al Jazeera in 2011 – show that Britain was mentoring the PA's security forces around this time. One 2004 document drawn up by British officials, reportedly in tandem with MI6, advocated the 'temporary internment' of senior figures from Hamas and Islamic Jihad 'with EU funding'.[45] A hotline would be established to connect the PA with the Israeli military with a view to preventing Palestinian violence. The PA's performance in implementing a 'security drive' would be verified by Britain and the USA, the document stated, adding 'we would ask Israel to judge it on results'.[46]

That British officials could draw up a plan for 'temporary internment' in the twenty-first century indicates that many of them remain wedded to the policies of the past. The British authorities had resorted to internment without trial in Palestine between the two world wars. More recently, internment was introduced in Northern Ireland during the 1970s. It was used as a weapon of discrimination: of 1,981 detained without trial between 1971 and 1975, all bar 107 were from the Catholic community. Many had no involvement in paramilitary activity.[47]

The 'temporary internment' plan was not implemented in Palestine – or at least not exactly in the way its drafters had urged. Blair's government stayed actively involved, though, in the discussions about policing the West Bank and Gaza. In 2004, Britain's department for international development hired Jonathan McIvor as its advisor on policing in Palestine.[48] It was the kind of appointment that should have led journalists to ask probing questions; yet the matter appears to have gone unnoticed by the press. McIvor had been the chief inspector in Plumstead, south-east London, during the 1990s. He was the most senior uniformed officer on duty in the area where Stephen Lawrence, a young black teenager, was murdered on 22 April 1993.

A public inquiry into that murder – chaired by William Macpherson, a retired judge – is best known for its finding that the London Metropolitan Police was affected by 'institutional racism'. McIvor was among those directly criticised. The inquiry report states that McIvor did not 'meet his responsibilities' on the night of the murder. It states that McIvor had regarded himself as 'superfluous' and 'concerned himself only with possible future public order implications' of the killing. His attitude came 'as a matter of considerable surprise since we regard Mr McIvor as an important person in the chain of command,' the report, published in 1999, states. Because of his seniority, McIvor should have 'taken charge' and ensured there was proper coordination between police officers, according to Macpherson's report. Conveying the impression he believed things 'were under control', McIvor was unaware of the most basic details. 'For example, he did not know there had been an eyewitness to the murder,' the report adds.

The report states, too, that McIvor defined himself as a 'manager' solely focused on public order. Accepting that he had only been in Plumstead for four months at that point, the report criticises him for appearing 'less aware than we would expect of other racist incidents and violence' in the area. 'He used the phrase and concept of "manager" rather like a shield to defend himself from any suggestion of operational responsibility,' the report states.[49]

Hilary Benn was Britain's secretary for international development in 2004. Asked if he had authorised McIvor's recruitment to the post of adviser on Palestine policing, Benn replied: 'As secretary of state, it was not my role to take decisions about the appointment of individual staff or consultants to the department.'[50] McIvor did not respond when asked if he underwent any training on racial equality or human rights before taking up his job as adviser.

McIvor was named the first head of an EU operation to support the PA's police in 2005. Known as COPPS – the EU Coordinating Office for Palestinian Police Support – it followed a disturbing agenda. A people living under occupation were being taught how to police their own occupation. The use of buzzwords such as 'peace' and 'ownership' could not disguise that fact.

COPPS fell under the rubric of the aforementioned 'roadmap'. A 'strategy' document for promotional activities relating to this 'mission' (as diplomats called it) stressed that its aim was to 'bring new practical weight to the EU's support for Israel's right to live in peace and security.' An 'adequate mechanism for coordination and cooperation with the relevant Israeli authorities will be established to ensure their acceptance and facilitation of mission activities,' the paper stated. Similarly, there would be 'close coordination' with a US military team also mentoring the PA's forces.[51]

McIvor was paid an annual salary of more than €200,000 ($224,000).[52] That made him part of a wealthy elite stationed in Ramallah at a time when nearly half of all Palestinians in the West Bank and Gaza had to make do with less than $2 a day.[53] Britain paid most of the operation's bills for its first year, according to a 'progress report' signed by McIvor. The report stated that McIvor and his team were assessing what 'public order' equipment was required by the PA's forces. A list of such equipment – categorised as 'defensive weapons' – included tear gas, water cannons, rubber bullets and smoke bombs. The EU wished to arrange training workshops on riot control techniques and 'move away the Israeli obstacles' to providing the PA with weapons. Spain, McIvor's paper noted, had already agreed to donate 1,500 batons, as well as two water cannon trucks and two armoured trucks for the PA's 'anti-riot personnel'.[54]

Six men have led the COPPS operation in the decade since its inception. Four of them, including McIvor, had previously served with the Royal Ulster Constabulary (RUC) in Northern Ireland. It is troubling that officers from the RUC should be tasked with devising plans for policing Palestine. For the Catholic community in Northern Ireland, the RUC is synonymous with repression. Its preferred method of crowd control was to fire plastic bullets liberally. Twelve-year-old Carol-Anne Kelly was doing nothing more threatening than carrying a carton of milk home from the shops when she was killed in 1981. She was among three children killed by plastic bullets in Northern Ireland that year.[55]

Asked whether it wished the PA's forces to replicate tactics used in Northern Ireland, a COPPS spokesman claimed the operation 'does not give any preference to any specific methods or models' of policing.[56] That claim seems to contradict what McIvor told the BBC in 2006: 'I think that many of the lessons learned from policing in Northern Ireland over the past 10 years – where policing is highly politicised, where it is contested – are directly transferable out here.'[57]

Paul Kernaghan, who became head of COPPS in 2009, has advocated that the RUC model should be exported to other conflict zones. As well as serving in Northern Ireland, he has undertaken 'missions' to Iraq and Afghanistan since their invasion by British and American troops.[58] While giving evidence to the Chilcot Inquiry in 2010, he said that at 'various stages in the RUC's existence, it had a fairly high level capability and, indeed at one stage, a light armoured capability.' He contended that 'you need something like that' in Iraq.[59]

Colin Smith, who succeeded McIvor as the COPPS chief in 2007, has spoken of how his work involved 'facilitating cooperation' between the PA and Israel. Such liaison was 'progressing', despite how Israel had curbed the PA forces' freedom of movement, Smith said in 2008.[60] Smith is an ex-RUC officer who was a top British police representative in Iraq before his stint in Palestine.[61] His assessment has been echoed by the Israeli authorities. Micky Rosenfeld, an Israeli police spokesman, has remarked that cooperation between the PA and Israel has deepened with help from the COPPS operation.[62]

A team from the British Army has also supported the work of the US 'security coordinator' for Israel and the Palestinian Authority.[63] Britain, Canada and the USA are the three key contributors of military personnel to the operation's headquarters, according to a 2010 study by America's Government Accountability Office.[64] Keith Dayton, the American military general who headed the operation from 2005 to 2010, has described the British and Canadians in his staff as 'my eyes and ears'. The British participants had more contacts with Palestinians than American soldiers, he indicated during a 2009 speech to the Washington Institute for Near East Policy, a pro-Israel lobby group. Dayton also stated that he was in daily contact with the COPPS headquarters and was 'well tied in with the efforts' made by Tony Blair (by then out of Downing Street and working as what London newspapers called a Middle East 'peace envoy').

Formed in 2005, the purpose of the US security coordinator's office was to 'allay Israeli fears' about the PA, Dayton said.[65] As part of that work, he trained the PA's forces to punish other Palestinians. That became apparent after Hamas won an election for the Palestinian Legislative Council in 2006. The Bush administration – supposedly dedicated to 'democracy promotion' in the Middle East – found it intolerable that Palestinians could vote for what it regarded as the wrong party. America actively worked to bring down a 'national unity government' formed by Fatah and Hamas in January 2007. The EU assisted the attempts to wreck that coalition by freezing direct aid to the PA. The result of that pressure was that the divisions between Gaza and the West Bank grew. Hamas assumed responsibility for the internal administration of Gaza, Fatah did so in the West Bank. America and the EU sided with Fatah. With America's connivance, cooperation between Israel and PA forces loyal to Fatah was stepped up. Some 1,500 people suspected of being involved with or supportive of Hamas were rounded up in the West Bank between mid-June and October 2007.[66]

Backed by Britain and America, the PA's forces turned the West Bank into a police state. When Israel attacked Gaza in late 2008 and 2009, Palestinians in the West Bank were denied the right to protest. Those who dared to defy a ban on protests were arrested.[67] Dayton has lauded the PA's forces for working in tandem with Israel to prevent major unrest in the West Bank. He has even inferred that the PA forces were effectively doing the work of the Israeli occupation. High-ranking Israeli soldiers left the West Bank to take part in the offensive against Gaza. Israeli soldiers could be absent from the West Bank, Dayton told the Washington Institute for Near East Policy, because 'they could trust' the PA forces.[68]

Torture of people arrested by PA forces has been widespread. In June 2009, Haitham Amer died after allegedly being tortured by PA security agents.[69] Eager to please their Western donors, Fatah politicians have even boasted of their willingness to approve violence against their own people. 'We have had to kill Palestinians to establish one authority, one gun and the rule of law,' Saeb Erekat, a prominent Fatah representative told a US delegation in September 2009. 'We continue to perform our obligations.'[70]

Bowing to Western pressure, the PA feels obliged to protect Israel. Mahmoud Abbas, the PA's president, has described 'security coordination' with Israel as 'sacred'. The coordination would be maintained 'whether we disagree or agree over policy,' he said in 2014.[71] Two years later, he boasted of how three young Palestinians allegedly planning an attack had been 'tracked down and arrested' by the PA's forces, offering proof that 'our security coordination with Israel is working well'.[72] Abbas did not name the three in question but he appears to have been referring to left-wing activists who have been detained without charge and beaten in custody.[73]

Suffering for Israel?

Tony Blair's memoirs give the impression that he was, in political terms, seduced by Sharon. Israel's 2005 withdrawal of its settlers from Gaza is almost universally perceived as a cynical manoeuvre. Dov Weisglass, an adviser to Sharon, admitted as much beforehand. He described the withdrawal plan as 'formaldehyde' in 2004. Its whole purpose was to freeze the 'peace process' and to remove discussions on Palestinian refugees and the prospect of a Palestinian state from the agenda. Weisglass said that he had 'effectively agreed' with the Bush administration that questions surrounding Israel's colonisation of the West Bank would not be addressed 'until the Palestinians turn into Finns'.[74] Apparently immune to such cynicism, Blair regarded it as an example of how Sharon was a 'real leader', albeit one who exasperated him. 'Whereas the international community, in its usual purblind way, saw disengagement from Gaza as a "unilateral" Israeli act and therefore wrong, I was emphatic that it could be presented as lifting the occupation and removing settlements,' Blair wrote in his memoirs.[75]

Blair went further than many of his acolytes in supporting Israel. Jack Straw, recently demoted from foreign secretary to leader of the Commons, issued quite a mild complaint about Israel's 2006 attack on Lebanon. Yet because he expressed some displeasure at an action of which Blair seemed to approve, the media appointed Straw as leader of an internal 'revolt'.[76] Blair's backing of an Israeli offensive that killed more than 1,000 Lebanese made him increasingly unpopular among Labour MPs and, to a greater extent, the general public. His stance contributed to his downfall. By his own admission, 'it probably did me more damage than anything since Iraq'. The 'damage' should not be exaggerated: he hung on in Downing Street for almost another year and none of his cabinet colleagues felt strongly enough about the Lebanon invasion to resign in protest. Blair seemed more aggrieved by how he 'suffered' (his precise word) than by the deaths and injuries of people in Lebanon. Blair even tried to paint a picture of moral Israeli soldiers – 'they do not target civilians,' he wrote in his memoirs – engaged in an epic struggle between what he called 'modernity and atavism'. He wrote:

At points I had wondered why I didn't just cave in and condemn Israel and call for them to stop unilaterally. The Israelis would have understood it and it would have been the proverbial safety valve for the fierce political criticism. But I had by now come to see the entire conventional approach to dealing with this problem as itself part of the problem. And, by the way, what was the problem? That was a good first question. To most people, in July 2006, looking at the news it was the Israel/Lebanon conflict. I didn't see it like that. I defined the problem as the wider struggle between the strain of religious extremism in Islam and the rest of us. To me, Lebanon was embroiled in something far bigger and more portentous than a temporary fight with Israel.[77]

By searching for portents, Blair was able to dodge the prosaic. Hezbollah was not posing any existential threat to Israel or to 'modernity'. Israel had used a Hezbollah raid on the boundary between Lebanon and Israel as the pretext for a massive military offensive. The Israeli spin on which Blair relied while searching for portents ignored the relentless assaults on Lebanese sovereignty. Although Israel had withdrawn from southern Lebanon in 2000, its warplanes had kept on flying over the country and spying on the Lebanese people.[78]

Blair's claim that Israel did not target civilians was at odds with what Israel's own generals said. Gadi Eisenkot, then head of the northern division in the Israeli army, acknowledged that a deliberate decision had been made to destroy the Dahiya neighbourhood of Beirut on the pretext that Hezbollah fighters lived there. Eisenkot told the Israeli newspaper *Yedioth Ahronoth*:

> What happened in the Dahiya quarter of Beirut will happen in every village from which Israel is fired on. We will apply disproportionate force on it [the village] and cause great damage and destruction there. From our standpoint, these are not civilian villages, they are military bases. This is not a recommendation. This is a plan. And it has been approved.[79]

The plan to which he alluded has become known as the Dahiya doctrine. It has been followed in subsequent attacks on Gaza – attacks that have enjoyed either tacit or explicit support from the British government.

Britain – by refusing to press for a ceasefire – did not just give Israel the breathing space it required to commit atrocities during 2006. It also provided Israel with practical assistance. Britain authorised arms sales worth £22.5 million to Israel in 2005, the year before the attack on Lebanon. That was almost twice the level for 2004.[80] Those figures do not tell the entire story. The British arms industry also benefited because of its connections to America, Israel's chief provider of military aid.

The American F16s used by Israel while attacking Lebanon contained electromagnetic components made by the Liverpool-based firm MPE. The Apache helicopters in Israel's arsenal were fitted with parts from eight British companies, including AgustaWestland and Smiths Industries.[81] Planes carrying bombs from America to Israel refuelled at Prestwick airport in Scotland. While Margaret Beckett, then the foreign secretary, expressed unease over the matter, she zoomed in on whether the correct procedures for the transport of hazardous cargo were being followed, rather than the obscenity of the arms trade.[82]

Blair's involvement with Palestine did not halt when he quit Downing Street. A few hours after he stood down as prime minister, it was announced that he would be the 'representative' of the Middle East 'quartet'. It was an appointment replete with irony. The Iraq invasion was arguably the worst crime committed so far this century. Two men were ultimately responsible for that invasion: George W. Bush and Tony Blair. One of them was now being rewarded with a high-profile conflict resolution job in the same region. Blair had become a 'peace envoy'.

At first glance, Blair's job description seemed to be limited. He was supposed to concentrate on such topics as coordinating aid to the Palestinians and promoting economic development in the West Bank and Gaza. On closer inspection, it appeared that he was being given *carte blanche* to act in Israel's interests. According to an official statement, Blair would 'liaise with other countries, as appropriate, in support of the agreed quartet objectives.'[83] All of the quartet's activities are supposed to abide by three 'principles'. They require Palestinians to recognise Israel (without requiring Israel to dismantle its apartheid system), respect the Oslo accords and renounce violence (without Israel being required to demilitarise).[84] Those principles amount to a recipe for the further humiliation of the Palestinians.

Having become acquainted with a number of Israeli politicians, Blair had begun echoing their tropes. In December 2007, he commented that 'facts on the ground' were needed to guarantee that 'what happens in the daily lives of Palestinians and Israelis is consistent with political talks and a Palestinian state.'[85] The term 'facts on the ground' has been used by Israeli strategists for decades. Settlements in the West Bank – including East Jerusalem – are viewed as 'facts on the ground', which the Israeli political elite wants to make irreversible.

One perception that developed about Blair's tenure as the 'quartet representative' is that he was something of an absentee, that he was too busy swanning around the world to give the quest for peace the attention it required. The perception had some truth in it: Blair, for example, seldom set foot in Gaza. Yet it would be wrong to judge Blair's record solely by the number of hours he spent at – or away from

– his desk in Jerusalem. The deeper significance of his appointment is that he was overseeing the normalisation of injustice.

That can be discerned from a policy document he published in 2008 titled *Towards a Palestinian State*. Though carefully phrased, the document smacked of bigotry. It recommended that various measures should be taken so that 'over time and progressively, the everyday life of Palestinians can be improved but in a way that does not put Israel's security at risk.'[86] Palestinians were thereby cast as an inherently dangerous people and Israel as benevolent. Israel, Blair announced, had granted permission for projects designed to benefit the Palestinians such as a children's park in Area C, the part of the West Bank being colonised relentlessly, and longer opening hours at the Allenby crossing, the Israeli-controlled boundary between the West Bank and Jordan.

Worse, the document implied that Israel was entitled to behave as it saw fit. 'Israel will retain overall responsibility in the West Bank and reserves the right to act where its security is at risk,' the document stated. Keith Dayton and James Jones, another US general, were 'working intensively to help develop the Palestinian capability to instil law and order and to combat terrorism,' it added. The generals were also liaising with Israel so that the PA 'will be given control of security under unique and different arrangements.' While the document stated that the details of these 'arrangements' were under constant discussion, subsequent events provide a clue as to how the discussions worked out.[87] As previously mentioned, the PA's forces became a proxy for the Israeli occupation – by rounding up Palestinians in the West Bank who protested against Israel's 2009 bombardment of Gaza.

That entire operation had been orchestrated by Israel. It had taken advantage of how the international media was fixated with a November 2008 presidential election in the USA to launch a raid on Gaza. Hamas' response of firing rockets into present-day Israel provided the pretext for a major offensive. The result was around 1,400 Palestinian deaths, mostly non-combatants, compared to 13 Israeli deaths, ten of whom were soldiers. Ordinary people around the world had no difficulty comprehending what had happened: protests were organised in many cities against how Israel was terrorising Gaza's 1.5 million inhabitants. Not for the first time, Blair was out of step with public opinion. Speaking on CNN, he urged that the 'smuggling issue – that is weapons and money coming through tunnels from Egypt to Gaza' be addressed through 'clear and definitive action'. At pains (again) to express understanding for Israel, he said: 'I think Israel would like to see a halt to this quickly but I think it is prepared to go on.'[88] Blair visited Gaza shortly after Operation Cast Lead, the code name for that Israeli offensive; the destruction he observed did not alter his perspective. He followed up his trip by attending a donors conference for Gaza's reconstruction in the Egyptian resort of Sharm el-Sheikh. From there, he gave another interview to CNN, his favourite TV channel judging by the number of times he has appeared on it. Answering a question on Hamas' 'missiles', he said: 'This violence coming out of Gaza should stop because it then, of course, means that Israel retaliates and then we go back into the whole cycle.'[89]

Just as Blair was willing to praise Ariel Sharon, he became something of a cheerleader for Benjamin Netanyahu. Ahead of the 2009 election that made him prime minister for the second time, Netanyahu discussed his idea for making 'economic peace' with 'moderate Palestinians'. It was not hard to work out what Netanyahu had in mind – bubbles of prosperity would be stimulated in parts of the West Bank. While Netanyahu said he wanted 'rapid economic growth that gives a stake for peace for the ordinary Palestinians', it was predictable that encouraging enterprise under a military occupation would only benefit an elite.[90] The wealth gap would widen between the elite and the 'ordinary Palestinians' about whom Netanyahu professed to be concerned. Few people could say with a straight face that Netanyahu was motivated by altruism, but Blair managed to; Blair told *Time* magazine that he believed Netanyahu wanted 'to build the [Palestinian] state from the bottom up'. Blair added: 'I understand and buy into that.'[91]

Equally, Blair's declared faith in America was not affected by the transition from George Bush to Barack Obama. When Obama offered a 'new beginning' in the relationship between the USA and 'Muslims around the world' during a visit to Cairo, Blair celebrated the president's typically polished speech as 'a huge event'. Ignoring the crucial issue of how an America that kept on giving billions in military aid to Israel each year was an enabler of apartheid and aggression, Blair said: 'I have no doubt at all of his [Obama's] sincerity or determination. So if everyone would commit themselves to a peaceful political negotiation and to a two-state solution, you could have this deal within the year.'[92]

Spindoctor for a siege

In May 2010, Britain's relations with Israel were, according to some accounts, tetchy. Gordon Brown's government expelled an Israeli diplomat because of how Mossad, the spying agency, used forged British passports while carrying out the assassination of Mahmoud al-Mabhouh, a leading Hamas figure, in Dubai earlier that year. Much less involved in British domestic politics than he had been for several years, Blair made no reference to the apparent frictions when he addressed the American Israel Public Affairs Committee's annual conference.[93] 'I am always described as a friend of Israel,' Blair told the event, organised by the top Zionist lobby group in Washington. 'It is true. I am proud of it.' He proceeded to delight his audience by condemning Hamas, while rhapsodising about how Israel should be regarded as a 'model' for the entire Middle East. According to Blair, the detention by Hamas of Gilad Shalit, an Israeli soldier, was a 'disgrace'. He did not use such unequivocal terms when referring to the siege of Gaza. Indeed, he did not even use the word 'siege'.[94] Anxious to empathise with an Israeli soldier (captured while enforcing an occupation), he did not see fit to express any anger over how more than 300 Palestinian children were then being held in Israeli military detention.[95] Many children are locked up for throwing stones at Israeli soldiers, a brave and risky way to insist that the occupation will never be accepted. Blair used his AIPAC speech to instruct Palestinians that their 'mentality has to move from resistance to governance'.[96]

Theoretically, Blair worked for a 'quartet'. In reality, one of its four members – the USA – pulled the strings. America was the main donor to his Jerusalem office, providing $13.5 million between 2007 and 2013.[97] Furthermore, he relied largely on American advice. From 2008 to 2010, that office was ran by Robert Danin, a US official who had previously worked at the State Department and the National Security Council.[98] Danin issued a series of statements favourable towards Israel. Commitments by Israel to allow a few extra trucks into Gaza were hailed by Danin as a 'positive step forward'. Like Blair, he avoided saying publicly that Gaza was under siege.[99]

On 31 May 2010, the Israeli military boarded the *Mavi Marmara*, a Turkish ship carrying activists who were attempting to break the maritime blockade of Gaza. Nine passengers were killed by Israel in international waters. Tony Blair, the man who regarded resistance directly targeting the Israeli military as a 'disgrace', merely described this attack on civilians as 'tragic'.[100] Blair's admiration for Netanyahu was sturdy enough to survive. 'I think he is sincere in his desire for peace,' Blair told *Newsweek* when asked a question about whether Netanyahu was endangering the 'peace process'.[101]

Dispensing with any pretense of impartiality, Blair effectively undertook 'public relations' work for Israel in the ensuing weeks. When Netanyahu agreed to an 'easing' of Gaza's siege, Blair went on a tour extolling the virtues of the Israeli commitment. Travelling to Luxembourg for a meeting of EU foreign ministers, he said that Netanyahu was prepared to allow civilian goods to enter Gaza, while maintaining a blockade on weapons. Blair was striving to build on this commitment so that 'we get a policy' that was, in his words, 'right for Israel's security and is humane to the people of Gaza'.[102] He was publicly thanked by Netanyahu for his 'statesmanship and friendship'. Part of that statesmanship involved using diplomatic niceties, it seemed. Blair would still not dare to utter the word 'siege'; instead he spoke of Israel's 'Gaza policy' and – using practically identical language to Netanyahu – demanded the release of Gilad Shalit 'now approaching four years in captivity'.[103]

Blair's work for the quartet was, in many respects, an extension of his work as prime minister. Having sponsored plans to put Palestinians in charge of policing their own occupation, he now advocated that they should be put in charge of supervising Gaza's siege. As part of the deal he worked out with Netanyahu, the PA was given a role monitoring the entry of goods into Gaza – without the blockade being lifted. 'Joint teams' were set up between Israel and the PA to expand operations at Karem Abu Salem (or Kerem Shalom in Hebrew), an Israeli-controlled goods crossing for Gaza. Although Blair conveyed the impression that all civilian goods were now permitted, Israel retained powers to stop or hamper imports of construction materials.[104]

Blair did not draw a salary for his quartet work. He did not need one. Through his activities as a business lobbyist, he used the networking opportunities open to a former prime minister to amass a vast fortune. His championing of economic development projects that would benefit major corporations inevitably raised questions about potential conflicts of interest.[105] In February 2011, Blair announced that he had reached an agreement with Israel on energy issues. Under it, Israel would start talks with the PA about exploiting gas reserves off Gaza's coast.[106] Twelve years earlier, the British Gas Group had been granted a licence to explore those gas fields by the PA. It was expected that Israel would be a major buyer of the gas. Yet negotiations on extracting the gas had stalled, reportedly because of Israel's insistence that it be allowed to buy the fuel at rates considerably lower than market prices.[107] The gas project was identified as a priority by Blair and his team. Another priority was winning a deal through which Israel would release electromagnetic frequencies to enable Wataniya, a Kuwaiti firm, to launch itself as a mobile phone operator in the West Bank.[108] Can it be a coincidence that both British Gas and Wataniya were clients of JP Morgan, the investment bank that had hired Blair as a lobbyist?[109]

One reason why Israel's siege of Gaza had such a devastating human impact was because Egypt cooperated in enforcing it. Hosni Mubarak, the Egyptian dictator, denied Palestinians the right to seek refuge by sealing his country's border with Gaza during Operation Cast Lead. That did not stop Blair from rallying to Mubarak's defence when Cairo's Tahrir Square was thronged with protesters demanding that he step down. Blair commended Mubarak for his supposedly positive attitude to the quest for 'peace' in Palestine, hailing him as 'immensely courageous and a force for good'.[110]

Throughout his time as the quartet representative, Blair recited his desire for a 'viable Palestinian state' so often that it became something of a mantra. He was adamant that a two-state solution was the only realistic way to achieve a durable peace. He did not spell out, though, what he meant by a 'viable' state. Was it one that comprised all of the West Bank and Gaza? In July 2011, he signalled that he believed Palestinians should be ready to accept far less than that. Visiting Washington for discussions with Hillary Clinton, then secretary of state, he said:

> I think the blueprint is to recognise you're obviously not going to go back to precisely the same borders as 1967 because of the changes that have taken place. But 1967 borders with mutually agreed land swaps is obviously the right way forward.[111]

Palestinians, he was effectively arguing, would have to regard much of the West Bank's colonisation as irreversible. Many Palestinian activists who are unaffiliated to either Hamas or Fatah are campaigning for a one-state solution covering all of historic Palestine, based on the principles of democracy and equality between people of all races and religions. Blair, however, has been dismissive of such calls.[112] He has even argued – without elaboration – that a one-state solution 'means, in the end, a nightmare for both sides'.[113]

Blair constantly implied that Palestinians must get cosy with their occupiers if the two-state solution was to be realized. In September 2011, Mahmoud Abbas, the PA's president, formally submitted an application for Palestine to be admitted as a member state of the United Nations. In protest at this move, Israel deployed a tactic it has repeatedly used to punish Palestinians. It blocked the transfer of tax and customs revenue to the PA. That is a fancy way of saying that Israel was stealing Palestinian money. Blair successfully pushed Netanyahu to unfreeze the revenue. The arguments he used were telling. He zoomed in on how Israel's decision was affecting the PA's 'security' personnel. 'Withholding these funds only benefits those who oppose peace and Israeli–Palestinian cooperation,' he said.[114]

Benjamin Netanyahu proved once again that he was not serious about peace in November 2012. His government launched a major offensive against Gaza, killing 167 Palestinians, more than 30 of whom were children.[115] As happened four years earlier, the attack was reported as an act of self-defence. The Western media parroted Israeli claims that it was caused by Palestinian armed groups firing rockets out of Gaza. Evidence that Israel had provoked the vast majority of incidents in which rockets were fired was ignored.[116] Blair was among those willing to spread Israeli myths. Speaking to the BBC, he repeated his desire to stop 'further armaments coming into Gaza [for resistance groups] because that is what is giving rise to the current situation.'[117] Israel apparently had nothing to do with it.

On at least one occasion, Blair implicitly blamed Hamas for a crime that its leadership did not authorise. In June 2014, three Israeli teenagers were kidnapped and murdered. One month later, Israeli police admitted that the chief suspects had Hamas connections but had not operated with Hamas' approval.[118] The kidnapping had been cynically exploited by Netanyahu – with Blair's cooperation. The two men recorded a joint message that June, in which Blair nodded solemnly as Netanyahu argued that 'the international community has to support Israel's right of self-defence' and called on Mahmoud Abbas to 'end his pact with Hamas' (a reference to a unity agreement that had recently been sealed between Hamas and Fatah). Blair followed by saying that Hamas had a 'very clear choice to make' between politics and violence.[119] It is noteworthy that he has never told Netanyahu to make such a choice.

Israel used the teenagers' abduction as a pretext for a wave of demolitions, arrests and bomb attacks against Palestinians. Having already acquiesced to Netanyahu's demand that he respect Israel's 'right to self-defence' – a euphemism for punishing the innocent – Blair's call for 'restraint' rang hollow.[120] When a 16-year-old Palestinian, Muhammad Abu Khdeir, was burnt to death by Israeli settlers in East Jerusalem, Blair contended that the 'fanatics must be sidelined'.[121] Conveniently, he overlooked how mainstream Israeli politicians – including Netanyahu – had stoked the flames of fanaticism.

Worse, Blair distorted the truth in a manner advantageous to Israel during its 51-day attack on Gaza in the summer of 2014. In an interview with the Israeli media outlet *Ynet* published on 10 July, he described the operation as one of 'retaliation' for Hamas' rockets, while saying there were 'many civilian deaths, as well, on the Palestinian side'.[122] The insinuation that Israelis had been killed, forcing Netanyahu's government to respond, was false. Another five days elapsed before any Israeli civilian was killed in the fighting.[123] Until then all the civilian deaths had been Palestinians. And Palestinians comprised the overwhelming majority of the civilian casualties throughout the operation. Of the 2,220 Palestinians killed, at least 1,492 were non-combatants. Five Israeli civilians and 67 Israeli soldiers were killed.[124]

Amid Israel's relentless violence, Blair perpetuated the fallacy that he was guiding the Palestinians towards greater autonomy. His oft-repeated message that Palestine needed investment was superficially plausible. The problems lay in the type of investment he was promoting. A bullet point inserted into a September 2014 paper that he presented to a Western-dominated committee coordinating aid to the PA was revealing. It stated that Blair's team was working to 'upgrade' Palestinian industrial estates into 'special economic zones'.[125] Such zones typically allow companies operating in them to pay less taxes and lower wages than those normally applying.

Although Blair's advisers have denied that he was seeking to worsen the conditions of Palestinian workers, there is ample reason to believe that is precisely what he was recommending.[126] The 'upgrade' proposal was part of the *Initiative for the Palestinian Economy*. That blueprint was drawn up by Blair's team in consultation with Palestinian and Israeli entrepreneurs. Another paper published by Blair under that rubric noted that Palestinian labour was 'well-educated, relatively inexpensive and abundant'.[127] That was a profound understatement: Palestinian workers are not simply 'inexpensive'; they are badly paid. According to data available around the time Blair's blueprint was drawn up, the average net daily wages for Palestinians in the West Bank and Gaza were $26 for men and $21 for women.[128] When Blair's then spokeswoman was asked if his initiative would lower those wages, she replied 'absolutely not'. She added that 'multinational companies would be a key driver' of proposals to boost Palestine's manufacturing industry.[129] That reply was not reassuring: major corporations are profit driven and averse to strong regulation. There was nothing in Blair's proposals to indicate that he was demanding that they pay a reasonable level of taxation or good wages. Rather, the available evidence (and the general economic philosophy that he espoused both as prime minister and in his subsequent career) points in the opposite direction.

The initiative was not actually Blair's idea. He had been tasked with devising the blueprint by John Kerry, America's secretary of state, in 2013.[130] Kerry announced that he had given that job to Blair during a conference involving top Palestinian and Israeli entrepreneurs hosted by Klaus Schwab, head of the World Economic Forum, an invitation-only club for the rich and powerful. Schwab's involvement should raise suspicions. One of Schwab's greatest triumphs – in his mind – was to persuade Nelson Mandela that the core tenets of the 1955 Freedom Charter be abandoned. That radical document contained a commitment to placing South Africa's industry under public ownership once apartheid was vanquished. By pressuring Mandela to repudiate the principles on which the struggle against minority white rule was waged, Schwab ensured that South Africa would be wedded to international capitalism and that racial inequality would persist.[131] Was he – abetted by Blair – advocating something similar for Palestine?

Blair made one of his rare trips to Gaza in February 2015. He used the occasion to write an opinion piece. While acknowledging that Gaza had been 'devastated', he avoided holding Israel responsible for that devastation. Rather, he shifted the focus by saying that Egypt was 'understandably' concerned about Hamas' connections to the Muslim Brotherhood. 'The international community need clarity from Hamas,' he wrote. 'Are they a Palestinian nationalist movement dedicated to the achievement of a Palestinian state or part of a broader Islamist movement with regional designs that impact governments outside of Gaza?'[132]

The 'international community' required no such clarity: Hamas has concentrated on Palestine since its inception. While it has connections in other countries, notably to the Muslim Brotherhood in Egypt, there is scant evidence of it having 'regional designs'. By empathising with Egypt, Blair was in effect giving his blessing to the brutal suppression of the Muslim Brotherhood at the behest of President Abdel Fatah al-Sisi. Around 900 people were killed at a Cairo rally in support of Muhammad Morsi – the deposed president – on 14 August 2013.[133] It was one of the bloodiest massacres of recent history. And now Blair wished to underscore how much he understood the concerns of the man who ordered it.

The Gaza trip was one of Blair's final engagements working for the 'quartet'. He stepped down from his post soon afterwards, though he still pops up on television screens offering his 'insights' on the Middle East. The consensus among the mainstream media on Blair's departure was that he had few results to show for his eight-year stretch as a 'peace envoy'.[134] That analysis overlooks how Blair had been given the job precisely because he had been a loyal lieutenant of the USA during his time in Downing Street. His job description implicitly required him to persuade the PA leadership that it accommodate Israeli apartheid. He enjoyed some success in that regard.

9
Partners in crime

The wars of the twenty-first century brought a sense of maturity and sophistication to Britain's relationship with Israel. Perhaps 2007 can be identified as the year when the relationship entered a new phase: that summer an Israeli-made drone was flown over the skies of Iraq and Afghanistan.[1] Britain operated these flights, signalling that its future 'defence' policy would rely, at least partly, on weapons that had been tested during Israel's attack on Lebanon the previous year and that would soon be used to inflict devastation on Gaza.[2]

Britain acquired a new prime minister that summer, too. Gordon Brown was Tony Blair's bitter rival, if the political correspondents in London were to be believed. Allegedly serious journalists had spent a decade fixated on the apparent struggle between the New Labour duo. The entourage of each man had briefed regularly against the other; the result was that acres of newsprint were filled with unattributed tittle-tattle. Once trivial issues of style and personality were removed, Brown and Blair differed little. On key dossiers of economic policy and international relations, there was no difference at all.

That was evident when Brown visited Jerusalem in 2008, becoming the first British prime minister to address Israel's parliament, the Knesset. Marking the sixtieth anniversary of Israel's foundation, Brown waxed lyrical about the state's achievements. He said:

From draining the swamps in the twentieth century to pioneering electric cars in the twenty-first, your history of ingenuity is a lesson in the boundless capacity of mind and spirit. No nation has achieved so much in so short a period of time. And to have accomplished all this in the face of the war, the terror, the violence, the threats, the intimidation and the insecurity is truly monumental.[3]

Brown's paean to Israel's technological prowess was incomplete. Some Israeli innovations undoubtedly have benign applications. Yet that cannot negate how Israel has turned its oppression of Palestinians and its general belligerence to its competitive advantage. Arms and surveillance equipment have emerged as key Israeli exports. And Britain is an avid buyer of Israel's cutting-edge weapons.

The drone flown in Iraq and Afghanistan was known as the Hermes 450. It has been used extensively by Britain in both of those wars. For most major undertakings in Afghanistan, the British Army had a Hermes 450 overhead, a defence committee meeting at the House of Commons was told in 2008.[4]

Designed and manufactured by the Israeli firm Elbit Systems, the Hermes 450 is the model on which the Watchkeeper programme, an initiative to equip the British Army with drones, was based. Elbit has been working on this initiative in tandem with Thales UK, a subsidiary of the French arms giant Thales.[5] The contract for this programme, awarded in 2005, was initially worth £800 million.[6] The project makes Britain a partner in Israel's crimes. Elbit's catalogues boast of how the drone is 'combat-proven', a euphemism for the fact it has been used to drop bombs on Palestinian families, and 'plays a major role, day after day, in the continuous war against terror around the globe.'[7]

The Watchkeeper is the largest drone programme in Europe. The drone's manufacturers contend that it will revolutionise the way the British Army fights. Just two people are needed to operate the vehicle; neither has to be a qualified pilot. One brochure for the drone uses the kind of language you would expect to see applied to a video game: 'The information generated by this technology allows commanders to detect, identify and track targets without the need to deploy troops into potentially sensitive or dangerous areas and also provides the ability to loiter while a target is engaged.'[8] A memo presented to the House of Commons' Defence Committee by Thales UK contended that drones perform the 'dull, dirty and dangerous jobs for which manned aircraft are not suitable' and that they enable 'more efficient war-fighting'. Although the memo predicts that the drones would lead to 'reduced numbers of UK casualties', it did not promise to cut civilian deaths or injuries.[9]

The Watchkeeper's maiden flight was over Megiddo in present-day Israel during April 2008. The drones are being produced by a firm called UAV Tactical Systems in Leicester.[10] Elbit owns more than half of that firm.[11] Part of the deal was that the first ten Watchkeeper drones would be made in present-day Israel, with production then being carried out at the Leicester plant.[12]

Engines for the drone are being made by a firm called UAV Engines near Birmingham; it is completely owned by Elbit.[13] In its 2009 annual report, Elbit named Britain and Israel as its main clients for drones. The aforementioned Hermes 450 was described as the 'backbone' of the pilotless warplane activities in the Israeli military. The drone had been 'fully operational' since 2000 and accumulated more than 140,000 flight hours.[14] That annual report failed to spell out that the Hermes was one of the two drones used in Operation Cast Lead, an attack that caused enormous suffering in Gaza during December 2008 and January 2009. Missiles were fired from those drones right from the very beginning of the offensive. On its first day, nine students and three other civilians were killed in a drone strike on Gaza City. The students were doing nothing more sinister than waiting for a bus.[15]

Devoted to drones

Such incidents did not dampen Britain's enthusiasm for Israeli drones. A few months after Operation Cast Lead, the defence ministry extended a contract for the use of the Hermes 450 by British troops.[16] Elbit's partner, Thales UK, had set up a team to advise the British Army on using the warplane in Afghanistan.[17] While defence ministers normally praise troops for their courage and dedication, Britain has slightly departed from that tradition by giving credit to technology. Quentin Davies, then a minister for 'defence equipment', stated in February 2010 that the Hermes 450 drone had done 'sterling work' in Afghanistan.[18] Two months later, the Watchkeeper was tested at Parc Aberporth in Wales; it was that drone's first British flight.[19]

The Conservative and Liberal Democrat coalition that took office in 2010 was just as devoted to drones as the Labour governments of Blair and Brown. In 2011, the defence ministry published a 'doctrine note' on how drones may contribute to Britain's military 'needs' between then and 2030. According to that paper, there was a general expectancy that the technology would become more prevalent following its use in Iraq and Afghanistan. While the USA dominated the 'high-end sector' of drone manufacturing, Israel had 'impressive worldwide sales' of smaller- and medium-sized drones. The paper acknowledged that there were ethical issues that needed to be addressed. Theoretically, it claimed, remote-controlled violence should be more moral than previous wars because 'a robot cannot be driven by anger to carry out illegal actions such as those at My Lai' during the Vietnam War. Despite a brief reference to press reports on 'killer drones' in Afghanistan, it failed to mention that drones had lately been used to commit war crimes in Gaza and that those crimes were ordered by military commanders (and politicians), not by robots.[20]

The arms industry has zealously promoted the Watchkeeper. After Philip Hammond, then Britain's defence secretary met his French counterpart Jean-Yves Le Drian in 2012, it was announced that France would soon begin trials of the drone and that it was interested in cooperating with Britain on the programme.[21] The drone was finally put to its intended use in 2014, when the British Army deployed it in Afghanistan.[22] The Watchkeeper did not see much action in the skies over Helmand province: the last British troops were withdrawn from Afghanistan in November that year.

The real picture was not as rosy as that painted by arms dealers. In 2015, the Bureau of Investigative Journalism published data indicating that the cost of the Watchkeeper programme had risen to £1.2 billion – around £400 million higher than that originally projected. Just 33 of the 54 drones ordered when the Watchkeeper contract was signed in 2005 had been delivered.[23] Characteristically, arms dealers have brazened out awkward questions about the programme. The very fact that the Watchkeeper was used for surveillance purposes in Afghanistan has enabled Thales and Elbit to declare the drone 'combat proven'.[24]

There is a wider significance to the Watchkeeper which the British press has generally overlooked. Fifty years ago, Israel began its military occupation of the West Bank and Gaza with the aid of Britain's weapons. Fifty years on, Britain is signalling that its future wars will use Israeli weaponry tested in the West Bank and Gaza. While Britain remains an exporter of arms to Israel, it has also become a lucrative client for the Israeli arms industry.

Replying to a parliamentary question, Britain's defence ministry has stated that it spent almost £16 million on Israeli products between 2014 and 2015.[25] The figure is more than likely an underestimate. According to Israel's official data, the value of its arms exports to Europe rose from $724 million in 2014 to more than $1.6 billion the following year.[26] Britain is the top military spender in Western Europe.[27]

Moreover, Israel's arms industry has invested heavily in Britain. Elbit, the leading Israeli weapons producer, has a number of subsidiaries headquartered in Britain, as well as being involved in joint ventures such as the Watchkeeper programme.

Ferranti Technologies, a firm based in Oldham, is fully owned by Elbit. It supplies components used by the Typhoon, one of the warplanes belonging to the Royal Air Force. One of the components boasts a suitably violent name: the throttle box controller.[28] Ferranti has also provided a helicopter freight service to British troops occupying Afghanistan, as well as making head-mounted displays for most of the combat helicopters in Britain's arsenal, according to the firm's website.[29] And it has developed a simulator for training drone operators.[30] Britain's defence ministry has signed several contracts with Ferranti. The firm has, for example, won an £11 million bid to supply the army with 'locator beacons' – technology used in rescuing military aircraft – between 2014 and 2021.[31]

Elbit does well from war and oppression: the value of its sales rose from $2.8 billion in 2011 to more than $3 billion in 2015.[32] The corporation has expanded its British operations in recent years. In 2011, it bought Elite Automotive Services (subsequently renamed Elite KL), a Staffordshire-based firm that makes air condition systems for drones and other military vehicles.[33] Meanwhile, a joint venture by Elbit and Kellogg, Brown and Root (KBR) opened for business in 2016.[34] Affinity, as the joint venture is called, was awarded a £500 million contract by Britain's defence ministry early that year. Under it, the firm will provide and maintain aircraft used in military training exercises. The contract is scheduled to last until 2033.[35]

Understandably – given the high level of public sympathy for Palestinians – the firm does not promote its Israeli connections. Although it names Elbit as a shareholder, the word 'Israel' is entirely absent from the firm's website at the time of writing. Rather, Affinity conveys the impression that it is a British company by congratulating itself for raffling a khaki-clad teddy bear to help an RAF charity.[36] Instro Precision, a firm based in Kent, is even more coy. Reading between the jargon on its homepage, it is possible to learn that the firm makes specialised cameras and other forms of surveillance technology.

Its location has allowed it to exhibit at the British pavilion of an international weapons fair in Turkey, a country that has had a somewhat strained relationship with Israel recently.[37] Papers that the firm is required to file with the registrar of companies for England and Wales contain details that cannot be found on its website. A document dating from December 2015 shows that five of its eight directors are Israelis; they include Elad Aharonson, a vice-president of Elbit.[38] The firm's Elbit connections were exposed by protesters who climbed onto the rooftop of its Kent factory on two separate days in 2015.[39]

Eyeing big orders

With sales exceeding $27 billion in 2014, the British firm BAE Systems is one of the top three largest weapons producers on the planet.[40] BAE has been intensifying its cooperation with Israel's arms industry. The trade magazine *IsraelDefense* reported in April 2012 that BAE and Elbit had teamed up with a view to developing new cannons for the USA and Israeli militaries. Operation Cast Lead, the major Israeli offensive in Gaza a few years earlier, had 'reaffirmed the importance of artillery', according to the magazine. Elbit and BAE were working on an 'entirely new' form of these traditional weapons and there was a strong prospect that Israel would be able to buy the new products with US military assistance, the magazine added.[41]

Later in 2012, BAE announced that it had been awarded a $400 million contract by the US Navy. Elbit was to be one of the main subcontractors on that project, which involved maintaining and servicing trainer aircraft.[42] The following year BAE stated that it had worked with Elbit on a portable 'precision-targeting' system for the US Army. Known as the Hammer, the system would reduce 'collateral damage', according to BAE's 'public relations' material.[43] 'Collateral damage' is the euphemism that military analysts use to describe civilian deaths.

Because of its strong transatlantic links, BAE has benefited considerably from America's military aid programme to Israel – a programme that reached unprecedented levels of 'generosity' under the Obama administration. BAE is a leading supplier of components for the warplanes assembled by Lockheed Martin, America (and the world's) largest arms company. Having long manufactured head-up displays for Lockheed's F16 fighters, BAE has more recently begun equipping them with 'advanced identification friend or foe systems'.[44] A Lockheed-manufactured F16 called the Fighting Falcon has been flown by the Israeli Air Force since 2004.[45] BAE's own brochures state that it has supplied technology fitted into the Fighting Falcon.[46]

The F16 is being replaced by the hugely expensive F35. BAE is being hailed as a 'major partner' in the consortium – headed by Lockheed Martin – behind these state-of-the-art killing machines. Most of the F35's rear section is being assembled by BAE in England and Australia, according to the firm.[47] Israel made a commitment in 2010 to buy 19 of these jets.[48]

BAE has also worked closely with Rafael, another Israeli arms producer. The two firms have been working on projects that could be described as sea-drones. In 2006, BAE, Rafael and Lockheed Martin joined forces to unveil the Protector, an unmanned naval vessel.[49] The Protector has subsequently been used to 'investigate suspicious fishing boats off the Gaza Strip coast,' the arms industry trade magazine *Israel-Defense* has reported.[50] That is a coded way of saying that the weapon is being used in enforcing a maritime blockade on Gaza. The Israeli Navy has imposed tight restrictions on Gaza's fishermen. Under the pretext of monitoring 'suspicious' activity, Israel has often arrested and fired at fishermen who were within the narrow zone in which they are permitted to work.[51]

As if that was not enough, BAE actually has a subsidiary named Rokar based in Jerusalem. Rokar has tried to fill a niche in Israel's expanding arsenal with the Silver Bullet, a project that reputedly transforms traditional artillery into 'smart' precision-guided weapons. The firm's selling points for the project are contradictory. Rokar claims that the Silver Bullet would both reduce 'collateral damage' and allow for 'increased firepower density and lethality' – in other words, that it could either be used to kill fewer or higher numbers of people.[52] The firm had a setback in 2016, when the Israeli military decided against signing a contract to buy the Silver Bullet.[53] However, the project is unlikely to be mothballed. Following the 2014 attack on Gaza, military analysts argued that Israel should acquire more advanced artillery.[54] It is entirely conceivable that Rokar will either sell such weapons to Israel in the future or that other clients will snatch up the firm's Israeli-designed products, which have been tested in the Naqab (Negev) region of historical Palestine. *Jane's Defence Weekly*, an arms industry magazine, has reported that the Silver Bullet is 'probably easier to sell internationally' than American weapons of a similar nature because it is not subject to US restrictions on arms exports.[55]

Clegg's crocodile tears

With Britain and Israel's arms industries becoming ever more interlinked, professions of concern by senior politicians need to be treated with scepticism. While Gaza was under attack in 2009, Nick Clegg, then the Liberal Democrats' leader, called for an embargo on weapons sales to Israel. Writing an opinion piece for *The Guardian*, Clegg noted that the value of approved British weapon exports to Israel had risen from £6 million for all of 2007 to £20 million for the first three months of 2008 alone.[56] The Labour government of the time effectively confessed later in 2009 that it had contributed to Israel's war crimes. David Miliband, then foreign secretary, said that British components had 'almost certainly' been fitted into weapons used in Gaza. His admission proved that the Labour government's declared policy of not allowing exports to Israel if they could be used 'aggressively' in Gaza and the West Bank was waffle.[57]

Little more than a year after making his embargo call, Clegg became deputy prime minister. He and his party were ideally placed to insist that weapons sales be halted. Vince Cable, the Lib Dems' intellectual guru, was appointed business secretary. Among his tasks were to decide whether or not export licences should be granted for weapons. Shamefully, Cable kept on rubber-stamping arms exports to Israel. In the six months before the 2014 attack on Gaza, Cable authorised the delivery of weapons and components worth £7 million to Israel. They included parts of drones and other warplanes and targeting equipment.[58]

Clegg and Cable tried to evade responsibility for their actions. After a number of UN schools had been bombed, they issued a joint statement in August 2014 urging that arms exports to Israel be suspended. Cable explicitly blamed the Conservatives for the failure to reach a coalition agreement on freezing arms exports.[59] The Tories were indeed culpable of assisting Israeli aggression, yet, contrary to what they implied, so were the Lib Dems. It is noteworthy that Clegg's 2009 embargo call had also been made following Israeli attacks on Gaza's schools. Why was it necessary to wait for more schools to be bombed before halting weapons sales?

Cable resorted to obfuscation later that August – when there was a temporary ceasefire in Gaza. He published another statement saying that 12 export licences to Israel would be blocked if there was a resumption of 'significant hostilities'. The decision had been taken, he stated, because the British government had not been able to clarify if the criteria for granting export licences had been met.[60] Contrary to what Cable implied, the situation was alarmingly clear. The criteria in question are part of a legally binding EU code on weapons exports. They require exporters to take into account whether or not a potential buyer respects international humanitarian law. Israel does not respect international law – its siege of Gaza violates the Fourth Geneva Convention. For that and many other reasons, there should be no arms sales to Israel whatsoever. Cable and his entourage have refused to allow any transparency over their decisions. A freedom of information request to see what advice had been provided to Cable on weapons sales to Israel met with the response that it was necessary to withhold the details. Disclosing them would increase the 'risk of protest against those companies that have exported military equipment to Israel,' the business department stated, citing demonstrations that had shut down some of Elbit's factories in Britain for a few days that summer.[61] Protecting the arms industry was deemed more important than protecting human rights.

The Liberal Democrats' approach to Israel was inconsistent. Although Clegg denounced Israeli atrocities in Gaza, he was more than accommodating towards the politicians who approved those atrocities. (The atrocities were not aberrations or mistakes – Tzipi Livni, Israel's foreign minister at the time, said in January 2009 it was a 'good thing' that Israeli troops were 'going wild' in Gaza).[62] Addressing the Lib Dems Friends of Israel in November 2010, Clegg called for changes to Britain's universal jurisdiction law – which allowed prosecution of crimes against humanity carried out abroad. Clegg argued that he wished to avoid 'accusations based on poorly justified grounds against visitors to the UK.'[63] It was clear that he was really talking about diluting the law to placate Israel. Campaigners had invoked the law (unsuccessfully) to try and have Ehud Barak arrested when he was invited to the British Labour Party's conference a year earlier. An attempt had similarly been made to arraign Shaul Mofaz, another military chief turned politician.[64] In both those cases, the accusations were amply justified; Barak had, as defence minister, overseen Operation Cast Lead. Mofaz had allegedly ordered commanders based in the West Bank to kill 70 Palestinians per day while an *intifada* was underway in 2001.[65] Lawyers seeking his prosecution had also documented how he had approved assassinations and house demolitions.[66]

Much to the Israeli government's relief, Britain altered the law in 2011. In the original law, anyone could ask the courts to issue an arrest warrant against a visitor suspected of war crimes. The bar has now been set far higher. The director of public prosecutions has to give the nod for an arrest warrant to be issued.[67] By raising the threshold, Britain has signalled that war criminals are, in certain cases, welcome.

Conservative cheerleading

Cheerleading for Israel has become something akin to official British policy. Philip Hammond, foreign secretary at the time, gave an extraordinary speech to Conservative Friends of Israel at his party's 2015 conference. Hammond admitted that David Cameron, then prime minister, George Osborne, then chancellor of the exchequer, and himself had collectively decided that Britain must support Israel's attack on Gaza the previous year. 'We took a bit of flack for it and we are proud of that,' Hammond said.[68]

Under normal circumstances, the chancellor is too busy with financial matters to have any significant say in foreign policy. By coordinating with Osborne, Hammond was emphasising that the three most powerful men in the government were fully behind Israel. What material had Osborne studied as he helped shape Britain's response to the Gaza invasion? In response to a freedom of information request, the treasury stated that Osborne was provided with a 'situation report' by the Foreign Office on 21 July 2014. The document described 20 July as 'the bloodiest day of the conflict so far'. More than 100 Palestinians were killed on that day, 60 of them in a massacre that Israel carried out in the Shujaiya neighbourhood of Gaza City. 'Displaced Gazans [are] struggling to find somewhere safe in an atmosphere of panic, fear and increased confusion,' the note added. 'With only three hours power per day in some areas, any semblance of normal life has been paralysed.'[69]

The triumvirate determining Britain's response evidently had access to comprehensive information about the destruction being wrought on Gaza. Not only did they resolve to back that destruction, they were, according to Hammond, proud to do so. Few within the Tories dissented. Sayeeda Warsi was an exception; she resigned as a Foreign Office minister, complaining that the 'government's approach and language during the current crisis in Gaza is morally indefensible.'[70] Warsi's protest was commendable, though it is hard to see how she can have been in any way surprised by how more senior ministers were behaving. The Tories had pledged ahead of the 2010 election that they would be resolutely pro-Israel in government. In 2008, William Hague, then shadow foreign secretary, said: 'The unbroken thread of Conservative Party support for Israel that has run for nearly a century from the Balfour Declaration to the present day will continue.'[71] The Tories did not break their promise. Cameron kept distorting the truth about Israel's 2014 offensive after it had concluded. In an interview with *The Jewish Chronicle* before the 2015 British general election, Cameron peddled the myth that Israel was merely responding to Hamas' rockets. He said: 'As PM, putting yourself in the shoes of the Israeli people, who want peace but have to put up with these indiscriminate attacks – that reinforces to me the importance of standing by Israel and Israel's right to defend itself.'[72]

Confounding the opinion polls, the Tories won enough seats in 2015 to govern on their own. The new administration has arguably proven even more favourably disposed towards Israel than the previous one. Countering the Palestinian solidarity movement has been prioritised.

Shortly after being appointed business secretary, Sajid Javid addressed the annual dinner of UK–Israel Business, a bilateral chamber of commerce. He had a simple recommendation to beat the Palestinian call for boycott, divestment and sanctions (BDS) against Israel: trade. According to data that he cited, Britain and Israel's commercial relations were worth more than £4.5 billion per year and Britain was the second largest importer of Israeli goods. Declaring his commitment to trade liberalisation, Javid said he believed 'freedom is an absolute concept' and pledged to do anything he could to promote increased business between Britain and Israel. The Tory government has tended to publicise cooperation of an apparently benign nature. A medical innovation project linking Britain's National Health Service and Israel's pharmaceutical industry has been lauded by Javid and other cabinet ministers.[73] Yet there is a darker side to the relationship: the British government is nurturing Israeli companies with strong military connections.

Britain's embassy in Tel Aviv hosts an initiative called the UK–Israel Tech Hub. It was launched by George Osborne on an official visit to Israel in 2011. After declaring that Israel's 'high-tech economy is one of the economic marvels of the world', Osborne contended that the scheme was making a simple offer. 'Britain can help Israeli innovation go global,' he said. One of the hub's stated objectives is to make Britain a 'partner of choice' for Israeli inventors.[74]

In pursuit of that goal, the British embassy has hired a team of Israeli advisers. The embassy has tried to put a positive spin on the team's skills by putting words like 'clean' and 'creative' in their titles.[75] Closer scrutiny of the advisers' experience reveals they are immersed in Israel's military culture. Haim Shani, chairman of the team at the time of writing, was appointed a director of Israel Aerospace Industries (IAI) in 2012. Together with Elbit and Rafael, IAI is one of Israel's top three arms manufacturers. Before joining IAI, he was a chief executive of NICE Systems, a maker of surveillance equipment.[76] NICE, considered a spin-off of Israeli intelligence, provides products used in wiretapping and other forms of espionage to police departments and corporations across the world.[77] Naomi Krieger Carmy, director of the UK–Israel Tech Hub at the time of writing, is referred to as an '8200 alumnus' on a website set up by the British embassy in Tel Aviv.[78] Unit 8200, part of the intelligence corps in the Israeli military, is dedicated to techno-logical development. *The Economist* magazine argued in 2015 that by investing considerable resources in innovation, the military has made Israel into one of the world's top ten exporters of 'internet-security software'.[79] Eden Shochat, an Israeli venture capitalist, has observed that Unit 8200 graduates focus on 'big data, deep learning and machine vision'.[80] This means that the future of the Internet and of technology more generally are being partly shaped by an army that deprives an entire people of its basic rights.

That is the reality behind the 'economic marvel' that dazzled George Osborne. It is also a trend that the British government wishes to persist. In 2016, the hub organised for a delegation of businesspeople working in Britain to visit Israel's 'cyber-security' industry. Lockheed

Martin, the weapons firm, was among the companies represented on that delegation. Matt Hancock, the Cabinet Office minister who took part in the trip, said that he wished to study how the partnership between private firms and public authorities that was deemed pivotal towards the success of Israel's technology sector could be replicated in Britain.[81]

Smearing solidarity

Britain's determination to boost 'security' cooperation with Israel exemplifies how there is a yawning gap between elite and public opinion. Far from desiring stronger ties with Israel, ordinary people in Britain wish to boycott its goods and institutions. An end to the weapons trade was one of the core demands made when an estimated 150,000 marched through London in protest at the 2014 attack on Gaza.[82]

The Tories' disdain for Palestine solidarity activism is not shared by all elected representatives. A local authority in Leicester has voted to boycott goods from Israel's settlements in the West Bank. Birmingham City Council has threatened Veolia, a corporation which has built a tramway for settlers in East Jerusalem, with loss of contracts.[83] The central government has refused to tolerate politicians who listen to concerns of their voters on Palestine. In his aforementioned address to Conservative Friends of Israel, Philip Hammond said: 'Under a Conservative government, our foreign policy will be made in the Foreign Office and not in hundreds of Labour-controlled town halls.'[84]

Boycotting has assumed a central importance in the Palestinian quest for justice. The growing boycott is perceived as a major threat by Israel and its supporters. Benjamin Netanyahu's government has devoted considerable resources towards trying to combat the boycott. Yisrael Katz, Israel's intelligence minister at the time of writing, has even advocated a policy of 'civil elimination' against Palestine solidarity activists. 'Civil elimination' is a euphemism for assassination.[85]

Israel fears the boycott because it is a potent form of unarmed resistance. The call for boycott, divestment and sanctions is one of moral clarity. It is based on three demands: an end to Israel's occupation of Arab land, full equality for Palestinian citizens of Israel and guaranteeing Palestinian refugees their right of return.[86]

It is not surprising that Britain's ruling elite is hostile to a campaign making those demands. Realizing the demands would put an end to the apartheid system that Britain helped to introduce in Palestine and that it still props up. The Tory governments led by David Cameron and his successor Theresa May have signalled their willingness to, in effect, insulate Israel from public outrage over its crimes.

In February 2016, the British government issued a policy paper directed at local authorities. Its objective was to prevent councils from taking decisions that were at odds with central government policy when voting on procurement and the provision of services. Councils would also not be allowed bar pension schemes that they ran from investing in corporations accused of pollution or human rights violations. The paper was described as guidance but it was really a diktat. Central government was giving itself the power to block measures that it did not like; local democracy was being stifled. A statement accompanying the paper singled out boycotts targeting Israel as measures that would not be tolerated.[87]

The government has been secretive about the circumstances in which the paper was drawn up. Asked for a list of contacts it had with Israeli diplomats and Zionist lobby groups in the twelve months prior to the publication of its guidance, Britain's communities and local government ministry claimed that it had no meetings with outside organisations on issues relating to the boycott of Israel within that period.[88]

It is true that a 'public consultation exercise' was held before the guidance was officially finalised. The exercise was a travesty of democracy. Participants were asked to comment on eight questions. None of them explicitly mentioned Israel, even though the whole initiative has been presented by the government as a response to Palestine solidarity activism. According to the government's report on the consultation, more than 23,000 of the respondents disagreed with the idea that a cabinet minister could thwart decisions taken by a local authority. As a total of 23,500 individuals and groups took part in the exercise, that means that they were almost unanimous in their opposition to the recommendations. Their concerns were treated with contempt. In September 2016, the Tory government stated that its guidance would not be altered.[89]

Benjamin Netanyahu's ruling coalition allocated around $26 million from the state's 2016 annual budget to tackling what it calls 'delegitimization' of Israel, principally the BDS movement.[90] As he prepared to visit London that year, Gilad Erdan, the minister overseeing that fightback, said:

> Great Britain is the world centre of the anti-Israel BDS campaign. I'm going there to battle the boycott and delegitimization in every arena and to discuss with members of the British government – which is also committed to fighting boycotts – ways to strengthen our cooperation against the anti-Semitic boycott campaign.[91]

It was not the first time that Britain was depicted as home to many of Israel's enemies. The Reut Institute, an Israeli think-tank, alleged in 2010 that London 'stands out as a hub of delegitimization'. Among the factors cited to back up the allegation were the strong level of concern about Palestine among trade unions, the sense that Israel had become a focus for the radical left similar to how South Africa was in the 1980s and the antipathy towards Israel among Britain's Muslims.[92]

Nor was it the first time that an Israeli government minister has openly accused Palestine solidarity campaigners of anti-Semitism. Smearing critics in this way has long been the default position for Israeli political figures. Back in 1973, Abba Eban, then Israel's foreign minister, advocated that Israel should systematically cast aspersions against opponents of Zionism, the state's ideology. 'One of the chief tasks of any dialogue with the gentile world is to prove that the distinction between anti-Zionism and anti-Semitism is not a distinction at all,' Eban argued.[93]

More than likely, the Tories will be in power when the centenary of the Balfour Declaration occurs in 1917. That declaration implicitly conflated Judaism and Zionism. It did so despite how Jews were never united in their support of Zionism and many were implacably opposed to the colonisation of Palestine. Today's Tories are less subtle than Balfour was. They explicitly conflate Zionism and Judaism and insist that if you are hostile to Zionism you harbour a general hatred of Jews. That argument can be found in official government statements. The Cabinet Office alleged in 2016 that boycotts of Israel were 'fuelling anti-Semitism'.[94] Abba Eban's wish of removing distinctions had come true.

A century ago, Britain's support for Zionism was somewhat tentative. A century later, it is so enthusiastic that Britain is outlawing certain expressions of solidarity with Zionism's victims, the indigenous Palestinians.

The results of Britain's embrace of Zionism have already been unsavoury. If recent trends continue, matters could get worse. One thing has remained constant over the past 100 years. With some exceptions, foreign policy has been the exclusive preserve of an elite; the British government wants to keep things that way. Ultimately, it may not be able to. Though the government might try to suffocate the boycott of Israel, it is unlikely to succeed. Unless Britain resorts to extremely draconian measures, nobody will be forced to put Israeli goods in their shopping basket. Weapons dealers and corporations that try to profit from Israeli apartheid will still be exposed through research and protest.

The Palestine solidarity is a grass-roots one. Unable to destroy it, senior politicians have instead tried to disparage it. Boris Johnson, foreign secretary at the time of writing, has called supporters of the boycott 'a bunch of corduroy-jacketed lefty academics'.[95] Teachers unconcerned with the whims of fashion can certainly be found in the Palestine solidarity movement but its support among ordinary people is much wider. If Britain is truly the world centre of Israel's critics, then Britain's rulers are out of touch with public opinion.

Postscript
Israel's greatest friend?

In June 2016, David Cameron bragged that Britain was 'Israel's greatest friend'.[1] A few days after making that claim – to a fundraiser for the organisation Jewish Care – Cameron resigned, having been on the losing side in the referendum on Britain's EU membership.

Being the 'greatest friend' requires Britain to downplay Israel's misconduct. At least, that was the impression soon conveyed by Cameron's Oxford peer-turned-political rival, Boris Johnson. A controversy erupted in January 2017 when Al Jazeera broadcast a documentary that showed a London-based Israeli diplomat telling an undercover reporter he wished to 'take down' Alan Duncan, a Foreign Office minister who had been critical of Israel's settlement activities in the West Bank.[2] Although there were many calls for a strong government response, Johnson (now foreign secretary) accepted an apology from the Israeli embassy and said that 'I think we should consider the matter closed.'[3]

Cameron's 'greatest friend' boast was contained in a plea for Britain to remain in the European Union so that it could exert a pro-Israel influence. It is certainly true that Britain's representatives had been accommodating towards Israel at EU level. One such representative, Catherine Ashton, was appointed the EU's foreign policy chief in 2009. She brokered a deal that allowed Israeli weapons firms to benefit from the Union's multi-billion euro scientific research programme.[4] To reach that deal, Ashton decided to disregard the salient fact that Israel's science ministry – which oversees Israel's participation in the programme – is headquartered in East Jerusalem.[5] Doing business with the ministry is tantamount to accepting Israel's annexation of East Jerusalem – despite how the EU has consistently refused to recognise that annexation.

Once Britain formally leaves the EU, it will obviously no longer have a direct say in the Union's policies. Theresa May has signalled, however, that close relations with Israel will remain a priority. When Benjamin Netanyahu visited Downing Street in February 2017, May voiced a desire to clinch a bilateral free trade agreement with Israel.[6] Eric Pickles, a veteran MP and a key player in the lobby group Conservative Friends of Israel, availed of the occasion to argue:

> Israel was one of the first countries to grasp that, post-Brexit, the UK will be stepping out into the world, and it would be fitting were the UK to sign its first trade deal with the Middle East's only true democracy. The building blocks are there.[7]

May rushed to see Donald Trump as soon as he had moved into the White House. This book was finalised in the early stages of Trump's presidency; given his irascibility, it would be foolish to predict what will happen to Anglo-American or Anglo-Israeli relations in the next few years. It is telling, though, that May gave early indications that her approach to the Middle East chimed with that of Trump – or at least was closer to Trump's than that of the Obama administration. In late 2016, John Kerry, about to leave office as US secretary of state, complained that Netanyahu headed the 'most right-wing government in Israeli history'. May's spokesman responded by telling the media that 'we do not believe it is appropriate to attack the composition of the democratically elected government of an ally.'[8]

The rebuke of Kerry was peculiar. Kerry had been part of an administration which approved record levels of military aid to Israel and even directly contributed to the 2014 attack on Gaza by replenishing some types of artillery in Israel's arsenal.[9] No serious analyst could conclude that he had been hostile to Israel.

Timing was probably one factor behind why May, in effect, came to Netanyahu's defence. Kerry's comments had been made after the UN Security Council approved a resolution condemning Israel's settlement activities. The vote drew a predictably hostile response from Israel. Although Britain had supported the resolution, May appeared determined to avoid any serious rift with Israel. Her affinity towards Netanyahu was plain to see when she hosted him in London around six weeks later. The visit coincided with an Israeli bombing attack on Gaza and a vote by the Knesset to confiscate large tracts of Palestinian land in the West Bank.[10] Bar a mild statement of 'opposition' to settlement activity, May refrained from any public denunciation of Israel.[11]

May's silence is symptomatic of a bigger problem. Her government has backed policies that conflate robust criticism of Israel with anti-Semitism. In December 2016, May stated that she wished to formally approve a definition of anti-Semitism, making Britain one of the first countries to do so.[12] The definition was part of a guidance paper from an organisation called the International Holocaust Remembrance Alliance; that paper cited a number of examples of what could be considered anti-Semitic. One of them was 'denying Jewish people their right to self-determination' by 'claiming that the existence of a state of Israel is a racist endeavour.'[13] Conceivably, this could mean that a historian or activist could be accused of anti-Semitism for writing – based on hard evidence – that the Zionists who oversaw the mass expulsion of Palestinians in 1948 were motivated by a sense of ethnic supremacy.

May's announcement about wishing to define anti-Semitism followed a report by the home affairs committee in House of Commons, published a few months earlier. That report recommended that use of the term 'Zionist' in an 'abusive or accusatory context' should be considered a hate crime.[14]

The backdrop to the recommendation was a public squabble within the Labour Party. A handful of injudicious comments about Zionism and Israel by a small number of Labour members had been exaggerated by the media and portrayed as an anti-Semitic crisis. The 'crisis' had been used by enemies of Jeremy Corbyn, the party's leader and a long-standing defender of Palestinian rights, to try and weaken him.[15] Although the 'crisis' did not damage Corbyn's popularity, it may have had an impact on his policies. Corbyn endorsed the same definition of anti-Semitism favoured by Theresa May in December 2016.[16] His willingness to do so contradicted with a remark he made in the autumn of that year, in which he said 'I do not accept' a virtually identical version of that definition.[17]

Hatred of Jews has never been the same thing as questioning whether it is legitimate for Israel to be constituted as a Jewish state, which discriminates against and oppresses Palestinians. By blurring the distinction between anti-Semitism and anti-Zionism, Britain's political leaders are effectively saying that condemnation of Israel must not stray beyond certain bounds. Describing settlement activities as 'unhelpful' is acceptable; asking if Israel practises apartheid is, in their view, not. The definition of anti-Semitism that May wants Britain to adopt could have a chilling effect on free speech.

This book began by noting some of Boris Johnson's comments on the Balfour Declaration. When Benjamin Netanyahu called to the Foreign Office in early 2017, Johnson acted as a tour guide. 'This is the desk where the Balfour Declaration was composed and written,' Johnson informed his guest, pointing behind him.[18] Johnson was now celebrating a document he had called 'tragicomically incoherent' not so long ago.

Whatever they may say in less guarded moments, Britain's top government ministers officially delight in their nation's support for Zionism and Israel. They display pride in how Britain laid Israel's foundations, despite how that construction work was undertaken at the Palestinians' expense.

Notes

Introduction

1. Boris Johnson, *The Churchill Factor: How One Man Made History* (London: Hodder & Stoughton, 2015), p. 319.
2. Justin Cohen, 'Boris Johnson: "World Would be Impoverished Without Israel"', *JewishNews*, 12 November 2015. www.jewishnews. timesofisrael.com
3. Stuart Littlewood, 'Hague's Diplomatic Double Standards', *Al Arabiya* English website, 2 June 2013. www.english.alarabiya.net
4. 'Full Text of British PM David Cameron's Knesset Speech', *The Times of Israel*, 12 March 2014. www.timesofisrael.com
5. 'Prime Minister Theresa May CFI Annual Business Lunch Full Speech', Conservative Friends of Israel website, 13 December 2016. www.cfoi. co.uk

1. Laying the foundations

1. 'The Balfour Declaration', *The Times*, 9 November 1917.
2. Doreen Ingrams, *Palestine Papers, 1917–1922: Seeds of Conflict* (London: Eland, 2009), p. 16.
3. Jonathan Schneer, 'How Anti-Semitism Helped Create Israel', *Foreign Policy*, 8 September 2010.
4. David Vital, *Zionism: The Crucial Phase* (Oxford: Oxford University Press, 1987), p. 190.
5. 'Bloody Balfour', *The Spectator*, 29 March 1963.
6. Ghada Karmi, *Married to Another Man: Israel's Dilemma in Palestine* (London: Pluto, 2007), p. 106.
7. Brian Klug, 'The Other Arthur Balfour "Protector of the Jews"', *The Balfour Project* website, 8 July 2013. www.balfourproject.org
8. Shlomo Sand, *The Invention of the Land of Israel: From Holy Land to Homeland* (London: Verso, 2012), p. 159.
9. Nahum Sokolov, *History of Zionism 1600–1918* (London: Longmans, Green and Co., 1919), as quoted in Victor Kattan, *From Coexistence to Conquest: International Law and the Origins of the Arab–Israeli Conflict, 1891–1949* (London: Pluto, 2009), pp. 20–21.

10. *The Times*, 23 November 1917, as quoted in Jon Kimche, *The Unromantics: The Great Powers and the Balfour Declaration* (London: Weidenfeld & Nicolson, 1968), p. 44.

11. Foreign Office file, Britain's National Archives, FO 141/805/12.

12. Vital, *Zionism*, p. 289.

13. Kimche, *The Unromantics*, p. 31.

14. 'Chaim Weizmann of Israel is Dead', *New York Times*, 9 November 1952.

15. Daphna Baram, *Disenchantment: The Guardian and Israel* (London: Guardian Books, 2008), pp. 33–43.

16. Foreign Office file, FO 141/805.

17. James Renton, 'Flawed Foundations: The Balfour Declaration and the Palestine Mandate', in Rory Miller (ed.), *Britain, Palestine and Empire: The Mandate Years* (Farnham: Ashgate, 2010), pp. 17–21.

18. Ingrams, *Palestine Papers*, p. 5.

19. Colonial Office file, CO 733/347/7.

20. Geoffrey Lewis, *Balfour and Weizmann: The Zionist, the Zealot and the Emergence of Israel* (London: Continuum, 2009), p. 164.

21. David Hirst, *The Gun and the Olive Branch: The Roots of Violence in the Middle East* (New York: Thunder's Mouth Press/Nation Books, 3rd edn, 2003), p. 161.

22. Tom Segev, *One Palestine, Complete: Jews and Arabs Under the British Mandate* (London: Abacus, 2001), p. 110.

23. David Lloyd George, *War Memoirs of David Lloyd George 1918* (Boston, MA: Little, Brown and Company, 1937), p. 280.

24. Ingrams, *Palestine Papers*, p. 73.

25. Leonard Stein, *The Balfour Declaration* (New York: Simon & Schuster, 1961), pp. 145–389.

26. John Rose, *The Myths of Zionism* (London: Pluto, 2004), p. 127.

27. Vital, *Zionism*, p. 251.

28. Lewis, *Balfour and Weizmann*, p. 143.

29. Kimche, *The Unromantics*, p. 58.

30. Ronald Storrs, *Orientations* (London: Nicholson & Watson, 2nd edn, 1945), p. 345.

31. Isaiah Friedman, *Palestine, a Twice-Promised Land?: The British, the Arabs and Zionism, 1915–1920* (New Brunswick, NJ: Transaction, 2000), p. 182.

32. James Barr, *A Line in the Sand: Britain, France and the Struggle that Shaped the Middle East* (London: Simon & Schuster, 2012), p. 32.

33. Ingrams, *Palestine Papers*, p. 4.

34. Greg Philo and Mike Berry, *More Bad News from Israel* (London: Pluto, 2011), p. 15.

35. Kimche, *The Unromantics*, p. 31.

36. Lewis, *Balfour and Weizmann*, p. 132.

37. Stein, *The Balfour Declaration*, p. 373.

38. Edwin Montagu, 'Memorandum of Edwin Montagu on the Anti-Semitism of the Present Government', August 1917. www.jewishvirtual library.org

39. Montagu, 'Memorandum of Edwin Montagu on the Anti-Semitism of the Present Government'.

40. Kattan, *From Coexistence to Conquest*, p. 74.

41. Treasury file, T1/12312/16987.

42. Sarah Irving, 'A Bitter-Sweet Glimpse into What Jerusalem Might Have Been'. *The Electronic Intifada*, 25 February 2014. www. electronicintifada.net

2. Bringing in the Black and Tans

1. Sahar Huneidi, *A Broken Trust: Herbert Samuel, Zionism and the Palestinians* (London: I.B. Tauris, 2001), pp. 29–33.

2. Doreen Ingrams, *Palestine Papers, 1917–1922: Seeds of Conflict* (London: Eland, 2009), pp. 84–85.

3. Norman Rose, *'A Senseless, Squalid War': Voices from Palestine 1890s–1948* (London: Pimlico, 2010), p. 18.

4. J.M.N. Jeffries, *The Palestine Deception 1915–1923: The McMahon-Hussein Correspondence, the Balfour Declaration and the Jewish National Home* (Washington, DC: Institute for Palestine Studies, 2014), p. 67.

5. Bernard Wasserstein, *Herbert Samuel: A Political Life* (Oxford: Oxford University Press, 1992), pp. 239–241.

6. Foreign Office file FO 141/439/1.

7. Nathan Weinstock, *Zionism: False Messiah* (London: Pluto, 2nd English-language edn, 1989), pp. 113–114.

8. Huneidi, *A Broken Trust*, p. 193.

9. Norman and Helen Bentwich, *Mandate Memories 1918–1948* (London: The Hogarth Press, 1965), p. 53.

10. Ingrams, *Palestine Papers*, p. 89.

11. Ronald Storrs, *Orientations* (London: Nicholson & Watson, 2nd edn, 1945), pp. 356–385.

12. Wasserstein, *Herbert Samuel*, p. 259.

13. Colonial Office file, CO 935/1/1.

14. Ibid.

15. Ibid.

16. Ibid.

17. Ibid.

18. Michael Makovsky, *Churchill's Promised Land: Zionism and Statecraft* (New Haven, CT and London: Yale University Press, 2007), pp. 121–126.

19. Colonial Office, *Palestine: Disturbances in May 1921. Reports of the Commission of Inquiry with Correspondence Relating Thereto.*

20. Huneidi, *A Broken Trust*, p. 128.

21. Tom Segev, *One Palestine, Complete: Jews and Arabs Under the British Mandate* (London: Abacus, 2001), p. 183.

22. Treasury file, T 161/21.

23. D.M. Leeson, *The Black and Tans: British Police and Auxiliaries in the Irish War of Independence, 1920–1921* (Oxford: Oxford University Press, 2011), pp. 31–32.

24. Padraig Yeates, 'The Black and Tans', *History Ireland*, January–February 2012. www.historyireland.com

25. Leeson, *The Black and Tans*, pp. 25–173.

26. Bentwich and Bentwich, *Mandate Memories*, p. 87.

27. Home Office file, HO 45/24727.

28. War Office file, WO 106/5720.

29. Edward Horne, *A Job Well Done: A History of the Palestine Police Force 1920–1948*, book published by the Palestine Police Old Comrades Benevolent Association, 1982, pp. 55–76.

30. Douglas V. Duff, *Bailing With a Teaspoon* (London: John Long, 1953), pp. 36–176.

31. Treasury file, T 172/1551.

32. Duff, *Bailing With a Teaspoon*, pp. 44–46.

33. Ibid.

34. *British White Paper of June 1922.* www.avalon.law.yale.edu

35. Segev, *One Palestine, Complete*, p. 229.

36. Mazin B. Qumsiyeh, *Popular Resistance in Palestine: A History of Hope and Empowerment* (London: Pluto, 2011), p. 60.

37. Edward Keith-Roach, *Pasha of Jerusalem: Memoirs of a District Commissioner Under the British Mandate* (London: The Radcliffe Press, 1994), pp. 122–124.

38. Colonial Office file, CO 733/175/3.

39. Colonial Office file, CO 733/282/3.

40. Colonial Office file, CO 733/175/3.

41. Ibid.

42. Colonial Office file, CO 733/175/4.

43. Colonial Office file, CO 733/176/2.

44. Nur Masalha, *Expulsion of the Palestinians: The Concept of 'Transfer' in Zionist Political Thought 1882–1948* (Washington, DC: Institute for Palestine Studies, 1992), pp. 32–33.

45. *Report of the Commission on the Palestine Disturbances of August 1929.* babel.hathitrust.org

46. Colonial Office file, CO 733/180/1.

47. Treasury file, T 161/1029.

48. Ibid.

49. House of Commons debate, 22 January 1930. www.hansard.millbanksystems.com

50. Colonial Office file, CO 733/181/1.

51. Colonial Office file, CO 733/181/5.

52. Colonial Office file, CO 733/180/6.

53. John Hope Simpson, *Palestine: Report on Immigration, Land Settlement and Development*, October 1930. www.jewishvirtuallibrary.org

54. *Palestine: Statement of Policy by His Majesty's Government*, October 1930. www.unispal.un.org

55. Canadians for Justice and Peace in the Middle East, *Palestine 1930: The Passfield White Paper*, fact sheet, August 2011. www.cjpmo.org

56. House of Commons debate, 17 November 1930. www.hansard.millbanksystems.com

57. 'History of the Jewish Agency for Israel', Jewish Agency website, no date. www.jewishagency.org

58. 'Jews Face Greatest Crisis', *The Jewish Criterion*, October 1930.

59. Ramsay MacDonald letter to Chaim Weizmann, 13 February 1931. www.jewishvirtuallibrary.org

60. Biography of Chaim Weizmann, Jewish Agency website, no date. www.jewishagency.org

61. Colonial Office file, CO 733/203/9.

62. Ibid.

63. Ibid.

64. Ibid.

65. Ibid.

66. *Report by His Majesty's Government in the United Kingdom of Great Britain and Northern Ireland to the Council of the League of Nations on the Administration of Palestine and Transjordan for the Year 1931*, 31 December 1931. www.unispal.un.org

67. 'New Palestine High Commissioner Sir Arthur Wauchope …', Jewish Telegraphic Agency, 22 October 1931.

68. Treasury file, T 161/754.

69. Horne, *A Job Well Done*, p. 186.
70. *Report by His Majesty's Government in the United Kingdom of Great Britain and Northern Ireland to the Council of the League of Nations.*
71. Colonial Office file, CO 733/239/5.
72. Qumsiyeh, *Popular Resistance in Palestine*, pp. 72–73.
73. Colonial Office file, CO 733/258/3.
74. Ibid.
75. Colonial Office file, CO 733/239/5.
76. Colonial Office file, CO 733/346/8.
77. Colonial Office file, CO 733.239/7.
78. Colonial Office file, CO 733/229/3.
79. Colonial Office file CO 733/268/7.

3. 'We must shoot to kill'

1. Colonial Office file, CO 733/310/3.
2. War Office file, WO 282/6.
3. Colonial Office file, CO 733/312/1.
4. War Office file, WO 32/4177.
5. Colonial Office file, CO 733/413/4.
6. Ted Swedenburg, *Memories of Revolt: The 1936–1939 Rebellion and the Palestinian National Past* (Fayetteville, AR: University of Arkansas Press, updated edn, 2003), p. 78.
7. Foreign Office file, FO 371/23242.
8. Ghassan Kanafani, *The 1936–39 Revolt in Palestine*, English translation published by Committee for a Democratic Palestine, New York, 1972. www.newjerseysolidarity.org/resources/kanafani/kanafani4.html
9. Colonial Office file, CO 733/311/2.
10. Matthew Hughes, 'Lawlessness was the Law: British Armed Forces, the Legal System and the Repression of the Arab Revolt in Palestine, 1936–1939', in Rory Miller (ed.), *Britain, Palestine and Empire: The Mandate Years* (Farnham: Ashgate, 2010), p. 141.
11. Beverley Milton-Edwards and Stephen Farrell, *Hamas: The Islamic Resistance Movement* (Cambridge: Polity, 2010), pp. 18–28.
12. Colonial Office file, CO 733/311/5.
13. Colonial Office file, CO 733/297/2.
14. Colonial Office file, CO 967/92.
15. Karl Sabbagh, *Britain in Palestine: The Story of British Rule in Palestine, 1917–48* (London: Skyscraper Publications, 2012), pp. 76–77.
16. Colonial Office file, CO 733/297/2.
17. Colonial Office file, CO 733/297/3.

18. Colonial Office file, CO 733/297/2.
19. Colonial Office file, CO 733/311/7.
20. Colonial Office file, CO 733/310/4.
21. Ibid.
22. Ibid.
23. Colonial Office file, CO 733/317/7.
24. Colonial Office file, CO 733/310/5.
25. House of Commons debate, 26 May 1936. www.hansard.millbank systems.com
26. Foreign Office file, FO 371/23245.
27. Colonial Office file, CO 859/18/13.
28. Ibid.
29. Colonial Office file, CO 733/328/10.
30. War Office file, WO 32/4562.
31. Colonial Office file, CO 733/303/3.
32. Colonial Office file, CO 733/317/1.
33. Colonial Office file, CO 733/311/3.
34. Colonial Office file, CO 733/315/6.
35. War Office file, WO 32/4177.
36. Colonial Office file, CO 733/313/6.
37. Colonial Office file, CO 733/313/1.
38. War Office file, WO 282/6.
39. Colonial Office file, CO 733/313/6.
40. Colonial Office file, CO 733/311/4.
41. Colonial Office file, CO 733/314/2.
42. Ibid.
43. Air Ministry file, AIR 2/1884.
44. Colonial Office file, CO 323/1395/26.
45. League of Nations, *Mandates Palestine Report of the Palestine Royal Commission.* www.jewishvirtuallibrary.org
46. Rosemary Sayigh, *Palestinians: From Peasants to Revolutionaries* (London: Zed, 1979), p. 39.
47. Edward Keith-Roach, *Pasha of Jerusalem: Memoirs of a District Commissioner Under the British Mandate* (London: The Radcliffe Press, 1994), p. 190.
48. Colonial Office file, CO 323/1424/11.
49. Colonial Office file, CO 733/389/18.
50. Matthew Hughes, *From Law and Order to Pacification: Britain's Suppression of the Arab Revolt in Palestine, 1936–39, Journal of Palestine Studies,* Winter 2010. www.palestine-studies.org
51. War Office file, WO 282/6.

52. Foreign Office file, FO 684/10.
53. Colonial Office file, CO 733/371/3.
54. Admiralty file, ADM 116/3690.
55. Edward Horne, *A Job Well Done: A History of the Palestine Police Force 1920–1948*, book published by the Palestine Police Old Comrades Benevolent Association, 1982, p. 228.
56. Ibid.
57. Admiralty file, ADM 116/3690.
58. Keith-Roach, *Pasha of Jerusalem*, p. 191.
59. Kevin Connolly, 'Charles Tegart and the Forts that Tower over Israel', BBC News, 10 September 2012. www.bbc.com
60. Colonial Office file, CO 733/383/3.
61. Sabbagh, *Britain in Palestine*, p. 78.
62. Colonial Office file, CO 733/383/1.
63. Colonial Office file, CO 733/413/3.
64. War Office file, WO 32/4562.
65. Colonial Office file, CO 733/371/2.
66. Colonial Office file, CO 733/413/5.
67. A.J. Sherman, *Mandate Days: British Lives in Palestine 1918–1948* (London: Thames & Hudson, 1997), p. 108.
68. Foreign Office file, FO 371/61938.
69. James Barr, *A Line in the Sand: Britain, France and the Struggle that Shaped the Middle East* (London: Simon & Schuster, 2012), p. 185.
70. Colonial Office file, CO 733/313/2.
71. Colonial Office file, CO 733/350/10.
72. Colonial Office file, CO 733/317/1.
73. Ibid.
74. Simon Anglim, *Orde Wingate: Unconventional Warrior, From the 1920s to the Twenty-First Century* (Barnsley: Pen & Sword, 2014), pp. 68–91.
75. Yigal Allon, *The Making of Israel's Army* (London: Sphere Books, 1971), pp. 20–23.
76. Ibid.
77. Tom Segev, *One Palestine, Complete: Jews and Arabs Under the British Mandate* (London: Abacus, updated edn, 2001), p. 430.
78. Matthew Hughes, *A British 'Foreign Legion'? The British Police in Mandate Palestine*, *Middle Eastern Studies*, Vol. 49 (5), 2013.
79. Colonial Office file, CO 733/379/3.
80. Norman and Helen Bentwich, *Mandate Memories 1918–1948* (London: The Hogarth Press, 1965), p. 160.
81. Elizabeth Monroe, *Britain's Moment in the Middle East, 1914–1956* (Baltimore, MD: Johns Hopkins, 1963), p. 87.

82. Colonial Office file, CO 733/316/8.
83. Colonial Office file, CO 733/413/2.
84. War Office file, WO 216/111.
85. Ibid.
86. War Office file, WO 216/46.
87. Mazin B. Qumsiyeh, *Popular Resistance in Palestine: A History of Hope and Empowerment* (London: Pluto, 2011), p. 85.
88. Foreign Office file, FO 371/61938.
89. Ibid.
90. John Newsinger, *The Blood Never Dried: A People's History of the British Empire* (London: Bookmarks, 2nd edn, 2013), p. 140.

4. Sowing the seeds of ethnic cleansing

1. Colonial Office file, CO 733/369/4.
2. Colonial Office file, CO 733/381/7.
3. Ibid.
4. 'British White Paper of 1939', Avalon Project website, no date. www.avalon.law.yale.edu
5. Rafael Medoff, '"A Death Sentence for the Jews": 75 Years Since the British White Paper', *Jewish News Service*, 4 May 2014. www.jns.org
6. Avi Shlaim, *The Iron Wall: Israel and the Arab World* (London: Penguin, 2001), p. 23.
7. Prime Minister's Office file, PREM 4/25/3.
8. Nathan Weinstock, *Zionism: False Messiah* (London: Pluto, 2nd English-language edn, 1989), pp. 219–220.
9. Paul Kelemen, *The British Left and Zionism: History of a Divorce* (Manchester: Manchester University Press, 2012), p. 36.
10. Nur Masalha, *Expulsion of the Palestinians: The Concept of 'Transfer' in Zionist Political Thought 1882–1948* (Washington, DC: Institute for Palestine Studies, 1992), p. 154.
11. Philip Brutton, *A Captain's Mandate: Palestine 1946–1948* (London: Leo Cooper, 1996), p. 28.
12. Anglo-American Committee of Inquiry, *Report to the United States Government and His Majesty's Government in the United Kingdom*, 20 April 1946. www.avalon.law.yale.edu
13. Ibid.
14. John B. Judis, *Genesis: Truman, American Jews and the Origins of the Arab/Israeli Conflict* (New York: Farrar, Strauss and Giroux, 2014), p. 211.
15. Morrison-Grady Plan text, 1946. www.ecf.org.il

16. Colonial Office file, CO 537/2296.
17. Colonial Office file, CO 537/2327.
18. Ibid.
19. Karl Sabbagh, *Britain in Palestine: The Story of British Rule in Palestine, 1917–48* (London: Skyscraper Publications, 2012), pp. 94–96.
20. Foreign Office file, FO 371/68501.
21. Hugh Stockwell papers, Liddell Hart Centre for Military Archives, King's College London.
22. Colonial Office file, CO 537/3901.
23. Nur Masalha, *The Palestine Nakba: Decolonising History, Narrating the Subaltern, Reclaiming Memory* (London: Zed, 2012), pp. 80–81.
24. Foreign Office file, FO 816/117.
25. Ibid.
26. Ibid.
27. Brutton, *A Captain's Mandate*, p.108.
28. Ilan Pappe, *The Making of the Arab–Israeli Conflict 1947–1951* (London: I.B. Tauris, revised edn, 2015), p. 65.
29. Ilan Pappe, *The Ethnic Cleansing of Palestine* (Oxford: Oneworld, 2007), pp. 87–99.
30. Norman Rose, *'A Senseless, Squalid War': Voices from Palestine 1890s–1948* (London: Pimlico, 2010), p. 185.
31. Colonial Office file, CO 537/3860.
32. Ibid.
33. Benny Morris, *The Birth of the Palestinian Refugee Problem Revisited* (Cambridge: Cambridge University Press, revised edn, 2004), pp. 186–188.
34. Hugh Stockwell papers, Liddell Hart Centre for Military Archives, King's College London.
35. Walid Khalidi, 'Selected Documents on the 1948 Palestine War', *Journal of Palestine Studies*, Spring 1988, www.palestine-studies.org
36. Stockwell papers.
37. Ibid.
38. Colonial Office file, CO 537/3926.
39. Morris, *The Birth of the Palestinian Refugee Problem Revisited*, p. 195.
40. Khalidi, 'Selected Documents on the 1948 Palestine War'.
41. Colonial Office file. CO 537/3926.
42. Colonial Office file, CO 537/3860.
43. Morris, *The Birth of the Palestinian Refugee Problem Revisited*, p. 196.
44. Foreign Office file, FO 371/68505.
45. Foreign Office file, FO 371/68507.
46. Ibid.

47. Simha Flapan, *The Birth of Israel: Myths and Realities* (New York: Pantheon, 1987), p. 99.
48. Foreign Office file, FO 371/68507.
49. Colonial Office file, CO 537/3860.
50. Colonial Office file, CO 537/3901.
51. Ibid.
52. Roger Hardy, *The Poisoned Well: Empire and its Legacy in the Middle East* (Oxford: Oxford University Press, 2016), advance reading copy, p. 95.
53. Foreign Office file, FO 492/1.
54. Ibid.
55. Pappe, *The Making of the Arab–Israeli Conflict 1947–1951*, p. 119.
56. Mary C. Wilson, *King Abdullah, Britain and the Making of Jordan* (Cambridge: Cambridge University Press, 1987), p. 2.
57. Morris, *The Birth of the Palestinian Refugee Problem Revisited*, p. 56.
58. Foreign Office file, FO 371/68852.
59. Foreign Office file, FO 371/68853.
60. Foreign Office file, FO 816/120.
61. Ibid.
62. Wilson, *King Abdullah, Britain and the Making of Jordan*, pp. 172–173.
63. Foreign Office file, FO 816/127.
64. Hardy, *The Poisoned Well*, p. 98.
65. Pappe, *The Ethnic Cleansing of Palestine*, pp. 166–167.
66. Foreign Office file, FO 492/2.
67. Ibid.
68. Foreign Office file, FO 371/68861.
69. United Nations, *Progress Report of the United Nations Mediator on Palestine*, 16 September 1948. www.ccf.org.il
70. Foreign Office file, FO 371/68861.
71. Foreign Office file, FO 371/68512.
72. Foreign Office file, FO 371/68862.
73. Foreign Office file, FO 371/68861.
74. Ibid.
75. Tony Greenstein, 'Palestinians Provoked Final Solution?', *Weekly Worker*, 29 October 2015. www.weeklyworker.co.uk
76. Foreign Office file, FO 816/128.
77. Johanna Caldwell, 'Inter-Arab Rivalry and the All-Palestine Government of 1948', *Jerusalem Quarterly*, Spring 2015. www.palestine-studies.org
78. Pappe, *The Making of the Arab-Israeli Conflict 1947–1951*, p. 254.
79. Flapan, *The Birth of Israel*, p. 84.
80. 'Who We Are', UNRWA website, no date. www.unrwa.org

5. *Arming Israel (1953–1956)*

1. Ilan Pappe, *Britain and the Arab–Israeli Conflict, 1948–51* (Basingstoke: Palgrave Macmillan, 1988), p. 69.
2. *Tripartite Declaration Regarding the Armistice Borders: Statement by the Governments of the United States, United Kingdom and France*, 25 May 1950. www.avalon.yale.edu
3. Foreign Office file, FO 371/104226.
4. Ibid.
5. Foreign Office file, FO 371/104224.
6. Foreign Office file, FO 371/115554.
7. Ibid.
8. Foreign Office file, FO 371/115558.
9. Ministry of Defence file, DEFE 7/207.
10. Foreign Office file, FO 371/115564.
11. Foreign Office file, FO 371/11567.
12. Ilan Pappe, *A History of Modern Palestine* (Cambridge: Cambridge University Press, 2nd edn, 2006), p. 154.
13. Foreign Office file, FO 371/115556.
14. Foreign Office file, FO 371/115564.
15. Ibid.
16. Baruch Kimmerling, *Politicide: The Real Legacy of Ariel Sharon* (London: Verso, updated edn, 2006), pp. 52–53.
17. Avi Shlaim, *The Iron Wall: Israel and the Arab World* (London: Penguin, 2001), pp. 149–154.
18. Ministry of Defence file, DEFE 7/209.
19. Foreign Office file, FO 371/121332.
20. Foreign Office file, FO 371/121334.
21. Foreign Office file, FO 371/121335.
22. Foreign Office file, FO 371/121341.
23. Saul Kelly, 'Transatlantic Diplomat: Sir Roger Matkins, Ambassador to Washington and Joint Permanent Secretary to the Treasury', in Saul Kelly and Anthony Gorst (eds), *Whitehall and the Suez Crisis* (London: Frank Cass, 2000), p. 162.
24. Scott Lucas (ed.), *Britain and Suez: The Lion's Last Roar* (Manchester: Manchester University Press, 1996), pp. 38–39.
25. Derek Varble, *The Suez Crisis 1956* (Oxford: Osprey, 2003), pp. 12–14.
26. Ollie Stone-Lee, 'Eden: A Man under Strain', BBC News website, 21 July 2006. http://news.bbc.co.uk/1/hi/uk_politics/5193202.stm
27. Shlaim, *The Iron Wall*, pp. 163–165.
28. Foreign Office file, FO 371/121351.

29. Ibid.
30. Ibid.
31. Ibid.
32. Lewis Johnman, 'Playing the Role of a Cassandra: Sir Gerald Fitzmaurice, Senior Legal Adviser to the Foreign Office', in Kelly and Gorst (eds), *Whitehall and the Suez Crisis* (London: Frank Cass, 2000), pp. 46–56.
33. Foreign Office file, FO 371/121746.
34. Foreign Office file, FO 371/121356.
35. Simon Hall, *1956: The World in Revolt* (London: Faber & Faber, 2016), pp. 264–267.
36. Foreign Office file, FO 371/121746.
37. Moshe Dayan, *Story of My Life* (London: Sphere, 1977), pp. 231–233.
38. Memorandum of a conference with the President, White House, Washington, 29 October 1956. www.history.state.gov
39. Varble, *The Suez Crisis 1956*, pp. 10–91.
40. Foreign Office file, FO 371/121752.
41. Joe Sacco, *Footnotes in Gaza* (London: Jonathan Cape, 2009), pp. 390–401.
42. House of Commons debate, 20 December 1956. www.hansard.millbanksystems.com
43. Biographical note on Anthony Eden, British government website, no date. www.gov.uk

6. Arming Israel (1957–1979)

1. Foreign Office file, FO 371/121359.
2. Ann Lane, 'The Past as Matrix: Sir Ivone Kirkpatrick, Permanent Under-Secretary for foreign Affairs', in Saul Kelly and Anthony Gorst (eds), *Whitehall and the Suez Crisis* (London: Frank Cass, 2000), p. 213.
3. Foreign Office file, FO 371/121751.
4. Foreign Office file, FO 371/142363.
5. Documents published on BBC website, 3 August 2005. www.news.bbc.co.uk
6. Michael Crick, 'How Britain Helped Israel get the Bomb', BBC website, 3 August 2005. http://news.bbc.co.uk/1/hi/programmes/newsnight/4743493.stm
7. 'Ceremony Marks Israel's Acquisition of First Submarine from Britain', Jewish Telegraphic Agency, 10 October 1958.
8. Ministry of Defence file, DEFE 6/51.
9. Ibid.

10. Ibid.
11. Foreign Office file, FO 371/142363.
12. Ibid.
13. Naval Forces file, ADM 1/29040.
14. Ibid.
15. Foreign and Commonwealth Office file, FCO 17/909.
16. 'Two More British Submarines for Israel', *Daily Telegraph*, 25 November 1964.
17. Naval Forces file, ADM 1/29040.
18. Naval Forces file, ADM 1/29040.
19. Foreign and Commonwealth Office file, FCO 17/579.
20. Ibid.
21. Foreign and Commonwealth Office file, FCO 93/2515.
22. Foreign and Commonwealth Office file, FCO 17/579.
23. Moshe Gat, 'Britain and the Occupied Territories after the 1967 War', *Middle East Review of International Affairs*, December 2006. www.rubincenter.org
24. Harold Wilson, *The Chariot of Israel: Britain, America and the State of Israel*, (London: George Weidenfeld & Nicolson, 1981), p. 343.
25. Jeremy Bowen, *Six Days: How the 1967 War Shaped the Middle East* (London: Simon & Schuster, 2003), pp. 89–171.
26. Foreign and Commonwealth Office file, FCO 17/580.
27. Nida al-Azza (ed), *Survey of Palestinian Refugees and Internally Displaced Persons 2010–2012*, Badil Resource Centre for Palestinian Residency and Refugee Rights. www.badil.org
28. Cabinet Office file, CAB 128/42/36.
29. Nigel Ashton, 'Searching for a Just and Lasting Peace? Anglo-American Relations and the Road to United Nations Security Council Resolution 242', *LSE Research Online*, February 2015. www.lse.ac.uk
30. Foreign and Commonwealth Office file, FCO 17/911.
31. Ibid.
32. Foreign and Commonwealth Office file, FCO 17/579.
33. Foreign and Commonwealth Office file, FCO 17/580.
34. Foreign and Commonwealth Office file, FCO 17/923/1.
35. Foreign and Commonwealth Office file, FCO 17/580.
36. United Nations Security Council Resolution 242, 22 November 1967. www.unispal.un.org
37. Foreign and Commonwealth Office file, FCO 17/580.
38. Ibid.
39. Ibid.
40. Bowen, *Six Days*, pp. 187–191.

41. Foreign and Commonwealth Office file, FCO 17/912.
42. Ibid.
43. Foreign and Commonwealth Office file, FCO 17/914.
44. Foreign and Commonwealth Office file, FCO 17/920.
45. Foreign and Commonwealth Office file, FCO 17/916.
46. Foreign and Commonwealth Office file, FCO 17/918.
47. 'Mrs Golda Meir in London', ITN Source, 11 June 1969. www.itnsource.com
48. Foreign and Commonwealth Office file, FCO 17/918.
49. Foreign and Commonwealth Office file, FCO 17/921.
50. Foreign and Commonwealth Office file, FCO 17/922.
51. Foreign and Commonwealth Office file, FCO 17/909.
52. Foreign and Commonwealth Office file, FCO 17/922.
53. Foreign and Commonwealth Office file, FCO 17/1304.
54. Foreign and Commonwealth Office file, FCO 17/1305.
55. Foreign and Commonwealth Office file, FCO 17/1303.
56. David Bocquelet, *Tanks Encyclopedia*, 1 December 2014. www.tanks-encyclopedia.com
57. Foreign and Commonwealth Office file, FCO 93/567.
58. Foreign and Commonwealth Office file, FCO 93/1606.
59. Human Rights Watch, *Flooding South Lebanon: Israel's Use of Cluster Munitions in Lebanon in July and August 2006*, February 2008. www.hrw.org
60. Prime Minister's Office file, PREM 15/497.
61. Foreign and Commonwealth Office file, FCO 17/1569.
62. Foreign and Commonwealth Office file, FCO 17/1308.
63. Prime Minister's Office file, PREM 15/497.
64. Foreign and Commonwealth Office file, FCO 17/1569.
65. Foreign and Commonwealth Office file, FCO 17/1571.
66. 'Gal Submarine', *Global Security* website, no date. www.globalsecurity.org
67. 'Arab Anger Over Subs', *Financial Times*, 8 March 1972.
68. Foreign and Commonwealth Office file, FCO 17/1753.
69. Foreign and Commonwealth Office file, FCO 55/1179.
70. 'About Us', Israel Atomic Energy Agency Commission website, no date. www.iaec.gov.il
71. William Greider, 'It's Official: The Pentagon Finally Admitted that Israel has Nuclear Weapons, Too', *The Nation*, 20 March 2015. www.thenation.com/article/its-official-pentagon-finally-admitted-israel-has-nuclear-weapons-too/

72. Azriel Bermant, 'How the Balfour Declaration Continues to Haunt Britain', *Haaretz*, 29 July 2016. www.haaretz.com/opinion/.premium-1.734178

73. House of Commons debate, 16 October 1973. www.hansard.millbanksystems.com

74. Simon C. Smith, 'Centurions and Chieftains: Tank Sales and British Policy Towards Israel in the Aftermath of the Six-Day War', *Contemporary British History*, 20 June 2014. www.tandfonline.com/doi/abs/10.1080/13619462.2014.930348

75. Foreign and Commonwealth Office file, FCO 93/2514.

76. Christopher Mayhew and Michael Adams, *Publish it Not: The Middle East Cover-Up* (Oxford: Signal, new edn, 2006), p. 42.

77. Robert Philpot, 'Wilson, True Friend of Israel', *The Jewish Chronicle Online*, 7 October 2014. www.thejc.com/comment/comment/wilson-true-friend-of-israel-1.58771

78. House of Commons debate, 18 October 1973. www.handsard.millbanksystems.com

79. Foreign and Commonwealth Office file, FCO 93/567.

80. Foreign and Commonwealth Office file, FCO 93/796.

81. Foreign and Commonwealth Office file, FCO 93/1606.

82. Foreign and Commonwealth Office file, FCO 66/1018.

83. Foreign and Commonwealth Office file, FCO 93/2105.

7. Sidelining the PLO

1. Foreign and Commonwealth Office file, FCO 93/182.

2. Shafiq al-Hout, *My Life in the PLO: The Inside Story of the Palestinian Struggle* (London: Pluto, 2011), p. 107.

3. Foreign and Commonwealth Office file, FCO 93/487.

4. Foreign and Commonwealth Office file, FCO 93/485.

5. The Palestinian National Charter: Resolutions of the Palestine National Council, 1–17 July 1968. www.avalon.law.yale.edu

6. Speech by Yasser Arafat to United Nations General Assembly, New York, 13 November 1974. www.badil.org

7. Foreign and Commonwealth Office file, FCO 93/488.

8. Foreign and Commonwealth Office file, FCO 93/745.

9. Foreign and Commonwealth Office file, FCO 93/488.

10. Al-Hout, *My Life in the PLO*, pp. 119–127.

11. Commonwealth Office file, FCO 93/746.

12. Ibid.

13. Ibid.

14. 'Kissinger: Aid to Israel is "Keystone" of US Policy in the Middle East', *Jewish Telegraphic Agency*, 7 November 1975. www.jta. org/1975/11/07/archive/kissinger-aid-to-israel-is-keystone-of-u-s-policy-in-the-middle-east

15. House of Lords debate, 26 November 1975. www.hansard.millbank systems.com

16. Foreign and Commonwealth Office file, FCO 93/747.

17. Agreement between the European Economic Community and Israel, 11 May 1975. www.mfa.gov.il

18. European Economic Community, Venice declaration, 13 June 1980. www.eeas.europa.eu

19. Treasury file, T 384/340.

20. Rosemary Hollis, *The Union and the Arab–Israeli Conflict: From Venice to Madrid*, seminar paper published by Palestinian Academic Society for the Study of International Affairs, 1995. www.passia.org

21. Letter from Peter Carrington to Yitzhak Shamir, 27 June 1980. www. margaretthatcher.org

22. Foreign and Commonwealth Office file, FCO 93/2572.

23. Foreign and Commonwealth Office file, FCO 93/2573.

24. Ibid.

25. Ibid.

26. Ibid.

27. Ibid.

28. Foreign and Commonwealth Office file, FCO 93/2476.

29. Foreign and Commonwealth Office file, FCO 93/2801.

30. Note from Michael Alexander to Margaret Thatcher, 1 May 1981. www. margaretthatcher.org

31. Foreign and Commonwealth Office file, FCO 93/2805.

32. 'Israel Bombs Baghdad Nuclear Reactor', BBC, 7 June 1981. www. news.bbc.co.uk

33. Foreign and Commonwealth Office file, FCO 8/4177.

34. Foreign and Commonwealth Office file, FCO 8/4178.

35. Foreign and Commonwealth Office file, FCO 93/2829.

36. United Nations Security Council Resolution 487, 19 June 1981. www. un.org

37. 'Origins', Multinational Force and Observers website, no date. www. mfo.org

38. 'Assembling the Force', Multinational Force and Observers website, no date. www.mfo.org

39. Foreign and Commonwealth Office file, FCO 93/2826.

40. Ibid.

41. Foreign and Commonwealth Office file, FCO 93/3192.

42. Foreign and Commonwealth Office file, FCO 151/8.

43. David K. Shipler, 'Israelis Dismiss Another Mayor in the West Bank', *New York Times*, 1 May 1982.

44. Foreign and Commonwealth Office file, FCO 93/3183.

45. Henry Kamm, 'Israel and Britain at Odds on Two Mayors', *New York Times*, 2 April 1982.

46. Foreign and Commonwealth Office file, FCO 93/3184.

47. Naomi Klein, *The Shock Doctrine: The Rise of Disaster Capitalism* (London: Penguin, 2007), pp. 137–138.

48. Foreign and Commonwealth Office file, FCO 93/3158.

49. David Blair, 'Israel Sold Weapons to Argentina at Height of Falklands War, Reveal Declassified Foreign Office Files', *The Telegraph*, 24 August 2016.

50. Foreign and Commonwealth Office file, FCO 93/3535.

51. Foreign and Commonwealth Office file, FCO 93/3177.

52. Message from Margaret Thatcher to Ronald Reagan, 15 June 1982. www.margaretthatcher.org

53. 'The Lebanon War: Operation Peace for Galilee (1982)', Israel's Ministry for Foreign Affairs website, no date. www.mfa.gov.il

54. 'Shlomo Argov, 73, Ex-Israeli Envoy, Dies', *New York Times*, 25 February 2003.

55. Foreign and Commonwealth Office file, FCO 93/1249.

56. Message from Margaret Thatcher to Ronald Reagan, 29 July 1982. www.margaretthatcher.org

57. Ronald Reagan, 'The Reagan Plan: US Policy for Peace in the Middle East', speech delivered on 1 September 1982. www.cfr.org

58. Ibid.

59. Prime Minister's office file, PREM 19/1088.

60. Jeff Halper, *War Against the People: Israel, the Palestinians and Global Pacification* (London: Pluto, 2015), pp. 41–42.

61. Foreign and Commonwealth Office file, FCO 93/2836.

62. Ibid.

63. Zeina Azzam, 'Why have the Killers of Sabra and Shatila Escaped Justice?', *The Electronic Intifada*, 15 September 2015. www.electronicintifada.net

64. Omar Karmi, 'West Turned Blind Eye to Israel's Involvement in Sabra and Shatila "Slaughter"', *The National*, 5 August 2013. www.thenational.ae

65. Foreign and Commonwealth Office file, FCO 93/3178.

66. Google search of Charles Moore, *Margaret Thatcher: The Authorised Biography, Volume II: Everything She Wants* (London: Penguin, 2015).

67. Prime Minister's Office file, PREM 19/1105.
68. Foreign and Commonwealth Office file, FCO 93/3515.
69. Foreign and Commonwealth Office file, FCO 93/2482.
70. Prime Minister's Office file, PREM 19/1105.
71. Foreign and Commonwealth Office file, FCO 93/3160.
72. Foreign and Commonwealth Office file, FCO 93/3536.
73. Ibid.
74. Ibid.
75. Prime Minister's office file, PREM 19/1106.
76. Foreign and Commonwealth Office file, FCO 93/3500.
77. Foreign and Commonwealth Office file, FCO 93/3536.
78. Foreign and Commonwealth Office file, FCO 93/3523.
79. Christopher Walker, 'Luce Visit Marred by Israeli Ban on Seeing Palestinians', *The Times*, 4 November 1983.
80. Foreign and Commonwealth Office file, FCO 93/3648.
81. Ibid.
82. Foreign and Commonwealth Office file, FCO 93/3500.
83. Foreign and Commonwealth Office file, FCO 93/4573.
84. Tom Wilkie, 'Israel Grabs British Uranium', *New Scientist*, 18 July 1985.
85. Foreign and Commonwealth Office file, FCO 151/3.
86. Prime Minister's Office file, PREM 19/1613.
87. Jo Thomas, 'Britain Calls Off a Meeting with Jordan–Palestine Unit', *New York Times*, 15 October 1985.
88. Prime Minister's Office file, PREM 19/1917.
89. Transcript of Margaret Thatcher's press conference, King David Hotel, Jerusalem, 27 May 1986. www.margaretthatcher.org
90. Prime Minister's Office file, PREM 19/1917.
91. Amanda Borschel-Dan, 'Missed Opportunity? The 1987 Peres–Hussein Deal that Wasn't', *Times of Israel*, 30 September 2016. www.timesofisrael.com
92. Letter from Riyad Mansour, Palestine Liberation Organization, to Javier Pérez de Cuéllar, secretary general of United Nations, 16 November 1988. www.unispal.un.org
93. House of Commons debate, 17 January 1989. www.hansard.millbanksystems.com
94. 'Global Reporter Round-Up: Thatcher Reaction', BBC website, 9 April 2013. www.bbc.com

8. The loyal lieutenant

1. Edward Said, 'The Morning After', *London Review of Books*, 21 October 1993. www.lrb.co.uk

2. House of Commons debate, 19 November 1993. www.hansard.millbanksystems.com

3. John Major's speech to Joint Israel Appeal and Jewish Continuity dinner, 21 November 1994. www.johnmajor.co.uk

4. 'Britain Lifts Arms Embargo Against Israel', *The Independent*, 27 May 1994.

5. Clyde Haberman, 'Israel Finishes Withdrawing Troops from the Gaza Strip', *New York Times*, 19 May 1994.

6. John Major's speech to Conservative Friends of Israel, 20 June 1995. www.johnmajor.co.uk

7. Profile of Bezeq, Who Profits? website, 21 March 2012. www.whoprofits.org

8. 'UN Condemns Israel's Settlement Plan', CNN website, 13 March 1997. www.edition.cnn.com

9. Toby Greene, *Blair, Labour and Palestine: Conflicting Views on Middle East Peace After 9/11* (New York: Bloomsbury Academic, 2014), p. 49.

10. Peter Oborne and James Jones, 'The Pro-Israel Lobby in Britain', *openDemocracy*, 13 November 2009. www.opendemocracy.net

11. Jenni Frazer, 'Lord Levy: Honours Even', *The Jewish Chronicle Online*, 16 May 2008. www.thejc.com

12. Paul Vallely, 'Michael Levy: Lord Cashpoint', *The Independent*, 18 March 2006.

13. Council of the European Union notes on 'proposed EU–Palestinian security cooperation', 6 April 1998. Documents obtained under EU freedom of information rules.

14. Wye River Memorandum, 23 October 1998. www.mfa.gov.il

15. Fawn Vrazo, 'A Push to Save Mideast Process: More Meetings Scheduled with Albright', *The Philadelphia Inquirer*, 5 May 1998.

16. House of Commons debate, 19 May 1999. www.hansard.millbanksystems.com

17. Jonathan Freedland, 'Blair's Latest Victory', *The Guardian*, 19 May 1999.

18. Profile of Ehud Barak, Israeli foreign ministry website, no date. www.mfa.gov.il

19. Avi Shlaim, *The Iron Wall: Israel and the Arab World* (London: Penguin, 2001), p. 608.

20. 'Britain has Role in Middle East Peace Process', *LFI News*, Autumn 1999.

21. Jonathan Cook, 'Ungenerous Occupier: Israel's Camp David Exposed', *The Electronic Intifada*, 1 January 2008. www.electronicintifada.net

22. 'Intifada Toll 2000–2005', BBC website, 8 February 2005. www.news.
bbc.co.uk

23. Jeff Halper, *War Against the People: Israel, the Palestinians and Global Pacification* (London: Pluto, 2015), p. 173.

24. 'Israel Seizes Palestinian Areas in Gaza Strip', *The Guardian*, 17 April 2001.

25. Ewan MacAskill, 'Israel Orders Army to Kill Suspects', *The Guardian*, 5 July 2001.

26. Suzanne Goldberg, 'Israeli Tanks Invade Two West Bank Towns', *The Guardian*, 13 September 2001.

27. Anita Fast, 'Hebron: Abu Sneineh Invaded by Israeli Forces', Christian Peacemaker Teams website, 5 October 2001. www.cpt.org

28. John Pilger, 'Blair's Meeting with Arafat Served to Disguise his Support for Sharon and the Zionist Project', 14 January 2002. www.johnpilger.com

29. House of Commons debate, 18 March 2002. www.hansard.millbanksystems.com

30. 'Ahmad Saadat must be Released and his Safety Ensured', Amnesty International website, 13 June 2002. www.amnesty.org

31. British government note on Jericho monitoring mission, 20 March 2006. www.gov.uk

32. Note from Tony Blair to George W. Bush, 28 July 2002. Document published as part of *The Report of the Iraq Inquiry*, 6 July 2016. www.iraqinquiry.org.uk

33. Tom Bower, *Broken Vows: Tony Blair, The Tragedy of Power* (London: Faber & Faber, 2016), p. 243.

34. 'Labour Friends of Israel', Powerbase website, 1 June 2015. www.powerbase.info

35. 'Did your MP Support the Government?', BBC website, 19 March 2003. www.news.bbc.co.uk

36. Human Rights Watch, *Off Target: The Conduct of the War and Civilian Casualties in Iraq*, December 2003. www.hrw.org

37. Colin King, Ove Dullum and Grethe Østern, *M85: An Analysis of Reliability*, report by Norwegian People's Aid, 2007. www.npaid.org

38. 'Munition Systems – Overview'. Israel Military Industries website, no date, www.imi-israel.com

39. Human Rights Watch, *Survey of Cluster Munition Policy and Practice*, February 2007. www.hrw.org

40. John Sloboda and Hamit Dardagan, 'How Many Civilians were Killed by Cluster Bombs?', Iraq Body Count website, 6 May 2003. www.iraqbodycount.org

41. Statement by John Chilcot, 6 July 2016. www.iraqinquiry.org.uk

42. Tony Blair, *A Journey* (London: Hutchinson, 2010), p. 403.

43. Suzanne Goldberg, 'Powell Insists Peace Envoy has not Abandoned the Middle East', *The Guardian*, 17 December 2001.

44. Middle East Quartet, *A Performance-Based Roadmap to a Permanent Two-State Solution to the Israeli–Palestinian Conflict*, document published 30 April 2003. www.un.org

45. Gregg Carlstom, 'MI6 Offered to Detain Hamas Figures', Al Jazeera website, 25 January 2011. www.aljazeera.com

46. 'Palestinian Security Plan', 2004 (precise date not given); document published on Al Jazeera website. www.aljazeera.com

47. Martin Melaugh, 'Internment – Summary of Main Events', Conflict Archive on the Internet, Ulster University website, no date. www.cain.ulst.ac.uk

48. Jonathan McIvor's profile on LinkedIn. www.linkedin.com

49. *The Stephen Lawrence Inquiry: Report of an Inquiry by Sir William Macpherson of Cluny*, February 1999. www.gov.uk

50. Exchange of email messages with Hilary Benn, September 2016.

51. Council of the European Union, 'Information Strategy for European Union Police Mission for the Palestinian Territories', November 2005. Document obtained under EU freedom of information rules.

52. Council of the European Union, note on 'European Union Police Mission for the Palestinian Territories', 26 October 2005. Document obtained under EU freedom of information rules.

53. Council of the European Union, note on 'European Union Police Mission for the Palestinian Territories', 2 December 2015. Document obtained under EU freedom of information rules.

54. EU Coordinating Office for Palestinian Police Support, 'Progress Report', April 2005. Document published on Al Jazeera website. www.aljazeera.net

55. Committee on the Administration of Justice, *Plastic Bullets: A Briefing Paper*, June 1998. www.caj.org.uk

56. David Cronin, 'Exporting Repression from Ulster to Palestine', *The Electronic Intifada*, 19 November 2014. www.electronicintifada.net

57. Matthew Price, 'Doubts over Palestinian Aid Schemes', BBC website, 21 February 2006. www.news.bbc.co.uk

58. 'Javier Solana, EU High Representative for the CFSP, Congratulates Paul Robert Kernaghan on Taking Office as Head of Mission of EUPOL COPPS', Council of the European Union website, 30 December 2008. www.consilium.europa.eu

59. Evidence by Paul Kernaghan to Iraq Inquiry, 23 July 2010. www. iraqinquiry.org.uk
60. Briefing by Colin Smith, Brussels, 23 June 2008. Video of briefing can be seen on www.youtube.com
61. 'Javier Solana, EU High Representative for CFSP, Welcomes Appointment of Head of EU Police Mission for the Palestinian Territories', Council of the European Union website, 3 January 2007. www.consilium.europa.eu
62. Dalia Hatuqa, 'Palestinians Police Israeli-Controlled Area', Al Jazeera website, 19 November 2013. www.aljazeera.net
63. House of Commons debate, 18 June 2009. www.parliament.uk
64. United States Government Accountability Office, *The Palestinian Authority: US Assistance is Training and Equipping the Security Forces but the Programme Needs to Measure Progress and Faces Logistical Constraints*, May 2010. www.gao.gov
65. Keith Dayton's speech to Washington Institute for Near East Policy, 7 May 2009. www.winep.org
66. Nathan Thrall, 'Our Man in Palestine', *New York Review of Books*, 14 October 2010. www.nybooks.com
67. Rachel Shabi, 'West Bank Despair over Gaza Assault', Al Jazeera website, 7 January 2009. www.aljazeera.net
68. Keith Dayton's speech to Washington Institute for Near East Policy, 7 May 2009.
69. 'Palestinian Authority: No Justice for Torture Death in Custody', Human Rights Watch website, 16 February 2011. www.hrw.org
70. Minutes of meeting between Saeb Erekat and David Hale, Jericho, 17 September 2009. Document published by Al Jazeera. www.aljazeera.net
71. Ali Abunimah, 'Mahmoud Abbas: Cooperation with Israeli Army, Secret Police is "Sacred"', *The Electronic Intifada*, 30 May 2014. www. electronicintifada.net
72. Nicola Abé, 'Palestinian President Abbas: "The World must not Forget Us"', *Spiegel Online*, 18 April 2016. www.spiegel.de
73. Charlotte Silver, 'Why is Mahmoud Abbas Boasting of Jailing Palestine's Youth?', *The Electronic Intifada*, 1 September 2016. www. electronicintifada.net
74. Ari Shavit, 'Top PM Aide: Gaza Plan Aims to Freeze the Peace Process', *Haaretz*, 6 October 2004.
75. Blair, *A Journey*, p. 515.
76. Patrick Hennessy, 'Straw Leads Revolt against Blair over Israel Crisis', *The Telegraph*, 30 July 2006.
77. Blair, *A Journey*, pp. 594–599.

78. Jonathan Cook, *Israel and the Clash of Civilisations: Iraq, Iran and the Plan to Remake the Middle East* (London: Pluto, 2008), pp. 53–54.

79. 'Israel Warns Hizbullah War would Invite Destruction', *Ynetnews*, 3 October 2008. www.ynetnews.com

80. Richard Norton-Taylor, 'British Arms Exports to Israel Double in a Year', *The Guardian*, 25 July 2006.

81. Benjamin Joffe-Walt, 'Made in the UK, Bringing Devastation to Lebanon – the British Parts in Israel's Deadly Attack Helicopters', *The Guardian*, 29 July 2006.

82. Matt Weaver, 'Beckett "Unhappy" with US Military Use of Scottish Airport', *The Guardian*, 27 July 2006.

83. 'Full text: Quartet statement', BBC website, 27 June 2007. www.news.bbc.com

84. Salam Fayyad, 'What Palestinians need to do to fulfill their quest for statehood', The Elders website, 3 March 2015. www.theelders.org

85. Jon Boyle, 'Palestinian Statehood Deal Possible in 2008: Blair', Reuters, 6 December 2007.

86. *Towards a Palestinian State*, document published by Tony Blair's office in Jerusalem, 13 May 2008. www.quartetrep.org

87. Ibid.

88. 'Blair on Gaza', CNN, 6 January 2009.

89. 'Blair: Politics Hinders Aid', CNN, 2 March 2009.

90. Raphael Aren, 'Netanyahu: Economics, Not Politics, is Key to Peace', *Haaretz*, 20 November 2008.

91. Tim McGirk, 'Tony Blair on Restarting the Middle East Peace Process', *Time*, 8 April 2009.

92. 'Video: Tony Blair Talks to Sir David Frost on Prospects for Middle East Peace on Al Jazeera English', Office of Tony Blair website, 19 June 2009. www.tonyblairoffice.org

93. Jay Solomon, 'Blair Wows AIPAC among UK–Israel Tensions', *Wall Street Journal*, 23 May 2010.

94. 'Tony Blair Addresses AIPAC Conference 2010', Office of Tony Blair website, 23 March 2010. www.tonyblairoffice.org

95. 'Number of Palestinian Children (12–17) in Israeli Military Detention', Defence for Children International – Palestine website. Data updated monthly. www.dci-palestine.org

96. 'Tony Blair Addresses AIPAC Conference 2010', Office of Tony Blair website, 23 March 2010. www.tonyblairoffice.org

97. David Cronin, 'Tony Blair Enables Israeli Raids in the West Bank', *The Electronic Intifada*, 5 November 2014. www.electronicintifada.net

98. Biographical note for Robert Danin, Council on Foreign Relations website, no date. www.cfr.org

99. 'Israel's Move to Allow More Goods into Gaza "Welcome"', Office of Tony Blair website, 19 April 2010, www.tonyblairoffice.org

100. 'Statement by Quartet Representative Tony Blair on the Gaza Flotilla', Office of Tony Blair website, 31 May 2010. www.tonyblairoffice.org

101. Anita Kirpalani, 'Gaza Crisis: Tony Blair on the Commando Raid', *Newsweek*, 4 June 2010.

102. 'Tony Blair Tells EU Foreign Ministers that Israel is Ready to Ease Gaza Blockade', Office of Tony Blair website, 14 June 2010. www.tonyblairoffice.org

103. 'Tony Blair Welcomes New Policy on Gaza', Office of Tony Blair website, 20 June 2010. www.tonyblairoffice.org

104. Israel's Ministry of Defence Coordinator of Government Activities in the Territories, *The Civilian Policy Towards the Gaza Strip: The Implementation of the Cabinet Decision*, June 2010. www.mfa.gov.il

105. Jonathan Cook, 'Tony Blair's Tangled Web: The Quartet Representative and the Peace Process', *Journal of Palestine Studies*, Winter 2013. www.palestine-studies.org

106. 'Package of Measures Agreed Between the Government of Israel and the Quartet Representative', Office of the Quartet website, 4 February 2011. www.quartetoffice.org

107. Victor Kattan, *The Gas Fields off Gaza: A Gift or a Curse?*, report by Al-Shabaka, 24 April 2012. www.al-shabaka.org

108. 'Tony Blair Welcomes Wataniya Mobile Phone Launch to Boost Palestinian Economy', Office of Tony Blair website, 1 November 2009. www.tonyblairoffice.org

109. Francis Beckett, David Hencke and Nick Kochan, *Blair Inc.: The Man Behind the Mask* (London: John Blake, 2015), pp. 22–23.

110. Chris McGreal, 'Tony Blair: Mubarak is "Immensely Courageous and a Force for Good"', *The Guardian*, 2 February 2011.

111. 'Quartet Principals Meet with Tony Blair in Washington DC to Promote Direct Negotiations', Office of Tony Blair website, 11 June 2011. www.tonyblairoffice.org

112. 'Tony Blair Addresses the American Task Force for Palestine in Washington DC', Office of Tony Blair website, 15 December 2010. www.tonyblairoffice.org

113. 'Tony Blair: We've got to Keep Pushing for Peace', Office of Tony Blair website, 4 December 2012. www.tonyblairoffice.org

114. 'Quartet Representative Welcomes Israeli Release of Funds to Palestinians, Urges Regular and Predictable Payments in Future',

Office of Tony Blair website, 30 November 2011. www.tonyblairoffice. org

115. Yael Stein, *Human Rights Violations during Operation Pillar of Defence, 14–21 November 2012*, report by B'Tselem, May 2013. www.btselem. org

116. 'Gaza Ceasefire Dynamics Explained: What Ceasefire will Work?', The Jerusalem Fund website, no date. www.thejerusalemfund.org

117. 'Tony Blair: Gaza Situation "Utterly Tragic"', BBC website, 19 November 2012. www.bbc.com

118. Adam Horowitz and Phil Weiss, 'Claim that Hamas Killed Three Teens is Turning Out to be the WMD of Gaza Onslaught', *Mondoweiss*, 26 July 2014. www.mondoweiss.net

119. 'Quartet Representative June 2014 Visit', Office of Tony Blair website, 19 June 2014. www.tonyblairoffice.org

120. 'Quartet Representative Statement on Current Situation', Office of Tony Blair website, 24 June 2014. www.tonyblairoffice.org

121. 'Blair Condemns Murder of Palestinian Teen', Office of Tony Blair website, 2 July 2014. www.tonyblairoffice.org

122. 'Blair: Israel Won't be Able to Destroy Hamas', *Ynet*, 10 July 2014. www.ynetnews.com

123. Jodi Rudoren and Anne Barnard, 'First Israeli Killed near Gaza Border', *New York Times*, 15 July 2014.

124. Mona Patel, Olivia Watson and Brad Parker, *Operation Protective Edge: A War Waged on Gaza's Children*, report by Defence for Children International – Palestine, April 2015. www.dci-palestine.org

125. Office of the Quartet Representative, *Report for the Meeting of the Ad-Hoc Liaison Committee on Action in Support of Palestinian State-Building*, 22 September 2014. www.quartetoffice.org

126. David Cronin, 'Tony Blair and the Corporate Capture of Palestine', *Middle East Eye*, 14 January 2015. www.middleasteye.net

127. Office of the Quartet Representative, *Initiative of the Palestinian Economy: Light Manufacturing*, no date. www.quartetoffice.org

128. Labour data published by Palestinian Central Bureau of Statistics. www. pcbs.gov.ps

129. Exchange of email messages between Office of Quartet Representative and the author, January 2015.

130. John Kerry's remarks to Special Programme on Breaking the Impasse, World Economic Forum, Dead Sea, Jordan, 26 May 2013. www.state. gov

131. Klaus Schwab, 'Nelson Mandela: Champion of Economic Freedom', *The Telegraph*, 6 December 2013.

132. 'Tony Blair Visits Gaza', Office of Tony Blair website, 15 February 2015. www.tonyblairoffice.org
133. Human Rights Watch, *All According to Plan: The Rabaa Massacre and Mass Killings of Protesters in Egypt*, 12 August 2014. www.hrw.org
134. John Reed and Roula Khalaf, 'Few Results to Show for Tony Blair in Contentious Middle East Role', *Financial Times*, 15 March 2015.

9. Partners in crime

1. Rob Coppinger, 'British Army's Elbit Hermes 450 UAVs Reach 7,000 Flight Hours', *FlightGlobal*, 14 April 2008. www.flightglobal.com
2. Arie Egozi, 'Israel Praises UAV Abilities during Operation Change of Direction Anti-Hezbollah Lebanon Campaign', *FlightGlobal*, 29 August 2006. www.flightglobal.com
3. Speech by Gordon Brown to Knesset, Jerusalem, 21 July 2008. www.ukpol.co.uk
4. Evidence to House of Commons Defence Committee, 3 June 2008. www.publications.parliament.uk
5. House of Commons Defence Committee, *Remote Control: Remotely-Piloted Air Systems – Current and Future UK Use*, March 2014. www.publications.parliament.uk
6. 'Watchkeeper Sensor Packages Announced', Thales Group website, 7 December 2015. www.thalesgroup.com
7. 'Hermes 450 – Tactical Long-Endurance UAS', Elbit Systems brochure, 2016. www.elbitsystems.com
8. 'UK MoD's Watchkeeper Programme', Thales Group website, 21 May 2007. www.thalesgroup.com
9. Memorandum from Thales UK to House of Commons Defence Committee, 25 April 2008.
10. 'Watchkeeper UAV Undertakes Maiden Flight', Thales Group website, 23 May 2008. www.thalesgroup.com
11. 'U-TacS Awarded $110 Million Order by Thales UK to Provide ISTAR Capability for UK Armed Forces', Elbit Systems website, 7 June 2007. www.elbitsystems.com
12. House of Commons, Defence Committee, *The Contribution of Unmanned Aerial Vehicles to ISTAR Capability*, August 2008. www.publications.parliament.uk
13. Mary Dobbing and Chris Cole, *Israel and the Drone Wars: Examining Israel's Production, Use and Proliferation of UAVs*, Drone Wars UK report, January 2014. www.dronewars.net

14. Elbit Systems' annual report to United States Security and Exchange Commission for the fiscal year ended 31 December 2009. www.elbitysystems.com

15. Human Rights Watch, *Precisely Wrong: Gaza Civilians Killed by Israeli-Drone Launched Missiles*, June 2009. www.hrw.org

16. 'The UK Ministry of Defence has Extended Thales UK's H-450 Unmanned Air System Contract', Thales Group website, 27 April 2009.

17. Evidence to House of Commons defence committee, 3 June 2008. www.publications.parliament.uk

18. House of Commons debate, 22 February 2010. www.parliament.uk

19. 'Watchkeeper Makes First UK Flight', Thales Group website, 15 April 2010. www.thalesgroup.com

20. Ministry of Defence, *The UK Approach to Unmanned Aircraft Systems*, March 2011. www.gov.uk

21. 'France and UK take a Significant Step Towards Watchkeeper Cooperation', Thales Group website, 25 July 2012. www.thalesgroup.com

22. 'Thales Welcomes Watchkeeper Operations for British Army in Afghanistan', Thales Group website, 29 September 2014. www.thalesgroup.com

23. Jack Serle and Alice Ross, 'Boxed Up, Barely Used and Four Years Late: Watchkeeper, the Army's "Affordable" £1.2 bn Drone Programme', Bureau of Investigative Journalism website, 2 October 2015. www.thebureauinvestigates.com

24. 'Thales Awarded Future Support Contract for Watchkeeper', Thales Group website, 29 June 2016. www.thalesgroup.com

25. Ministry of Defence reply to parliamentary question, 13 January 2006. www.parliament.uk

26. Gili Cohen, 'Israel's Weapons Sales to Europe More than Double Amid Refugee Crisis', *Haaretz*, 6 April 2016.

27. Stockholm International Peace Research Institute, *Trends in World Military Expenditure, 2015*, April 2016. www.sipri.org

28. 'Ferranti Technologies Visit RAF Coningsby', Royal Air Force website, 12 February 2016. www.raf.mod.uk

29. 'Ferranti Technologies Expands Helicopter Business', Ferranti Technologies website, 31 August 2013. www.ferranti-technologies.co.uk

30. 'Resource UAS Showcases Generic UAS Mission Simulator', Ferranti Technologies website, 17 September 2012. www.ferranti-technologies.co.uk

31. Response by Ministry of Defence to freedom of information request, 29 August 2014. www.gov.uk

32. Elbit Systems' annual report to United States Security and Exchange Commission for the fiscal year ended 31 December 2015. www.elbitysystems.com

33. 'About Us', Elite KL website, no date. www.elitekl.co.uk

34. Elbit Systems' annual report to United States Security and Exchange Commission for the fiscal year ended 31 December 2015. www.elbitysystems.com

35. 'Affinity Selected to Deliver Fixed Wing Military Flying Training Services to the UK's Ministry of Defence', Affinity Flying Training Services website, 2 February 2016. www.affinityfts.co.uk

36. 'Affinity Raffles Pilot Bear for Forces Charity', 25 August 2016. www.affinityfts.co.uk

37. 'Instro to Exhibit at IDEF "15 Istanbul"', Instro Precision website, no date. www.instro.com

38. Annual return of Instro Precision, 9 December 2015. Document filed with Companies House. www.companieshouse.gov.uk

39. 'What is Instro Hiding?', East Kent Campaign Against the Arms Trade, 13 July 2015. www.caatekent.wordpress.com

40. Stockholm International Peace Research Institute, *The SIPRI Top 100 Arms-Producing and Military Services*, December 2015. www.sipri.org

41. 'Elbit and BAE Offer the IDF a New Cannon', *IsraelDefense*, 26 April 2012. www.israeldefense.co.il

42. '$400 Million US Navy Aircraft Maintenance Contract Awarded', BAE Systems website, 13 December 2012. www.baesystems.com

43. 'New Precision Targeting System to Increase Accuracy of US Army's Threat Detection and Response Capabilities', BAE Systems website, 16 April 2013. www.baesystems.com

44. 'Lockheed Martin Aeronautics Recognises Top Performing Suppliers', Lockheed Martin website, 25 May 2016. www.lockheedmartin.com

45. 'Lockheed F-16I "Fighting Falcon" Suha', Israeli Air Force website, no date. www.iaf.org.il

46. BAE Systems, *Head-Up Displays: See-Through Display for Military Aviation*, 2013 brochure. www.baesystems.com

47. 'F-35', BAE Systems website, no date. www.baesystems.com

48. 'US, Lockheed Martin Reach Deal on Israeli F-35 Fighter Jets', *Haaretz*, 26 July 2012.

49. '"Protector" Unmanned Surface Vehicle Demonstrated to US Navy and Coast Guard for Force Protection', *Businesswire*, 16 August 2006. www.businesswire.com

50. '"Protector" – the Electronic Warfare Version', *IsraelDefense*, 20 June 2011. www.israeldefense.com

51. 'Israeli Attacks on Fishermen in the Gaza Sea', Palestinian Centre for Human Rights website, 14 January 2016. www.pchrgaza.org

52. BAE Systems, *Silver Bullet: Standard Artillery Transformed into Precision-Guided Weapons*, May 2014. www.baesystems.com

53. Barbara Opall-Rome, 'Israeli Army Taps IAI's Topgun for Precision Artillery Project', *DefenseNews*, 20 July 2016. www.defensenews.com

54. 'Precision Guidance Fuze for IDF's Artillery', *IsraelDefense*, 13 December 2014. www.israeldefense.co.il

55. Christopher F. Foss, 'Smart Ammo: Precision-Guided Munitions for Field Artillery', *IHS Jane's Defence Weekly*, 9 September 2015. www.janes.com

56. Nick Clegg, 'We Must Stop Arming Israel', *The Guardian*, 7 January 2009.

57. Yasmin Khan, 'UK Campaigners Score Victory Towards Arms Embargo', War on Want website, 24 April 2009. www.waronwant.org

58. 'UK Licensed £7m Worth of Arms to Israel in Lead-Up to the Bombing of Gaza', Campaign Against the Arms Trade website, 24 November 2014. www.caat.org.uk

59. 'Nick Clegg Calls for Suspension of Licenses for Arms Exports to Israel', Liberal Democrats website, 5 August 2014. www.libdems.org.uk

60. 'Government Announces Findings of Review of Licensed Exports to Israel', British government website, 12 August 2014. www.gov.uk

61. Email message to the author from Department of Business, Innovation and Skills, 5 May 2015.

62. Kim Sengupta and Donald Macintyre, 'Israeli Cabinet Divided over Fresh Gaza Surge', *The Independent*, 13 January 2009.

63. 'Nick Clegg: Full Speech to Lib Dem Friends of Israel', *The Jewish Chronicle Online*, 11 November 2010. www.thejc.com

64. Leon Symons and Anshel Pfeffer, 'Miliband Dismissed Barak "War Crimes" Prosecution Bid', *The Jewish Chronicle Online*, 1 October 2009. www.thejc.com

65. Donald Macintyre, 'Candidate Who Wants Olmert's Job Once "Sought Deaths of 70 Palestinians a Day"', *The Independent*, 1 August 2008.

66. Donald Macintyre, 'Olmert Indicted as Deputy is Accused of War Crimes', *The Independent*, 8 September 2008.

67. 'Universal Jurisdiction', British government website, 15 September 2011. www.gov.uk

68. 'Foreign Secretary Philip Hammond Addresses 500 Delegates at CFI Party Conference Reception', Conservative Friends of Israel website, 7 October 2015. www.cfoi.co.uk

69. Treasury's response to freedom of information request, 24 November 2015.

70. Patrick Wintour and Rowena Mason, 'Lady Warsi Resigns over UK's "Morally Indefensible" Stance on Gaza', *The Guardian*, 5 August 2014.

71. Stuart Littlewood, 'Israel's Friends at Westminster', *The Palestine Chronicle*, 25 July 2010. www.palestinechronicle.com

72. Stephen Pollard, 'David Cameron: Israel was Right was to Defend Itself over Gaza – and I Feel that Very Clearly', *The Jewish Chronicle Online*, 30 April 2015. www.thejc.com

73. Sajid Javid's speech to UK–Israel Business annual dinner, 8 June 2015. www.gov.uk

74. 'Overview of the Hub', UK–Israel Tech Hub, no date. www.gov.uk

75. 'Meet the Team', UK–Israel Tech Hub website, no date. www.ukisraelhub.com

76. Yuval Azulai, 'Haim Shani Appointed IAI Director', *Globes*, 21 March 2012. www.globes.co.il

77. Jeff Halper, *War Against the People: Israel, the Palestinians and Global Pacification* (London: Pluto, 2015), pp. 267–269.

78. 'Meet the Team', UK–Israel Tech Hub website, no date. www.ukisraelhub.com

79. 'Cyber-Boom or Cyber-Bubble', *The Economist*, 1 August 2015.

80. Neal Ungerleider, 'Beyond Meerkat: What's Next for Israel's Entrepreneurs?', *Fast Company*, 3 April 2015. www.fastcompany.com

81. Lauren Blanchard, 'UK Deepens Cyber-Security Cooperation with Israel During Cabinet Minister Visit', *NoCamels*, 16 February 2016. www.nocamels.com

82. Natasha Culzac, 'Israel-Gaza Conflict: 150,000 Protest in London for End to "Massacre and Arms Trade"', *The Independent*, 9 August 2014.

83. Matt Payton, 'Israel Boycott Ban: The Local Authorities that Imposed Unofficial Sanctions Against "Unethical Companies"', *The Independent*, 15 February 2016.

84. 'Foreign Secretary Philip Hammond Addresses 500 Delegates at CFI Party Conference Reception', Conservative Friends of Israel website, 7 October 2015. www.cfoi.co.uk

85. Mairav Zonszein, 'In Israel, BDS is Winning', *+972 Magazine*, 28 March 2016. www.972mag.com

86. 'Palestinian Civil Society Call for BDS', Palestinian BDS National Committee website, 9 July 2005. www.bdsmovement.net

87. 'Putting a Stop to Public Procurement Boycotts', British government website, 17 February 2016. www.gov.uk

88. Reply from Department for Communities and Local Government to freedom of information request, 16 March 2016.

89. Department for Communities and Local Government, *Revoking and Replacing the Local Government Pension Scheme (Management and Investment of Funds) Regulations 2009: Government Response to Consultation*, September 2016. www.gov.uk

90. Daniel Estrin, 'Covertly, Israel Prepares to Fight Boycott Activists Online', Associated Press, 17 February 2016.

91. Lahav Harkov, 'Israel's Strategic Affairs Minister Heads to London on BDS-Fighting Mission', *The Jerusalem Post*, 4 September 2016.

92. The Reut Institute, *Building a Firewall Against the Assault on Israel's Legitimacy: London as a Case Study*, November 2010. www.reut-institute.org

93. Philip Weiss, 'Abba Eban said Chomsky was "Guilty" over Jews' Refusal to Disappear', *Mondoweiss*, 3 June 2007. www.mondoweiss.net

94. 'Cabinet Office Minister Announces Proposals to Curb Anti-Israel Boycotts', Conservative Friends of Israel website, 17 February 2016. www.cfoi.co.uk

95. Channel 4 News video, 9 November 2015.

Postscript: Israel's greatest friend?

1. Josh Jackman, 'David Cameron calls on Jewish Community to Vote Remain so Britain can Support Israel "From Inside the Room"', *The Jewish Chronicle Online*, 21 June 2016. www.thejc.com

2. 'Israel's Parliamentary Plot Against UK Politicians', Al Jazeera website, 8 January 2017. www.aljazeera.com

3. House of Commons debate, 10 January 2017. www.hansard.parliament.uk

4. 'Joint Statement by EU High Representative Catherine Ashton and Israeli Minister of Justice Tzipi Livni on Israel's Participation in the Horizon 2020 Programme', European External Action Service website, 26 November 2013. www.eeas.europa.eu

5. European Commission briefing note for Catherine Ashton on 'Israel and EU Funding Instruments', 24 July 2013. Document obtained under EU freedom of information rules.

6. 'Prime Minister Theresa May met with Prime Minister Benjamin Netanyahu of Israel and Discussed Free Trade, Security and Iran', British government website, 6 February 2017. www.gov.uk

7. Eric Pickles, 'Netanyahu's Visit. It Would be Fitting were Britain Later to Sign its First Free Trade Deal with the Middle East's Only True Democracy', *ConservativeHome*, 6 February 2017. www.conservativehome.com

8. Heather Stewart, 'Theresa May's Criticism of John Kerry Israel Speech Sparks Blunt US Reply', *The Guardian*, 29 December 2016.

9. Phil Stewart, 'US Defends Supplying Israel Ammunition During Gaza Conflict', Reuters, 31 July 2014.

10. 'Knesset Set to Vote on Law that Lets Israel Expropriate Vast Tracts of Private Palestinian Land', Adalah website, 5 February 2017. www.adalah.org

11. 'Prime Minister Theresa May met with Prime Minister Benjamin Netanyahu of Israel and Discussed Free Trade, Security and Iran', British government website, 6 February 2017. www.gov.uk

12. 'Government Leads the Way in Tackling Anti-Semitism', British government website, 12 December 2016. www.gov.uk

13. 'Working Definition of Anti-Semitism', International Holocaust Remembrance Alliance website, 27 June 2016. www.holocaustremembrance.com

14. House of Commons Home Affairs Committee, *Anti-Semitism in the UK*, 13 December 2016. www.publications.parliament.uk

15. Asa Winstanley, 'How Israel Lobby Manufactured UK Labour Party's Anti-Semitism Crisis', *The Electronic Intifada*, 28 April 2016. www.electronicintifada.net

16. Peter Edwards, 'Corbyn Backs Official Definition to Stamp out "Repugnant" Anti-Semitism', *LabourList*, 12 December 2016. www.labourlist.org

17. Video of Labour Party leadership hustings uploaded to YouTube on 18 September 2016.

18. 'BoJo Shows Netanyahu his Office', video uploaded to RT UK channel on YouTube, 7 February 2017.

Acknowledgements

The idea for this book was planted in my head on a warm spring evening six years ago. After chairing a public meeting at which I spoke in London, Karma Nabulsi asked me if I knew that Winston Churchill had recommended sending members of the Black and Tans to Palestine. That nugget of information fascinated me; the Black and Tans and the Auxiliaries were British forces that had behaved in a ruthless manner during Ireland's war of independence. Some of their most infamous crimes were committed in my hometown – Balbriggan, County Dublin.

Thanks to Karma for alerting me to a vital fact.

Journalists have, in my view, a duty to cause trouble for the powerful. Not every publication is willing to allow its writers fulfil that duty. I am lucky to work for one that does: *The Electronic Intifada*. Huge thanks to Ali Abunimah and Maureen Murphy for hiring me as a contributing editor and to my colleagues Asa Winstanley, Nora Barrows-Friedman, Omar Karmi and Michael Brown.

Special thanks, also, to David Shulman, Melanie Patrick, Neda Tehrani and everyone at Pluto Press.

Much of the information contained this book comes from documents that I scoured at Britain's National Archives in Kew. I would like to thank the staff there for being helpful and friendly at all times. I wish to express similar appreciation to the staff at the Liddel Hart Centre for Military Archives in King's College London.

My biggest thanks go to my wife Susan, who never (or almost never) complained about my weekly research trips to England, and to our families.

David Cronin
February 2017

Index

Printed and bound by CPI Group (UK) Ltd, Croydon, CR0 4YY

25/03/2025

14647331-0002